the herdsmen at the south end, and the in another direction, causing considerable inconvenience to the herdsmen.

All in all the cavalry did an excellent job, caring for the parks, formulating rules, laying down precedents, and training men, thus laying the foundations for what became in 1916 the National Park Service. Indeed, many of the first Park Rangers were former cavalrymen.

The book also describes the many efforts of staunch conservationists such as John Muir, Theodore Roosevelt, Frederick Law Olmstead, George G. Vest, and Robert Underwood Johnson to induce Congress to provide appropriations and to establish laws and legal machinery for the preservation of the parks. The long and often discouraging fight for laws and legal machinery at last succeeded in 1894, twenty-two years after the first National Park was established. Many of the same men were simultaneously engaged in successfully defending Yellowstone Park from the introduction of a railroad. Mr. Hampton has delved into Congressional records, National Archives, and Park records. His book is an impeccable piece of research as well as a little known chapter in the history of the conservation movement.

H. DUANE HAMPTON is Associate Professor of History at the University of Montana. His interest in conservation and the American West has made him a frequent contributor to such journals as *Montana, the Magazine of Western History, Arizona and the West, Colorado Magazine, Forest History,* and others.

How the U.S. Cavalry Saved

OUR NATIONAL PARKS

The Three Brothers, Yosemite Valley

How the U.S. Cavalry Saved

OUR NATIONAL PARKS

H. DUANE HAMPTON

INDIANA UNIVERSITY PRESS

Bloomington / London

For Ander, Weed, and Beef

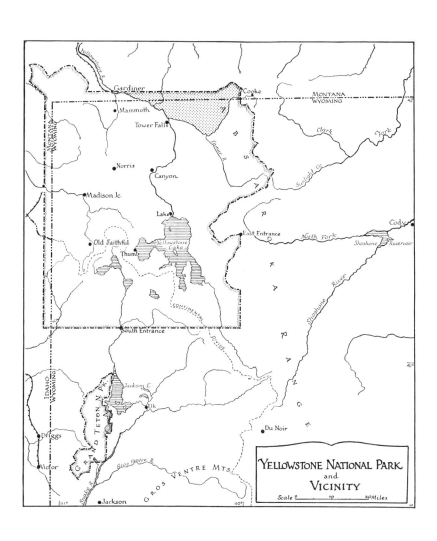

YELLOWSTONE NATIONAL PARK
and
VICINITY

Scale 0   10   20 Miles

CONTENTS

ACKNOWLEDGMENTS

MY FRIEND, Jerome DeSanto, first called my attention to the events described herein and assisted me in collecting some of the materials that appear in this book. Aubrey Haines, former Yellowstone Park Historian, guided my way through the Yellowstone Archives; Douglass Hubbard, former Chief Naturalist, Yosemite, contributed direction on the California Parks. Sara Jackson, National Archives, and Robert Athearn, University of Colorado, took an active, personal interest in my research and tendered the proper amount of encouragement. A few institutions and many individuals made my research possible and pleasant. To Suzanne Hampton, Lucile Fry, Howard Scamehorn, and Carl Ubbelohde I extend special thanks. The Yellowstone Library and Museum Association, the University of Colorado, and the University of Montana Research Council provided financial assistance. Mackey Brown, Missoula, Montana, and especially Miriam S. Farley, Indiana University Press, contributed many helpful suggestions.

How the U.S. Cavalry Saved

OUR NATIONAL PARKS

Old Faithful, Yellowstone Park

Introduction

LATE IN THE EVENING OF AUGUST 17, 1886, Troop "M," First United States Cavalry, marched into the Yellowstone National Park. Three days later the military commander relieved the Park Superintendent of his duties and inaugurated a new era of National Park administration. Established in 1872 in response to the urgings of a few dedicated men, the Park had been administered by civilian appointees who were provided with neither physical nor legal force to stop the endemic vandalism, poaching, and trespassing which threatened its existence. Some Congressmen, faced with this apparent administrative failure, labeled the park concept an absurdity. Congress declined to appropriate money for the continued operation of the Park in 1886, and the Secretary of the Interior was forced to request sufficient troops to protect the Park. The resulting military management was extended to the Yosemite, General Grant, and Sequoia National Parks, and continued in the Yellowstone until 1918. Thus these parks were preserved for posterity, and thus were laid the foundations of the National Park Service.

The present-day interest in conservation and preservation of natural resources and natural beauty is a direct legacy from those farsighted individuals who were responsible for the formation and protection of these early national parks. That these persons were few in number is not surprising; the predominant nineteenth-century attitude toward natural resources was one of use and not preservation. Unfortunately, we have an almost overwhelming tendency to judge our forebears by the standards of the present. Today we accuse the men responsible for the extinction of the passenger pigeon, the near extinction of the bison, and the virtual destruction of millions of acres of virgin timber for thoughtless or even malicious destruction of the nation's resources. Yet the many persons who cut the forests, or allowed them to burn, or who indiscriminately killed the game, did not consider themselves either criminal or immoral. Most of them were sincere in their belief that America's natural resources were, in fact, unlimited. Fortunately, attitudes toward land and forests changed, and so did governmental policies. In late nineteenth-century America, *laissez faire* was the predominant philosophy; exploitation of the nation's resources was a way of life. Americans worshiped the practical and the useful, and generally held altruism and aestheticism in disdain. Their governments traditionally reacted to environmental crises rather than anticipating and avoiding them, and their laws not only lagged behind new needs but resisted change when those needs were outmoded.

Given this background, it is surprising that a mere handful of prescient men could convince Congress, and ultimately the people, that some elements of the nation's natural heritage were worth preserving.

The period of military administration of the National Parks is unique in American history. Before 1894 in the Yellowstone, and throughout its administrative career in the

California Parks, the cavalry operated without a legal framework or means of law enforcement. Yet during the thirty-two years of military guardianship a National Park policy was evolved and administrative procedures were formulated. Moreover, when the National Park Service began operating in 1918, it took over from the military a previously trained cadre of men. Even more important, the National Park Service, when organized, had something to administer: the Yellowstone, the Yosemite, the General Grant, and the Sequoia National Park. In a very real sense, the cavalry saved these parks, and in so doing, saved the National Park idea.

I

The Genesis of an Idea

CITIZENS OF BABYLON, Greece, and Rome set aside parks, and the development of formal gardens was revived during the Renaissance. The idea of preserving tracts of land for recreation and pleasure gained force in feudal England when the nobility began using forests as a source of game as well as timber, and later the townspeople instigated the practice of segregating a section of a township for the use of all residents in "common." This custom was transported across the Atlantic by the earliest English colonists, and though surrounded by forests and unsettled land, they, too, formed their town commons, small plots of uncultivated land set amid the villages and tilled fields. Such areas were originally established for common pasturage, but eventually their recreational values became apparent and many exist today in the form of city parks.

The early settlers of this country made some attempts to preserve lands solely for recreation. A few early laws were designed to prevent the wanton killing of game and the wasteful cutting of timber, but these were atypical. Before man could convince himself of the propriety of preserving nature, he had first to change his attitude toward nature itself.[1] This was accomplished in part through the efforts of poets, writers, and artists.

Readers of Coleridge, Southey, and Wordsworth imbibed their romantic view of nature. Influenced by both the Romantic mood and the English poets, William Cullen Bryant eulogized the American landscape and praised nature for its aesthetic, not economic, value. In 1823 the publication of James Fenimore Cooper's *The Pioneers* gave the American public a new approach to nature through an unsentimental yet accurate description of the world of the woods. Cooper made disparaging remarks about the wasteful ways of the white man, condemned the wanton destruction of the pigeon, the bass, and the tree, and subtly warned that some elements of nature should be saved for future generations lest a desolate landscape be their legacy. Though neither Bryant nor Cooper directly advocated the setting aside of wilderness preserves, both influenced public opinion and directed thoughts toward the household of nature.[2]

George Catlin, the noted artist, explorer, and admirer of the Plains Indian, had, after a visit to the Indian country of the upper Missouri in 1832, written a series of letters describing what he had seen. In one of these letters, first published in the New York *Daily Commercial Advertiser* the following year, Catlin foresaw the probable extinction of both buffalo and Indian and, alluding to that area of unsettled land which extended "from the province of Mexico to Lake Winnepeg," proposed that these regions

might in future be seen, (by some great protecting policy of government) preserved in their pristine beauty and wilderness, in a *magnificent park,* where the world could see for ages to come, the native Indian in his classic attire, galloping his wild horse, with sinewy bow, and shield and lance, amid the fleeting herds of elks and buffaloes. What a beautiful and thrilling specimen for America to preserve and hold up to the view of her refined citizens and the world, in future ages! A *nation's park,* containing man and beast, in all the wild and freshness of their nature's beauty.[3]

Among other things, Catlin wrote that park land could be preserved "without detriment to the country" since these areas were "uniformly sterile, and of no available use to cultivating man."[4] The artist desired "no other monument" to his memory "than the reputation of having been the founder of such an institution." Thus, some forty years before Congress was willing to accept the idea, Catlin advocated the setting aside of land for its inherent aesthetic values.

Catlin's was not the only voice advocating preservation. After outlining a philosophy of nature, Ralph Waldo Emerson recommended that "The interminable forests should become graceful parks, for use and delight. . . ." Later, Henry David Thoreau enthralled Americans with his *Walden* and in "Chesuncook," published in the *Atlantic Monthly,* he questioned:

Why should not we . . . have our national preserves . . . in which the bear and panther and some even of the hunter race, may still exist, and not be 'civilized off the face of the earth' . . . for inspiration and our true re-creation? Or should we, like villains, grub them all up for poaching on our own national domains?[5]

Artists, also, were showing Americans the glories of nature in their land. Landscape painting, before 1800, was almost nonexistent in this country; the majority of practicing artists devoted themselves almost entirely to historical paintings or to portraits of the rich and famous. But even as Cooper and Bryant were describing the great out-of-doors in verse and prose, a new movement was taking shape in painting. The first exploratory steps were made by Washington Allston, John Trumbull, and John Vanderlyn, but only after the successful showing of Thomas Cole's paintings in 1825 did the public become interested in the paintings of what was later known as the Hudson River School. Under Cole's leadership the American artist looked to the great falls of the Niagara, the hills of New England, and eventually to the majestic mountains of the West for inspiration. Cole, though he had never seen the Western plains and mountains, realized that "Americans have a strong desire for excellence . . . a love of nature" and, recognizing that even then such wilderness was passing away, he called attention to the "necessity of saving and perpetuating its features."[6]

Prompted by such writing and painting, townspeople began to venture forth into the country. Camping parties became fashionable for the more sturdy; vacations in the newly established mountain resorts or weekends at the seashore became the vogue. But the summer migration to the Eastern seaboard and to the cool forests of the North only moved the congestion of the city to such previously tranquil areas as Saratoga, White Sulphur Springs, the Adirondacks, Madison-on-Lakes, Nahant, Newport, Appledore, Mount Desert, and Mount Holyoke. It may even have seemed to some that there was not enough country to go around. The completion of the transcontinental railroad in 1869, and the development of other railroad lines west of the Mississippi River, prompted promoters to extol the vacation attractions of the Rocky Mountain area. One far-seeing Englishman, commenting on the Pike's Peak area, thought that "when Colorado becomes a populous state, the Springs of the Fountaine qui Bouille will constitute its spa . . . no more glorious summer residence could be imagined." He firmly believed that "the Coloradoan of the future . . . will have little cause to envy us Easterners our Saratoga."[7]

On July 3, 1844, an editorial appeared in the New York *Evening Post* under the title "A New Park" over the signature of William Cullen Bryant. Bryant had discovered, during his own quest for fresh air, that it was no longer possible, in half

National Park Service

Mammoth Terraces, Yellowstone Park

an hour's walk, for the city dweller to reach open country. The time was approaching, he said, when the city would no longer be able to purchase suitable land for recreation and pleasure, and he advocated the creation of a park within the city. This editorial set the spark to the movement that was to end some years later with the creation of Central Park. Enlisting the aid of Andrew Jackson Downing, the great landscape architect, Bryant argued his case before the people, and in 1851 an act was passed providing for the purchase of some of the necessary land. Realization of the idea was delayed by political bickering, but the appointment of Frederick Law Olmsted, the well-known landscape architect, as superintendent of the project, and later as architect-in-chief, brought the park to completion in 1858.[8]

The transition of the park idea from that of an urban plot set aside for weary city-dwellers to that of a large area maintained in a natural setting for the use of all citizens of the nation was slow in coming. In 1832 an act was passed authorizing the governor of the Territory of Arkansas to lease salt springs located in the Territory; it further provided that four sections of land in the Ouachita Mountains, in which were centered mineral hot springs, "shall be reserved for the future disposal of the United States."[9] This did not, however, mean that Congress recognized the scenic or aesthetic values of nature. The springs had potential commercial value, and at least one bathhouse had been constructed in the area. Congress simply had responded to the cries of territorial constituents who wanted the area maintained for free public use.

The canals and railroads that made summer vacations at various resort areas feasible were still confined to the East. While the tourist could journey to the White Mountains or the Eastern seaboard with fair comfort, he could not travel very far west of the Alleghenies without discomfort. Many arcadian reports of the Western regions had filtered back to Eastern readers in the form of travel accounts, books, lectures, and articles. The Reverend Timothy Flint, in his *Recollections of the Last Ten Years,* published in 1826, likened the Mississippi Valley to the Garden of Eden, while his contemporary Judge James Hall thought Ohio and the land west was truly the Promised Land. C. W. Dana, presaging the railroad brochures of a later date and representing the then planned Pacific Railway, published a handbook under the title *The Garden of the World; or, The Great West,* in an attempt to entice potential immigrants to settle in the area between the Mississippi River and the Pacific Ocean.[10]

But by 1850 many people had returned from the frontier region bringing tales of discomfort that discouraged less hardy travelers. Washington Irving's *Tour of the Prairies* (1835) described the bleak, far-reaching prairies quite realistically, and *Astoria* (1836) declared that the Western region was "vast and trackless as the ocean . . . the great American desert . . . where no man permanently abides." In the first edition of Francis Parkman's *Oregon Trail* (1849) the plains region was again described as the great American desert. Government explorers also traversed sections of the West and brought back descriptions. Lewis and Clark had chronicled their trip to the Columbia River in 1805–1806, and earlier the report of Lieutenant Zebulon Montgomery Pike had appeared describing the region south of the Lewis and Clark route. Pike predicted that the area might "become in time as celebrated as the sandy deserts of Africa," and the report of Major Stephen Long in 1820 gave credence to such a prediction.[11]

The reports of travelers were thus conflicting as to the true character of the area beyond the Mississippi; government reports were both verbose and technical, and, while the literary output whetted the curiosity of those residing in the East, it was perhaps the painters and photographers who best publicized the region. Among them were John James Audubon, George Catlin, Karl Bodmer, Alfred Miller, and Albert Bierstadt. Continuing the tradition pioneered by Cole, Audubon reproduced in painstaking detail the wildlife of the Western regions, while Catlin, Miller, Bodmer, and Bierstadt portrayed the scenic splendor of the West on huge, spectacular canvases. Landscape views were also reproduced by photography, which had been introduced into this country in 1839. John Mix Stanley had accompanied as photographer one of the several government surveys sent out to determine a route for the Pacific railroad, and John C. Fremont's Utah expedition of 1854 included the Baltimore painter turned photographer, S. N. Carvalho.[12] Many of the photographs of Western scenes taken on these early explorations were transposed into lithographs or woodcuts and given wide circulation in the East.[13]

Such reports, verbal and pictorial, may have stimulated public interest. Ultimately, Congress took the next step toward conservation when in 1864 it granted to California a portion of the public domain that included the Yosemite Valley and the Mariposa Big Tree Grove.

Four years after gold was found at Sutter's mill in California, Eastern newspaper readers learned of another discovery in that far-off land. In the spring of 1852 a hunter stumbled into an area forested with giant trees *(Sequoia gigantea)* and the reports of this discovery spread rapidly. With an eye to possible profit, two men stripped the bark from one of the giants and shipped the specimen East for exhibition. After touring the Eastern seaboard cities, the entrepreneurs set up their exhibit at the Crystal Palace in London, where wary Londoners soon branded the exhibit as a "humbug," refusing to believe that the bark could have come from one tree. But while the exhibition was a financial failure, it raised valuable voices of protest. One irate Californian sent a letter to *Gleason's Pictorial* protesting the desecration of "such a splendid tree," stating that while in Europe such wonders of nature would be protected by law, "in this money-making-go-ahead community, thirty or forty thousand dollars are paid for it and the purchaser chops it down and ships it off for a shilling show." The writer hoped that "no one will conceive the idea of purchasing Niagara Falls with the same purpose."[14] James Russell Lowell added his protest against the destruction of the big tree when, in his article "Humanity to Trees," he proposed the establishment of a "society for the prevention of cruelty to trees." The danger to these unique giants of the California forests was underlined by an article in *Harper's Weekly* which claimed that the tree stripped of its bark was rapidly decaying, having been skinned "with as much neatness and industry as a troup of jackals would display in clearing the bones of a dead lion."[15]

While the mutilation of the big trees in California had gained widespread publicity in the East, the discovery of the Yosemite Valley passed almost unnoticed. As early as 1827 Jedediah Strong Smith had led a party of fur trappers from Salt Lake through the Sierra Nevadas to the Pacific. In 1833 Joseph Reddeford Walker, a trapper and explorer in the company of Captain B. L. E. Bonneville, led a similar band of adventurers directly into the area that was to become the Yosemite National Park. Trails were blazed, and some knowledge of the California region was gained, but little publicity was given to these early discoveries.[16] In 1851 an expeditionary force, led by James D. Savage, was sent to discipline the various tribes of Indians who roamed the California mountains. During the campaign Savage's battalion explored the entire course of the Yosemite Valley, and while they failed to subdue the "Yosemitos," the volunteers agreed to name the Valley after the tribe of Indians for which they searched.[17] The scenic wonders of the Valley were described in the *Daily Alta California,* but the story was not picked up by Eastern publications.[18]

Eastern readers became aware of the Valley's existence in 1856, however, when an article from the *California Christian Advocate* was reproduced in the *Country Gentleman.* It declared that the "Yo-hem-i-ty" valley was "the most striking natural wonder on the Pacific" and predicted that this region would, in the future, become a great resort area. The first sketches of the Valley, by Thomas A. Ayres, were distributed in lithograph form throughout the East, and Horace Greeley termed the Valley the "most unique and majestic of nature's marvels."[19] The first photographs of the Valley were taken in 1859 by C. L. Weed and R. H. Vance,[20] and four years later C. E. Watkins' photographs were exhibited at Goupil's art gallery in New York. Residents of the Eastern seaboard were further made aware of the Western splendors when, in a series of eight articles published by the *Boston Evening Tran-*

National Park Service

President Taft's party at Wawona Tree,
Mariposa Grove, 1909. This tree toppled
in 1969.

script, the writer Starr King described the scenery of the Valley in glowing terms.[21]

Public interest in the West, and particularly in the Yosemite Valley and the California big trees, was thus aroused, but the trip to California from the East was still a hazardous and expensive undertaking. The residents of California, however, foresaw that the Yosemite Valley might become for the West what the great falls of the Niagara were for the East, and some realized that private interests would soon attempt to capitalize upon its natural wonders. Experienced leadership was needed to preserve the scenic grandeur of the mountain fastness, and fortunately such leadership was available.

At the close of the Mexican War, Colonel John C. Fremont had purchased the Rancho Las Mariposas, a vast estate of some 44,000 acres lying south and east of the Yosemite Valley. With the discovery of gold north of his estate in 1848, Fremont extended his rancho to include the mining claims, and invested money in a vain attempt to develop the mines. Bankruptcy followed and the Fremont Grant was purchased by a group of Wall Street financiers at a sheriff's sale. The nonresident owners employed the architect-in-chief of the newly formed New York City Central Park, Frederick Law Olmstead, to superintend their investment. Olmsted arrived in California in the fall of 1863 to assume his new duties and remained until 1865. During this time he was the leader of a small group of men who instigated and pushed to fulfillment the movement to reserve the Yosemite Valley and to preserve the giant trees from destruction.[22]

On March 28, 1864, the California Senator, John Conness, introduced into the Senate a bill providing that the Yosemite Valley and the area embracing the "Mariposa Big Tree Grove" be granted to the state of California, on condition that the area "shall be held for public use, resort, and recreation . . . for all time." The area was to be managed by the governor of the state and eight commissioners appointed by him, none of whom were to receive compensation for their services.[23] In this novel legislation an idea, suggested by Catlin, advocated by Thoreau and others, was acknowledged.

Olmsted, soon after his arrival in California, had visited the Yosemite Valley in the autumn, when the streams were reduced to a mere trickle, the great falls dried up, and the vegetation sparse and brown. Yet he was overcome by the "union of the deepest sublimity with the deepest beauty" and he thought "Yo Semite the greatest glory of nature."[24] He was so convinced of the necessity of preserving the unique Valley that he immediately set about persuading others to join him in a crusade to have the area removed from the public domain. Though opposed by some, he managed to enlist the aid of the San Francisco physician Professor John F. Morse and the California representative of the Central American Steamship Transit Company of New York, Israel Ward Raymond. It was Raymond who, on February 20, 1864, wrote to Senator Conness, enclosing some "views" of the Valley and stating that he thought "it important to obtain the proprietorship soon, to prevent occupation and especially to preserve the trees in the valley from destruction," and advocated the passage of the necessary legislation by Congress.[25] Senator Conness forwarded the letter to the General Land Office and requested that a bill incorporating Raymond's suggestions be prepared and returned to the Senate.[26]

The resulting bill was introduced by Conness and reported by the Senate Committee on Public Lands without amendment on May 17, 1864. Conness reassured the Senate that the lands to be granted were "for all public purposes worthless" and that the entire grant was "a matter involving no appropriation whatever." Senator Foster of Connecticut wondered if the state of California would accept the grant, but Conness replied that the application came from gentlemen of fortune, taste, and refinement in California, that the Commissioner of the General Land Office had taken a great interest in the preservation of the Valley and the Big Tree Grove, and that he, Conness, could speak for the state. In the course of debate strong argument was made for the preservation of the big trees by recalling the bark stripping episode some twelve years before. The purpose of the bill was stated to be the preservation of these trees from further "devastation and injury." The preservation of the Yosemite Valley was not mentioned and it appears to have had importance only in its relation to the sequoias. The bill was read a third time and passed by the Senate.[27]

The bill appeared upon the floor of the House with the unanimous approval of the Committee on Public Lands. Again, the Valley received little attention; replying to a query, the Chairman of the Public Lands Committee said, "Well, it is about a mile [long]; it is a gorge in the mountains." One Representative objected that there was no specific stipulation in the bill concerning preservation of the giant trees, but Representative Cole of California erroneously assured him that the state would "take good care of these trees." The measure passed the House on June 29, 1864, and was signed by President Lincoln the following day.[28]

The areas thus set aside were to be administered by the state of California; Congress and the Federal Government accepted no responsibility for their preservation or improvement. The Act provided that portions of the granted lands could be leased for a maximum of ten years, the resulting revenue to be expended in the building of roads to, and the preservation and improvement of, the grants.[29] Since the 1864 Legislature of California had already adjourned, it was not until some three months later that Governor F. F. Low proclaimed the grant to the state and appointed himself and eight others as a Board to manage the grant. Frederick Law Olmsted became chairman of the Board and immediately began organizing the new "parks."[30] But the State's attempt to preserve and protect the park areas ended, eventually, in abject failure, and when, in 1890, National Parks were formed in and around the grants, civilian control and mismanagement gave way to military control. Later the grants themselves were ceded back to the national government and placed under military supervision.

The passage of the Act of 1864, granting to California the two tracts of land, did not establish a "national park." No national laws were enacted for administration of the areas, and, after the passage of the Act, Congress seems to have dismissed the areas from its collective mind. The significance of the legislation lies in the fact that it provided for land to be reserved for strictly nonutilitarian purposes, thus establishing a precedent for the later reservation of the Yellowstone region. It is probable that if Congress had not then been preoccupied with the Civil War the opponents of the bill would have combined to defeat its passage. The public mind was not yet directed toward the preservation and conservation of the aesthetic elements of nature.

National Park Service

George S. Anderson and pet bear cub

II

The Nation's First National Park

THE FIRST GROUP of white men to visit the area that later became Yellowstone National Park were the fur trappers, followed by the traders, and, with the discovery of minerals, the prospectors. The United States Army was there, as it was in most of the Western frontier area, but instead of facilitating settlement and exploitation as it did elsewhere, here it prevented it.

Until 1869—a scant three years before Congress created Yellowstone Park—knowledge of the natural curiosities and wonders of the region was based principally upon the tales of the occasional trapper or explorer. Probably the first white man to visit the Yellowstone region was John Colter, who, during the winter of 1807–1808, traveled through the wilderness area that was to become the first National Park.[1] Colter reported seeing geysers and other evidences of hydrothermal activity around the headwaters of the Yellowstone River, but it was not the reports of natural curiosities that aroused interest in this Western country; it was the news brought back by the Lewis and Clark Expedition—reports of mountain streams teeming with beaver, and an all-water route along the Missouri River that would lead the trapper to those streams.

During the winter of 1806–1807, St. Louis was the scene of much activity and excitement as traders and trappers congregated to await the spring thaw that would clear the Missouri of ice and allow their passage into the mountainous regions to the west. One such trader was the Spaniard, Manuel Lisa, who, with a group of forty-two frontiersmen, journeyed up the Missouri and Yellowstone Rivers in 1807 to the mouth of the Big Horn, where a timbered blockhouse was constructed. From here the men dispersed in various directions to trap, trade, and hunt. The indomitable John Colter was one of these trappers, and it was from Fort Manuel, as the blockhouse was named, that he started his trip into the Yellowstone region. The success of this group's first venture led to the formation of the Missouri Fur Company in 1809. Soon trappers representing Astor's American Fur Company, the Hudson's Bay Company, and later the Rocky Mountain Fur Company spread throughout the northern and central Rockies, and some six hundred trappers searched the many streams for "sign," traded with the Indians, and explored vast areas of what, until their arrival, had been unknown to white men.

It is probable that many of these explorers wandered into the Yellowstone region, but only a few left reports of their findings; initials carved in trees and remnants of campsites indicate that they were there.[2] It is generally believed that trappers working for England's North West Company and, later, the Hudson's Bay Company visited the area in 1818 and again in 1824, and it is quite likely that famous "mountain men" like James Bridger, Thomas Fitzpatrick, and Jedediah S. Smith were familiar with the geyser region as early as 1824. The first printed account of the "infernal region" appeared in the *Philadelphia Gazette and Daily Advertizer* on September 27, 1827, and was reprinted in the *Niles Weekly*

Register on October 6, 1827. This report of the natural phenomena found at the headwaters of the Yellowstone contains an accurate description of Yellowstone Lake and some of the thermal springs located near it.[3] During the 1830's, when the American fur trade was approaching its apogee, many trappers and traders ventured into the area, and some of their descriptions were placed in journals or later published in book form.[4]

Actually the geyser areas were best described by the trappers, who considered their talents as storytellers second only to their prowess in killing game. Naturally their stories were often embellished, exaggerated, and sometimes totally untrue. The stories Jim Bridger is said to have told best exemplify this process, and though fact is to be found in many of these tales of the Yellowstone region, they were far from literal truth. Bridger told of glass mountains, of geysers spouting water seventy feet into the air, of petrified birds perched on petrified trees singing petrified songs.[5] Perhaps the most accurate and descriptive diarist among the early trappers was Osborne Russell, who visited the Yellowstone area at least three different times between 1835 and 1839, but his competent observations failed to replace the tall tales of Bridger and others.[6] But by the 1840's the days of the trader and trapper were ending and the white man was seen less frequently in this portion of the West.[7]

In some instances the trails blazed by the trapper were followed by prospectors searching for a trace of "color" that might indicate a large ore body, but precious minerals were scarce in the Yellowstone region, and for the most part this area was bypassed. Some parties who ventured into the geyser basins left a few place names and influenced later and larger explorations of the area, but fortunately for the preservation of the later National Park, the only big strikes discovered were located to the north and east of the present boundaries of the park.

The tales of the early trappers did generate some further

interest in the unexplained phenomena referred to by these early explorers. In 1859 Captain W. F. Raynolds of the Corps of Topographical Engineers, United States Army, was directed to head an expedition to investigate the character and habits of the Indians and the possibilities of agriculture and settlement of the area surrounding the headwaters of the Missouri River—including sources of the Yellowstone, Gallatin, and Madison Rivers. This was the first effort by the government to ascertain the validity of the fabled stories. The expedition failed to explore the area because of the combined obstacles of snow and mountains. It did, however, link up the past and future. Jim Bridger was the guide for the party, and Dr. Ferdinand V. Hayden, who later saw and described the phenomena in scientific terms, was the geologist.[8] The formal report of the expedition was not published until 1868, too late to provide any real impetus to further exploration. Chittenden considers Raynolds' failure to fully explore the Yellowstone region "a fact quite as fortunate as any other" in the region's history, since a full report authenticating what had previously been discounted as myth and fantasy would surely have drawn speculators and settlers into the area.[9] Before Bridger's tales reached the public in the form of a government document a few private individuals were developing plans for the "rediscovery" of the Yellowstone wonderland.[10]

A year before the publication of the Raynolds report there was talk among the people of Montana Territory about organizing an exploring party to journey into the Yellowstone country and either confirm or refute the accounts of volcanic phenomena earlier reported by the trappers and miners; however, no expedition was formed that year.[11] Plans were again made in 1868, and while these, too, failed to materialize, the interest aroused was sufficient to prompt three men to ascend the Yellowstone River and thoroughly explore the regions surrounding its headwaters. David E. Folsom, C. W. Cook, and William Peterson, in 1869, made the first purposeful exploration of the area with the sole objective of determining its actual character. Upon their return the explorers were hesitant to make known their discoveries, for, unlike Bridger, they wished to maintain their reputations as honest men. Some time later, however, Folsom, aided by Cook, prepared an article accurately describing the wonders the small party had seen; after being rejected by several Eastern publications, it was finally published in July, 1870, by the Lakeside Publishing Company of Chicago in their *Western Monthly.* [12]

The lucid and articulate reports of Folsom, Cook, and Peterson served to stimulate some interest in the heretofore rumored wonderland and in the spring of 1870 two leading citizens of the Montana Territory appealed to General Winfield S. Hancock, Commanding Officer, Department of Dakota, for military escort for a projected Yellowstone exploration party. One of these men, Nathaniel P. Langford, famous for his part in the vigilante days of 1863 and 1864 in the Territory, later wrote that he "indulged, for several years, a great curiosity to see the upper valley of the Yellowstone," his curiosity having been aroused by the stories told "by trappers and mountaineers of the natural phenomena of that region." As a result of his urging a group was formed who "determined to make the journey." [13]

Under the leadership of Henry D. Washburn, Surveyor-General of Public Lands for Montana Territory, Langford, Samuel T. Hauser, Cornelius Hedges, Warren C. Gillette, Truman C. Everts, Walter Trumbull, Benjamin F. Stickney, and Jacob Smith, accompanied by Lieutenant Gustavus C. Doane and six cavalrymen, departed from Fort Ellis on August 22, 1870, for the Yellowstone Region. The expedition made an extensive and thorough exploration of the geysers, hot springs, and towering falls and through its efforts the unique wonders of the region were at last reported in detail. Upon their return several members of the party prepared articles for magazines and newspapers, [14] and Langford gave lectures in Helena, Minneapolis, New York City, and Washington, D. C. Through these descriptions the public was at last made aware of this remarkable mountain wilderness. The official report of the expedition, prepared by Lieutenant Doane, was described by Dr. F. V. Hayden as being "remarkable . . . written under the inspiration of the wonderful physical phenomena" and "that for graphic descriptions and thrilling interest it has not been surpassed by any official report . . . since the time of Lewis and Clark."[15]

The immediate result of the Washburn-Langford-Doane Expedition was the organization, a year later, of two government expeditions to secure further official scientific information on the area. The sources of the Yellowstone River were explored and plotted by the Barlow-Heap Expedition, a party of Army Engineers that was sent out in 1871 under direct orders from Lieutenant General Philip Sheridan, Commanding Officer of the Division of the Missouri. At the same time the region was canvassed by the Hayden Expedition sent out by the Interior Department.[16] The ultimate results of the three exploration parties into the Yellowstone region between 1869 and 1871 was the establishment of the Yellowstone National Park in 1872.

The idea of establishing the geyser region and its environs as a national park has been credited to many. Chittenden admitted that "no special credit for originality should attach to the matter," then proceeded to state categorically that the source of the idea could be found in "the Washburn Expedition of 1870"; the place of conception was at a campsite near the junction of the Firehole and Gibbons Rivers, the date was September 19, 1870, and the man responsible was Cornelius' Hedges.[17] In 1904 Hedges published his diary, to which he appended a note maintaining that it "was at the first camp after leaving the lower Geyser Basin when all were speculating which point in the region we had been through, would become most notable that I first suggested the uniting all our efforts to get it made a National Park."[18] Lieutenant Doane made no reference to this suggestion in his official report, nor did Langford or Trumbull in the articles they published in May and June, 1871, in *Scribner's* and the *Overland Monthly.*

Even though the suggestion may have been made by Hedges at the now famous campfire, the idea of establishing national parks did not originate there. Chittenden's statement concerning the birth of the national park idea has been repeated in almost every book dealing with the origins of national parks despite evidence to the contrary. Cramton, writing in 1932, and Huth in 1950, effectively demolished the historical basis for the National Park Service's campfire vignette, presented annually on the banks of the Madison; finally, in 1964, the Park historian was able to end the historical travesty.[19]

While members of the Washburn Expedition worked in many ways to promote the establishment of the Yellowstone area as a national park, the suggestion of setting that region apart for the use of the public at large seems to have been made before 1870. As early as 1865 a young Jesuit priest, Father Francis X. Kuppens, visited the Yellowstone region and described the wonders he had seen to a group of men, among whom were Cornelius Hedges and the Acting Governor of Montana Territory, Thomas F. Meagher. Kuppens later wrote that the Acting Governor, upon hearing a description of the area, stated that the area should be reserved as a park by the government, if indeed "things were as described," and agreed with the rest of the company that further explorations should be made.[20] Others suggest that David Folsom, upon returning from the 1869 exploration, "discussed with General Washburn the project of creating a park" in order to preserve the natural wonders of the region,[21] and that he incorporated in the article submitted to the *Western Monthly* a similar suggestion.[22]

But regardless of all of these "suggestions," one must speculate that the park idea did not originate in the Yellowstone area, but in the act of Congress in 1864 granting the

Yosemite Valley to the State of California "for public use, resort and recreation." Yosemite was soon referred to as a National Park.[23] In 1871 an editor, referring to Yosemite, went on to describe the Yellowstone area and stated, "Let this, too, be set apart by Congress as a domain retained unto all mankind . . . and let it be *esta perpetua.*"[24]

The legislation creating the California grant had established a precedent; but since the Yellowstone region embraced parts of three Territories, it could not be given in trusteeship to one state. The only way to preserve the area was to place it directly under Federal control.

One of the most influential events that led to the park legislation was the expedition led by F. V. Hayden, head of the United States Geological Survey of the Territories. Through his efforts an item appropriating $40,000 for survey work around the sources of the Missouri and Yellowstone Rivers was included in the sundry civil act of March 3, 1871. Since he had not had the money or opportunity to thoroughly explore the region in 1860 when he was attached as geologist to the Raynolds Expedition, Hayden organized a comprehensive group of scientists, artists, and photographers, and during the summer of 1871 they thoroughly surveyed the Yellowstone region, compiling extensive data on its geology, zoology, botany, paleontology, and meteorology.[25] In addition to the scientific reports, visual reproductions of the natural curiosities were prepared by W. H. Jackson, the frontier photographer, and the artist Thomas Moran.[26]

When he returned to Washington, Hayden was met by Nathaniel Langford, Cornelius Hedges, and Samuel Hauser, Helena bank president and a member of the 1870 expedition. This small group feared that if some action were not taken to preserve the Yellowstone area, it would soon be claimed by homesteaders. Langford and Hedges had already enlisted the aid of William H. Clagett, newly elected Delegate from Montana Territory. Working under the guidance of Congressman Henry L. Dawes,[27] Chairman of the Ways and Means Committee, these men began to frame legislation that would establish a national park in the Yellowstone region.[28]

A bill to "set aside a certain tract of land lying near the headwaters of the Yellowstone River as a public park" was introduced in the two houses of Congress on December 18, 1871, and was immediately referred to the committees on public lands.[29] The Senate bill was reported back on January 22, 1872, by Senator Samuel C. Pomeroy of Kansas, who, speaking for the Committee, recommended its passage. After a series of minor legislative delays, the bill finally came up for consideration on January 30, 1872.[30] The only serious opposition to its passage was voiced by Senator Cornelius Cole of California, Chairman of the Senate Committee on Appropriations, who, in a speech representing the attitude of many 19th-century men, stated:

> I have grave doubts about the propriety of passing this bill.
> . . . The geysers will remain, no matter where the ownership
> of the land may be, and I do not know why settlers should be
> excluded from a tract of land forty miles square. . . . I cannot
> see how the natural curiosities can be interfered with if settlers
> are allowed to appropriate them. . . . I do not see the reason
> or propriety of setting apart a large tract of land . . . in the
> Territories of the United States for a public park.[31]

Nevertheless the Senate passed the measure without a call for ayes and noes and it went to the House, where it remained on the Speaker's table until February 27.[32]

While the bill was being considered by Congress, its proponents were far from idle. Langford was busy writing, lecturing, and attempting to influence any member of Congress with whom he came in contact. Four hundred copies of *Scribner's Magazine,* in which his articles describing the Yellowstone area had appeared the previous May and June, were obtained and placed upon Congressional desks.[33] Hayden, with the aid of the Secretary of the Interior, exhibited Jackson's photographs, maps, and specimens acquired on his expedition in the lobbies of Congress and personally expounded the wonders of the region in interviews with Congressmen.[34] He wrote another article for *Scribner's*[35] and one for the *American Journal of Science and Arts.* In this he asserted that the speedy passage of the park bill would "prevent squatters from taking possession of the springs and destroying the beautiful decorations."[36]

Further pressure for the preservation of the area came from the legislature of the Territory of Montana, which, however, proposed that the new park be placed under Territorial control. These Montana frontiersmen exhibited the same desire for local control as had been shown by the residents of California in respect to the Yosemite Valley. Settlers in Wyoming Territory, fearing ejection from the Yellowstone region, opposed the formation of a park, but the editor of the *Rocky Mountain Gazette* criticized their position. A desire for preservation of forests was also present in Montana Territory even at this early date. Noting the existence of forest fires, the editor of the *Helena Daily Herald* stated, "The loss to us is trifling, but the value of these timber lands to future generations is incalculable."[37]

When, on February 27, 1872, the Senate bill providing for the establishment of the park came before the House for consideration, attempts were made to delay the measure by referring it to either the Committee on Public Lands or the Committee on Territories. Representative Henry L. Dawes of Massachusetts recommended immediate consideration and explained its purpose:

This bill follows the analogy of the bill passed by Congress six or eight years ago, setting apart the Yosemite valley . . . for the public park, with this difference: that bill granted to the State of California the jurisdiction over that land beyond the control of the United States. This bill reserves the control over the land and preserves the control over it to the United States. Nobody can dwell upon it for the purpose of agriculture . . . it will infringe upon no vested rights, the title to it will still remain in the United States. . . . This bill treads upon no rights of the settler . . . and it receives the urgent and ardent support of the Legislature of that Territory [Montana] and of the Delegate himself. . . .[38]

In part because of assurances that the land to be set aside was economically worthless, and the fact that the bill provided for the reservation of land already belonging to the government and contained no appropriation, no speech was made in the House in opposition to the Yellowstone bill. On the roll call, 115 representatives favored the bill, 65 opposed, and 60 failed to vote.[39] The bill was promptly signed by President Grant and became operative on March 1, 1872.

The editors of *Scribner's* assured their readers that the Yellowstone bill would call attention to the "unexampled richness" of Montana and Wyoming Territories, enticing both the artist and the pleasure tourist, "while it aims to ensure that the region in question shall be kept in the most favorable condition to attract travel and gratify a cultivated and intelligent curiosity. By the Act, some 2,500 square miles of territory . . . are set apart as a National Park (!) . . . Verily a colossal sort of junketing-place!"[40]

Thus, through the efforts of an energetic and zealous group of men, the long, though sometimes faint, tradition of conservation in the United States was finally recognized. The setting apart "as a public park or pleasuring-ground for the benefit and enjoyment of the people" of more than two million acres of land with a wealth of timber, game, grass, water power, and possible minerals was a dramatic departure from the general public land policy previously followed by Congress. This occurred during a period when public opinion was more materialistic than idealistic; when millions of acres were being reserved not for the public but for the railroads; when vast areas of timber in the old Northwest were being slashed and cut by greedy lumbermen, without thought of reforestation; when cattlemen were spreading their herds over the public domain and resisting any efforts toward conservation that might interfere with the development of power and riches; when the frontier military commanders claimed that the Indians could be brought to terms only when their main subsistence was destroyed, urged the slaughter of buffalo, and resisted through Congress any effort to protect and preserve them.

The new Yellowstone Park was fortunately situated somewhat to the west of most private activity, so when the bill came before Congress an attitude of indifference prevailed on the part of both Congressmen and the public. However, this historic Act did not mean that the public had suddenly become aware of its wasteful habits. It did not mean the end of exploitation of the country's resources; the ravages of uncontrolled enterprise continued unabated for at least two decades, and Congress wavered constantly on the advisability of even maintaining the nation's one park. On several occasions members of Congress, representing the views of their constituents, advocated selling the area to private parties as had been done with other public lands, and getting out of the "show business," since it was not the purpose of the government to "raise wild animals" nor was it the government's duty to establish a hunting reserve for the "wealthy and traveling foreign dignitaries."

III

The Early Years

in Yellowstone:

1872–1882

Hopes for the new park were high, but the Act which had brought it into being failed to provide for all contingencies. The major difficulties that beset the administration of the Yellowstone National Park during the first decade and a half of its existence can be traced to the ambiguities and omissions of that legislation.

The administrative structure provided for the nation's first park was a ramshackle affair. Congress vested exclusive control of the Park's administration in the Secretary of the Interior, who was enjoined to make and enforce all regulations necessary to prevent trespassing; to insure the preservation of the Park from injury or despoilment; to retain in their natural condition "all timber, mineral deposits, natural curiosities, or wonders" within the Park, and to guard against the "wanton destruction of the fish and game . . . and against their capture or destruction for the purposes of merchandise or profit."[1]

Unfortunately the Act provided no specific laws for the government of the region; it neither specified offenses nor provided punishment or legal machinery for the enforcement of such rules as might be promulgated by the Secretary of the Interior. No appropriation was made for administering the Park, for constructing roads, or for protecting the Park from vandalism. One result of this parsimony was that the first Superintendent was forced to serve without remuneration and, except for his infrequent visits, the Park was entirely without supervision.

Nathaniel P. Langford, member and chronicler of the 1870 exploring party, was appropriately appointed the first Superintendent of the new National Park. He was advised that no attempt should be made to "beautify or adorn" the reservation, but that he was at liberty to "apply any moneys which may be received from leases to carrying out the object of the Act of Congress."[2] No such moneys were forthcoming.

Langford spent several weeks in the Park and the adjacent country during the summer of 1872 as a member of the Stevenson division of the Hayden Geological Survey. In tendering a report of his activities, he urged that all hunting, fishing, and trapping within the Park, "except for purposes of recreation by visitors and tourists, or for use by actual residents" be prohibited "under severe penalties." He realized that no laws or regulations could be enforced without the aid of courts, and recommended that the Park be attached to Gallatin County, Montana Territory, for judicial purposes and that the laws of the Territory be made operative and enforced within Park boundaries.[3] Had this suggestion been followed, the early administration of the Park might well have been more successful. Unfortunately, it was ignored by officials in Washington.

The winter following his appointment as Superintendent, Langford traveled to Washington in a vain attempt to secure an appropriation from Congress to use in organizing the administration and instituting improvements within the Park. W. H. Clagett, delegate in Congress from Montana

Territory, listened to Langford's plea and recommended to the Secretary of the Interior that he request from Congress an appropriation of $15,000. Both Clagett and Langford thought that this amount, coupled with the expected revenue from leases, would be sufficient for some years to come, and Clagett pledged his full support in obtaining the requested funds.[4] Only a year before, while the bill establishing the Park was pending in Congress, Hayden, in order to overcome the argument that annual appropriations would be required for its care and improvement, had been "compelled to give a distinct pledge" that he would not "apply for an appropriation for several years at least."[5] Apparently Langford and Clagett were not so compelled.

In February, 1873, Acting Secretary of the Interior B. R. Cowen duly requested that Congress appropriate $15,000 to be used in constructing wagon roads within the Park, making the area more attractive to visitors and prospective lessees. Letters from both Clagett and Langford, explaining the necessity for such an appropriation, were appended to the request, but their pleas were ignored by Congress; no appropriation was made, and no government official resided in the Park during its first winter of existence.[6]

Since the position of Superintendent carried no salary, Langford devoted most of his activities and time to his position as National Bank Examiner for the Pacific States and Territories. In the spring of 1873, he appointed David E. Folsom to the nonpaying position of Assistant Superintendent. Folsom had been a member of the 1869 expedition and evidently revisited the Park several times during the summer following his appointment. Through reports received from Folsom, Langford learned that visitors to the Park had "broken off and carried away . . . many of the most beautiful formations." Writing to Secretary Delano, Langford suggested that leases be given to responsible persons to build roads and hotels. The leaseholders might then aid in protecting the various wonders from further vandalism, but the development of roads would first be necessary to lure such responsible persons to the Park. The absence of any law enforcement machinery was again mentioned and the first of many pleas for the appointment of a U. S. Commissioner and "one or two . . . Deputy U. S. Marshals with power to compel obedience to the Park regulations" was set forth.[7]

Folsom's reports of destruction within the Park were substantiated by letters from other sources. The culprits included rich sportsmen like the Earl of Dunraven, who visited the Park in 1874; hunters who came after meat to sell in neighboring towns; and tourists from the adjoining Territories. H. R. Horr, a resident within the Park, wrote that parties were ruthlessly slaughtering deer and elk, taking only the skin and tongues of the slain animals, and suggested that Jack Baronett, another settler within the Park, be authorized to "keep hunters from slaughtering the game," adding, "Besides myself he is the only one who will hibernate in this National Domain." Governor B. F. Potts of Montana Territory thought that "national pride should . . . induce Congress to make a liberal appropriation to employ a resident Superintendent of the Park and make such roads as are necessary and preserve from spoliation the numberless curiosities of that wonderful region." Governor Campbell of Wyoming Territory urged an appropriation for the survey of the boundaries of the Park.[8] An article appeared in the *Avant Courier* (Bozeman), September 26, 1873, claiming that there had been serious multilation of the various curiosities and, in a petition to the Secretary of the Interior, citizens of Montana Territory "residing near the line of the Yellowstone National Park" requested that a Committee of Congress be appointed to visit the Park in order to better appraise the need for an appropriation to protect the Park from destruction.[9]

Early in 1874 a rather bizarre plan for the survey and improvement of the Park was presented to the Secretary of the Interior by a European-trained landscape architect, Knut Forsberg. Forsberg recommended a project including several maps, two relief models of the Park, locations for a National Observatory, Forest Institute, a National Swimming School, Race Grounds, National Rowing Clubs, Botanical Gardens, Zoological Gardens, Geological Museums, Health "Cliniques," the Graffenberger Watercure Institution, and "thousands of grounds for erecting private villas"—the cost he estimated at $132,000. Hayden thought the plans "too elaborate for the needs of the present time," and James A. Garfield, Chairman of the House Committee on Appropriations and later President of the United States, reported that in the committee's opinion Mr. Forsberg's scheme was "wholly beyond the range of improvements that the Government ought to undertake," adding, however, that something should be done to preserve the park area and that, if any appropriation was necessary, a request for one should be presented soon.[10]

In response to this suggestion, Secretary Delano prepared and submitted the draft of a bill that would have extended the lease period from ten to twenty years, allowed toll roads to be constructed, and appropriated $100,000 for the construction of public roads, for a survey of boundaries, and "for such other purposes as may be deemed necessary." The proposed bill would also have provided a punishment by fine or imprisonment for any person found violating the rules or regulations of the Park. Court jurisdiction would be placed with any judge or commissioner of the federal courts of Montana or Wyoming Territory and authority to arrest violators was put in the hands of the U. S. Marshals of the two territories. Accompanying the proposed bill were letters showing the necessity of such action from Langford, Hayden, the Governors of Wyoming and Montana Territories, and a petition signed by seventy-two residents of the Montana Territory.[11]

Clagett's successor, Martin Maginnis, introduced Secretary Delano's bill into the House, and a like measure was presented to the Senate by Senator William Windom of Minnesota. The Senate Committee on Public Lands favorably reported a bill appropriating $25,000, but neither branch of Congress took further action.[12]

A tour of the Park in the summer of 1874 convinced Langford that preservation of the area could not be accomplished "without moneyed aid"; consequently, he once again implored the Secretary of the Interior to include in his annual estimate for the Department an appropriation to enable him to construct roads and survey the boundaries. This time he requested $100,000, and once again he gave reassurance that such an appropriation would suffice for several years. Langford's letter was forwarded by the Secretary to James G. Blaine, Speaker of the House, accompanied by a formal request for $100,000. Again, an appropriation of $25,000 was recommended by the Senate Committee on Public Lands, but once again, no appropriation was forthcoming.[13]

Thus far, no appropriation bill for the Yellowstone National Park had reached the floor of Congress. But in March, 1875, a vigorous effort was made on the floor of the House by Representative Mark H. Dunnell of Minnesota to obtain the much needed appropriation. Dunnell, who had rendered valuable service in the passage of the original Yellowstone bill by the House in 1872, now offered a sundry civil bill amendment which called for an appropriation of $25,000 for the construction of roads, the surveying of Park boundaries, and such other purposes as might be deemed necessary by the Secretary of the Interior. Dunnell's amendment was defeated, with Chairman Garfield opposing it as being "too early."[14]

On August 28, 1875, Superintendent Langford penned a last appeal for an appropriation for the Park and asked that such appropriation be made available for immediate use in order to preserve the Park from further vandalism. Delegate Maginnis "heartily approved" the request and added that he had learned from members of the Secretary of War Belknap's party who had recently toured the Park that "the spoliations in the Park" were great and that in his opinion, "the Government should take some action to preserve these wonderful and beautiful curiosities before it is too late."[15] But once again Congress failed to heed the request.

Attempting to supervise a large tract of wilderness with no funds at his disposal for protection or improvement, and no code of laws by which he could regulate the conduct of visitors to the Park, Langford found his position as Superintendent largely nominal. The act establishing the Park clearly defined the purposes for which it was created: withdrawal of the land from the public domain to prevent private occupancy and its reservation "for the benefit and enjoyment of the people," preservation of the natural curiosities, forests, and game found within its borders, and the allowance of leases and privileges to provide for the comfort and convenience of visitors. No legal machinery was provided, no legal code was drawn, no offenses were defined, and no punishments were decreed. However, the Secretary of the Interior was authorized to "take all such measures as shall be necessary or proper to fully carry out the objects and purposes" of the act. With this provision in mind, Langford forwarded to the Secretary what he considered to be a comprehensive set of rules and regulations, designed to prohibit all hunting, fishing, or trapping within the Park; the cutting of timber without the permission of the Superintendent; the mutilation of formations or the collection of specimens without the permission of the Superintendent; it also stipulated that all persons residing within the Park were to vacate their holdings upon an order to that effect by the Superintendent. No fires were to be kindled except when necessary and these were to be fully extinguished. Any violation of these rules was to be punished with "severe penalties."[16] The "severe penalties" were not enumerated because there were none.

Langford realized that he was powerless to prevent violations of the new rules and regulations, and he knew also that no leases, and hence no money, would be forthcoming until the Park was made more attractive to prospective lessees. This could be done only with the aid of appropriations from Congress. Since he served without pay, he never suggested the use of paid police or assistants to enforce the rules. Instead, he thought that once the places of interest were leased to responsible parties, it would be to their benefit and profit to stop the vandalism themselves. But responsible parties seeking leases did not appear. Not until roads were constructed and hotel facilities completed would travelers venture into the "Wonderland." Left thus without the necessary appropriations and with no means of enforcing the few prohibitory rules and regulations, the Park's first Superintendent moved to St. Paul, Minnesota, and devoted his attention to his duties as bank examiner for the Pacific States and Territories. He made no annual report to the Secretary of the Interior after 1872, and his last official letter to the Department was written in 1875. Langford's greatest contribution to the National Park System is not to be found in those five years he was the chief administrator of the Yellowstone, but rather in the few years preceding the establishment of the Park. He was one of the organizers of the expedition that discovered the wonders of the area in 1870, and it was he who, through a series of magazine articles and lectures, made them known to the world. He is entitled to great credit for his efforts in the creation and preservation of the Park. If his administration seemed inept and inefficient, the blame rests not upon him, but upon Congress.

Langford's prohibitory rules did not prevent or reduce the acts of destruction then under way within the Park. General W. E. Strong, traveling with Secretary of War Belknap in 1875, noted the disappearance of elk, deer, and mountain sheep from within the Park, and stated that "During the last five years the game has been slaughtered by the thousands of hunters who killed them for their hides alone"—an elk skin bringing about six dollars on the market at that time. After observing that "over four thousand [elk] were killed last winter by professional hunters in the Mammoth Springs basin alone, their carcasses and branching antlers can be seen on every hillside and in every valley," Strong thought it an outrage and "a crying shame that this indiscriminate slaughter . . . should be permitted." Recalling the fact that the laws of the Park authorized the Secretary of the Interior to protect the "game against wanton destruction," the indignant General joined the growing list of critics who were blaming the hapless Langford for the conditions in the Park by adding, "Even those who were so active in the creation of the Park seem to have forgotten their child."[17] The report of another military figure visiting the Park at this time gave credence to the General's remarks. Captain William Ludlow wrote:

> Hunters have for years devoted themselves to the slaughter of game, until within the limits of the park it is hardly to be found. I was credibly informed . . . that during the winter of 1874 and 1875 . . . no less than from 1,500 to 2,000 of these [elk] were destroyed within a radius of 15 miles of Mammoth Springs . . . the skins only were taken . . . a continuance of this wholesale and wasteful butchery can have but one effect, viz, the extermination of the animal.[18]

The attractions of the Park were being decimated by more than skin hunters, however. Members of the Ludlow party witnessed the destructive propensities of visitors who, despite the absence of facilities, had come (mostly on horseback with pack animals) to view the marvels of the region. In his journal entry of August 23, 1875, Captain Ludlow described the wonders of an unnamed geyser and stated:

> The only blemish on this artistic handiwork had been occasioned by the rude hand of man. The ornamental work about the crater and the pools had been broken and defaced in the most prominent places by visitors, and the pebbles were inscribed in pencil with the names of great numbers of the most unimportant persons. . . . The visitors prowled about with

shovel and ax, chopping and hacking and prying up great pieces of the most ornamental work they could find; women and men alike joining in the barbarous pastime.

At another geyser formation, the party came upon "two women, with tucked-up skirts and rubber shoes, armed, one with an ax, the other with a spade, who were climbing about." Upon returning to their camp, they were "just in time to prevent the fall of an uplifted ax, which a woman was evidently about to bring straight down on the summit" of another geyser cone. Ludlow noted that there was no one present in the geyser basins "with authority to stop the devastation."

Not satisfied with merely describing the wholesale destruction of game and vandalism to the geysers, Captain Ludlow set forth some suggestions for the management and administration of the Park. He urged that Congress appropriate funds to survey the boundary of the Park and to construct roads and bridges. Visitors to the Park area should be strictly forbidden to kill any game and any hunters apprehended "should have their arms and spoils confiscated," besides being liable to prosecution. More important was his suggestion that the Yellowstone National Park be turned over to the United States Army for needed protection. He believed that:

> The cure for . . . unlawful practices and undoubted evils can only be found in a thorough mounted police of the park. In the absence of any legislative provision for this, recourse can most readily be had to the already-existing facilities afforded by the presence of troops in the vicinity and by the transfer of the park to the control of the War Department. Troops should be stationed to act as guards at the lake, the Mammoth Springs, and especially in the Geyser Basin.

This recommendation came six years before General W. T. Sherman made a similar suggestion, eight years before its Congressional recognition, and eleven years before it became a fact. Looking to the future, Captain Ludlow prophetically added, "the day will come, and it cannot be far distant, when this most interesting region . . . will be rendered accessible to all; and then, thronged with visitors from all over the world, it will be what nature and Congress, for once working together in unison, have declared it should be, a national park."[19]

Ludlow's suggestion for military control of the Park was seconded by Secretary of the War Belknap, who stated in his report that "it is the wish and desire of this Department to unite with the Secretary of the Interior," in order to open and survey the region, and "if authority were given to the War Department . . . to station one or two companies of troops in or near the park for the purpose of preventing spoliation . . . the result would be satisfactory."[20] The military plea for control was not immediately acknowledged; an inept civilian administration was to continue eleven more years before cavalry troops were assigned to the Yellowstone.

President Rutherford B. Hayes took office in March, 1877, and immediately appointed Carl Schurz to replace Columbus Delano as Secretary of the Interior. Schurz became a close friend of the new National Park; he visited the area in 1880, and gave full support to every measure put forth on its behalf. During his administration, and in part because of his support, the first appropriation was made for the Park by Congress. The new Secretary of the Interior notified Langford on April 18, 1877, that the order appointing him as Superintendent was revoked and that the Department "avails itself of the gratuitous services of a gentleman . . . who visits the park in the interests of science" and who was to be the new Superintendent.[21] This man with the scientific bent was Philetus W. Norris.

Norris had applied for the appointment as Superintendent in a letter accompanied by recommendations written by Governor C. M. Croswell of Michigan; Morrison R. Waite,

Chief Justice of the Supreme Court; and Governor William Dennison of Ohio. In this letter Norris declared that in a recent exploration of the park area he had found "no Superintendent or other agent of the Government" present to prevent destruction of game and vandalism to the geysers. He was appointed to the post April 18, 1877, his pay subject to future appropriations that might be made by Congress.[22]

Born at Palmyra, New York, August 17, 1821, Norris was a guide at Portage Falls on the Genesee River when he was eight years old. At the age of seventeen he was employed by the Hudson's Bay Company in Manitoba, and at twenty-one he founded the town of Pioneer in northwestern Ohio. His service with the Union troops during the Civil War was broken by a term served in the Ohio legislature, and after the war he established the town of Norris, now within the limits of Detroit. Here he edited and published a newspaper called the *Norris Suburban*. In 1870 he made a trip overland to the Pacific Ocean, and in 1875 he visited Yellowstone Park. Endowed with more than average curiosity, perseverance, and enthusiasm, Norris was later criticized for being a visionary. His later writings in both prose and verse exemplify not the doer, but the dreamer; and yet his real accomplishments were many. Although he was unable to do all that he hoped for in Yellowstone, his contribution can still be considered substantial.

In his first act as Superintendent, Norris appointed J. C. McCartney, a resident of the Park, to the new position of Assistant Superintendent. Norris advised his new assistant not only to guard the Park against vandalism, but to enjoin others to do the same; he also informed him that he would arrive in the Park sometime in June "if not too much annoyed by Indians" on his way out. McCartney was also made to understand that, since there was no money with which to pay him, his services would necessarily be unpaid and "mainly in the interest of science."[23]

An issue of the *Norris Suburban* carried on its editorial page an announcement of Norris' appointment, a copy of the existing Rules and Regulations for Yellowstone Park, and a reminder from the editor to all of his "old mountain comrades and friends" to aid him in stopping the acts of vandalism then being perpetrated within the Park.[24]

When Norris arrived in the Park that summer, he had printed on cloth and posted in surrounding towns five hundred copies of a notice specifying acts which were in violation of Park rules. "Law, public sentiment, . . . and the good fame of Montana alike" he added, "forbid violation of this notice." There was, however, no effective law and very little public sentiment.[25]

Norris' first summer in the Park was given over to exploration of those areas not yet visited by Department officials. Returning to his home in Michigan in September, he stated that he felt no "salaried obligation" to remain longer in the Park since he was being constantly informed of matters there by his assistant. His annual report urged an appropriation to cover the cost of boundary survey, salaries, and road construction.[26]

This again raised the question of money for the Park, and support for the needed appropriations now came from a new quarter. At the twenty-sixth Annual Meeting of the American Association for the Advancement of Science, a resolution was adopted asking Congress to direct its attention to the destruction that had taken place within the Park. A committee of five prominent members was appointed to memorialize Congress and was authorized to use all legitimate means at their disposal to obtain appropriations for protection of the Park.[27] Some 181 residents of Bozeman, Montana Territory, had also signed a petition requesting that the Secretary of the Interior recommend to Congress an appropriation sufficient to cover the needed protection and improvement within the Park.[28]

Secretary Schurz sent to Congress on March 6, 1878, a

request for an appropriation of $15,000, which he declared necessary to enable his Department to carry out the intention and provisions of the enabling act of 1872. He called attention to the fact that no appropriation of any kind had been legislated and appended to his letter those of Norris and Hayden, along with the resolution passed by the American Association for the Advancement of Science and the Montana petition.[29] In response to the Secretary's request, Representative Alpheus Williams of Michigan introduced a bill to appropriate moneys for the protection and improvement of the Park, but the Committee on Appropriations failed to take any action. When the sundry civil bill was reported without an appropriation for Yellowstone National Park, Representative Williams proposed on June 13, 1878, an amendment to appropriate $10,000 to "protect, preserve, and improve" the Park. This amendment was enacted into law, and thus became the first Congressional appropriation for national park purposes.[30]

Six days after the appropriation became effective, Norris was reappointed Superintendent with compensation at the rate of $1,500 per annum, effective July 1, 1878.[31] On July 17 he employed Benjamin P. Bush as his assistant at a salary of $50 per month. Spending the latter part of the summer in the Park, Norris organized construction of wagon roads and bridges, and continued his explorations into various parts of the Park. He recommended the construction of a plain but comfortable building for use by the Superintendent and earnestly urged the Secretary to make leases to responsible parties, who, he assumed, would then become agents of the government and aid in the protection of the curiosities and animals of the Park. An appropriation of $25,000 was requested so that he might complete roads and bridle paths "necessary to effect leases of Hotel, Ranch and Yacht sites."[32]

Roving bands of Bannock Indians sighted on the western boundary of the Park prompted Norris to advocate the establishment of "a small military post" within the Park, but there is no evidence that he desired more from the military than protection from the Indians.[33] Hayden, however, had earlier suggested the establishment of a military post, and he, like Captain Ludlow before him, recommended the use of the military not so much for protection from any Indian menace as for prevention of vandalism and skin hunters. Hayden realized that the size and isolated position of the Park combined to prevent any civilian supervision over visitors, and thought that until the Park became more accessible by the construction of roads and the western extension of the Northern Pacific Railroad, it would "require the establishment of a military Post within its boundaries . . . garrisoned by one or more companies of soldiers who could be sent out over various portions of the Park from time to time on police duty."[34] The lawmakers of the country paid no heed to the statement by either Norris or Hayden.

Upon returning to the Park in June, 1879, Norris confirmed his predecessor's feeling that the title of Superintendent carried with it no authoritative power. His former assistant, J. C. McCartney, had erected a cabin and outbuildings within the Park, where he engaged in the liquor trade. His presence there was in violation of rule number five, which provided that no person was to reside permanently within the Park without express permission of the Secretary of the Interior. When ordered to vacate the premises by the Superintendent, McCartney declined to do so. The Secretary advised Norris to first offer McCartney a one-year lease and, if this was refused, to utilize the "aid of the Military" in forcibly ejecting him. The lease was offered and refused. Fearing reprisals from either McCartney or his friends, who included Professor Hayden, Martin Maginnis, Congressional Delegate from Montana Territory, and "the most drunken and debased portion of the Mountaineers," as well as many of the soldiers stationed at Fort Ellis, Norris hesitated to call for help from the Army. Instead, he suggested that if "there be no general law or rule prohibiting sale of stimulants upon all national reservations that the Hon. Secretary of the Interior add it to the rules for my special guidance." Thus armed, he hoped to persuade McCartney to sell his holdings to Congress since, if forbidden to sell liquor, McCartney would have no reason for staying. Subsequently, Rule Number Six was added, which read: "The sale of intoxicating liquors is strictly prohibited." McCartney later made a settlement with the government and his buildings were destroyed.[35]

An appropriation of $10,000 for the improvement and protection of the Park was included in the sundry civil bill for the fiscal year 1880,[36] and with this Norris continued his road building and trail cutting. He also constructed at Mammoth Hot Springs a blockhouse complete with loopholes and a turret. The Superintendent was still wary of Indians, but he found, much to his chagrin, that it was not the Indian who troubled him but the occasional tourist who destroyed the signboards which he had placed around the various geysers and other points of interest.[37]

The presence of the Superintendent in the Park may have checked the vandalism, but it did not stop it. Visitors reported that many of the small natural reservoirs along the terraces of the Old Faithful geyser had been converted into "stationary card baskets" by previous visitors who wrote their names on the mineral deposits; subsequent deposits formed a "transparent glaze over the lines" that served to "preserve them forever." One group of tourists even enlisted the aid of Superintendent Norris in "making a fine collection of specimens," and in selecting their camping places while the men of the party hunted; his assistance, however, did not serve to stay their criticism of his work. They claimed that there were no adjectives "in our language that can properly define the public highway that was cut through heavy timber . . . with the stumps left from two to twenty inches above the ground," which made it impossible to get their wagon over the stumpy road; they also found it pretty hard to see "what had been done with the Government funds." In addition, they found Norris's trails very difficult to follow and claimed to have often lost their way. Theirs was evidently not the only party that found the roads in the Park less than satisfying, for one group preceding them had penned their critical (but incorrect) thoughts upon a sign bordering the stumpy path, "Government appropriations for public improvements in the park in 1872, $35,000. Surplus on hand October 1, 1880, $34,500." A longtime resident of the Park, writing of Norris and his roads, maintained that only the best wagons could navigate over the stumps.[38]

Game was still being slaughtered in the Park, and even Superintendent Norris, taking advantage of the elk and deer that had been driven into sheltered glens, was able to secure an "abundant winter's supply of fresh meat," in addition to the hides of bear, wolf, and wolverine. He thought hunting in the Park was "excellent sport," though he found it rather severe and dangerous. This did not exactly jibe with the ideas of Secretary Schurz, who had recommended in April that a portion of the Park be reserved solely for the protection and preservation of game animals, for if such protection was not afforded, the bison, elk, moose, deer, and mountain sheep would soon be exterminated.[39] A different conservation plan was set forth by one who was more familiar with the Park than was the Secretary of the Interior: Harry Yount, "Gamekeeper of the Yellowstone National Park," twice urged, for the purpose of game protection, "the appointment of a small active, reliable police force," members of which would receive regular pay allocated from the Congressional appropriation for the Park. He thought that such a force could, "in addition to the protection of game, assist the superintendent of the Park in enforcing the laws, rules and regulations for protection of guide-boards and bridges, and the preservation of the countless . . . geyser cones."[40] Congress failed to take cognizance of either suggestion.

While protection of the Park lagged, some progress was made toward improvements within it. In his annual report to the Secretary of the Interior for the year 1881, Norris reported that he had completed some 153 miles of roads, 213 miles of bridle paths, and cut eight miles of trails through heavy forests within the Park.[41] His efforts were both praised and ridiculed by military officers who had had the opportunity to use his roads. Lieutenant Colonel James F. Gregory, aide-de-camp to General Sheridan, noted in his journal entry of August 26, 1881, that "Mr. Norris . . . is doing a good work in making wagon roads to the principal points of interest and trails to the less important ones,"[42] but Lieutenant G. C. Doane, 2nd Cavalry, then stationed at Fort Ellis, dismissed the improvements made by Norris as "ridiculous." Both men were unhappy with the lack of protection afforded the game and curiosities. Doane maintained that the "protection has been one of spoliation—and the preservation of game has been by running it with hounds, and otherwise destroying it." He thought that military protection would be the ultimate and only sure resort, and to this end the Park "should be guarded by a detachment of Cavalry."[43] While not necessarily recommending a change of administration, Gregory speculated that some means should be devised to prevent the vandalism and "restrain his or her, especially *her,* propensities to hammer and chip off rocks, to break down and destroy every growing thing, and to fill up with trees, sticks, &c., the wonderful craters." He reported seeing persons armed with hatchets "hammering and cracking the beautiful tracery around the geysers," apparently merely for the pleasure of destruction, for the broken fragments were left lying where they fell.[44]

Norris realized that all was not as it should be, and sought to strengthen his position by amending the existing regulations in an attempt to make them enforceable. The following set of rules was forwarded to Secretary of the Interior S. J. Kirkwood, approved by him on May 4, 1881, and continued in force for the duration of the early civilian administration:

1. Cutting of timber within the Park was strictly forbidden, also removal of mineral deposits or natural curiosities without the Superintendent's permission.

2. Fires should be kindled only when actually necessary, and immediately extinguished when no longer required.

3. Hunting, trapping, and fishing, except to procure food for visitors or actual residents, were prohibited.

4. No person would be permitted to reside permanently within the Park without permission from the Department of the Interior.

5. *The sale of intoxicating liquors was prohibited.*

6. Trespassers or violators of any of the foregoing rules would be summarily removed from the Park by the Superintendent and his employees, who were authorized to seize "prohibited articles" in case of resistance to their authority or repetition of any offence.[45]

The frontiersman and tourist found it impossible to draw a line between killing of game for food and for sport. Norris realized that his means of enforcement were negligible and requested that "Additional provisions by Congress, by the council of Wyoming Territory, or by both of them" be made to establish legal machinery for his use. He thought, also, that the "proposed organization of a county of Wyoming, with a seat of justice near enough to insure legal cooperation and assistance in the management of the park" should be given Departmental support, since he found "it neither desirable nor in accordance with the spirit of our institutions . . . to continue the control of so vast a region . . . by mere moral suasion, occasionally sustained by more potent appeals from the muzzles of Winchester rifles."[46]

Members of Congress, while failing to act upon suggestions for the establishment of legal machinery in the Park, did give ear to the critics of Norris, and consequently of the Department of the Interior's management, or nonmanagement, of Park affairs. On January 30, 1882, Samuel S. Cox, Representative from New York, introduced H. R. 3751, which provided that from June 20, 1882, the Yellowstone National Park would be "under the exclusive care, control and government of the War Department" and, with the exception of the winter months, "a military encampment, to consist of at least one company of cavalry and one company of infantry" would be stationed in the Park. The bill provided punishment for violation of the rules in the form of a fine or imprisonment, and placed the legal jurisdiction of the Park in the District Courts of Montana Territory. The bill also granted a right of way to any "existing Railroad Company duly chartered" to build within the Park, suggesting that persons interested in more than preservation of the Park might have been behind the measure.[47]

National Park Service

Soldiers on rifle range, about 1900

In reply to a request from the Chairman of the Committee on Public Lands for his views on the proposed bill, Interior Secretary S. J. Kirkwood stated that he did not believe the War Department could accomplish more, "with the same expenditure of funds, toward carrying out the objects for which the Park was set aside than could be accomplished by the Department of the Interior."[48] The bill was not reported out of committee. The proposed bill raised no stir outside of Congress, and very little within. But four years later military government came to the Park. Twelve years of debate intervened before the establishment of federal law for the Park; and the attempt to franchise a railroad within the Park was not defeated until after fifteen years of strenuous and eventually successful opposition.

In an effort to circumvent the charges against his department and the Park, Secretary Kirkwood relieved Norris of his position as Superintendent and appointed in his stead Patrick H. Conger. The results of this change were to be quite contrary to those desired by the Secretary, however. Norris continued in government service, exploring the remains of old Indian villages and burial grounds and collecting specimens and artifacts for the National Museum. He made his last visit to the Park in 1883 and two years later died at Rocky Hill, Kentucky. He had failed, as had Langford, to stop the depredations and slaughter of game within the Park, but he had succeeded in obtaining what were to be annual appropriations; he had constructed roads, bridges, and buildings, explored vast areas, studied the history, and examined the antiquities of the Park. He left his name on a peak, a pass, and a geyser basin within the Park, and a year after his dismissal, he appended to a book of his poems what was to become a model for all later guidebooks of the Park.[49] His administration stands out in admirable contrast to the three Superintendents who were to follow.

IV

The Early Years

in Yellowstone:

1882–1886

ON APRIL 1, 1882, ten years and one month after the passage of the Act creating the Park, Patrick H. Conger replaced Norris as Superintendent.[1] Conger had been a Deputy United States Marshal in Dubuque, Iowa, but his appointment as Superintendent of the Yellowstone was due more to the fact that he was an Iowa Republican. Secretary of the Interior S. J. Kirkwood was a Republican; he was also from Iowa. Conger was faced by a problem unknown to the two Superintendents who preceded him, a problem that frustrated his attempts to enforce the few regulatory rules: monopoly power in the Park. His administration was a stormy one, fraught with charges of incompetence and maladministration. Unfortunately, some historians have given too much credence to the reports of his enemies and paid too little attention either to his refutation of the many malicious charges made against him or to the political atmosphere in which such charges were made.

In the fall of 1882 the Northern Pacific Railroad had laid track as far west as Livingston, Montana Territory, and a branch line south to the Park was anticipated. Since this transportation promised an increase in the number of tourists, concessions within the Park became more attractive. Henry M. Teller of Colorado had been appointed Secretary of the Interior by President Arthur, and under his auspices, in 1882, a tentative agreement was reached granting exclusive privileges on 4,400 acres of Park land to Carroll T. Hobart of Fargo, Henry F. Douglas of Fort Yates, Dakota Territory, and Rufus Hatch, a New York stockbroker.[2] The new Superintendent established a basis for the later enmity between him and the expectant lessees when, asked by the Secretary for his opinion on the advisability of granting the proposed lease, he replied with some foresight that he thought the lease covered entirely too much ground, it would in the future be worth "a very large sum of money" because of increased tourism, and the public would be "restive" if all the proposed privileges were granted to a single party or corporation.[3]

The proposed lease would have given a ten-year monopoly for the erection of hotels, the operation of a stage line, and the construction of telegraph lines within the Park. The lease would be granted to a newly formed corporation, the Yellowstone National Park Improvement Company, which would pay an annual rental of two dollars per acre.

The Act establishing the Park had authorized the Secretary of the Interior to grant ten-year leases "of small parcels of ground" for the erection of hotels. When the Hobart-Hatch lease was proposed by Secretary Teller in 1882, some members of the Senate thought that 4,400 acres failed to qualify as a small parcel of land and directed the Secretary to transmit to the Senate available information pertaining to leases in the Park. In doing so Teller deliberately ignored Conger's written opposition and defended the proposed lease, claiming that since "no means to protect the curiosities within the park from injury" had been stipulated in the organic Act, such leases were proper and necessary to provide

the needed protection "with the least possible expense to the government." Prompted by Conger's adverse opinion, Senator George C. Vest of Missouri, in a report from the Committee on Territories, maintained that the entire business was contrary to the Act establishing the Park. The proposed monopolistic lease was therefore defeated, but the antagonism between Conger and C. T. Hobart increased with later developments.[4]

Lieutenant-General P. H. Sheridan toured the Park in the summer of 1882 and in his annual report to the War Department he attacked the Hobart-Hatch contract, regretting "exceedingly to learn that the National Park had been rented out to private parties," and advised the extension of the boundaries of the Park. He made another suggestion that materialized four years later. Noting that large numbers of deer, elk, moose, and mountain sheep had been slaughtered in the Park, he stated: "If authorized to do so, I will engage to keep out skin hunters and all other hunters, by use of troops from Forts Washakie on the south, Custer on the east, and Ellis on the north, and, if necessary, I can keep sufficient troops in the Park to accomplish this object."[5] His remarks were seconded by the Governor of Montana Territory, John Schuyler Crosby, who further suggested the appointment of an "engineer officer of the Army" as general superintendent of the Park with means to lay out roads and make improvements; this officer should be vested with authority to "call upon the military stationed in the neighborhood" for aid in enforcing such laws as might be passed for protection of the Park.[6] The Inspector General of the Army, Brigadier General D. B. Sacket, thought that a single troop of cavalry assigned to duty in the Park during the summer months would afford all the protection needed against fire and vandalism, and the assignment of such a unit could be accomplished with little expense to the War Department and none to the Department of the Interior.[7]

In response to Sheridan's plea that some action be taken

toward protecting the Park, and fearing that the area might be transferred from civil control if some remedial action were not soon taken, Senator George C. Vest[8] undertook the leadership of the movement in Congress for national park development and protection. He secured the adoption of a resolution by the Senate on December 12, 1882, calling upon the Committee on Territories to review possible legislation needed to afford protection to the Park. On January 5, 1883, as Chairman of this committee, he reported a bill (S. 2317) to amend the original Park Act of 1872. Noting that the annual appropriation for the Park was too small to furnish the Superintendent with a sufficient number of men to adequately protect the Park, Vest proposed the "employment of one or two companies of cavalry," as suggested by General Sheridan, to "exclude the mercenary wretches" who were then reportedly killing the game within the Park. The bill as submitted extended the area of the Park, placed it within the criminal jurisdiction of the Montana Territorial courts for offenses against life or property, and created within the Park a police jurisdiction for the arrest, examination, and punishment of violators of regulations made by the Secretary of the Interior. A similar bill was introduced in the House, but no action was taken on either.[9]

Unable to obtain the desired Congressional action, Vest informed the Secretary of the Interior that he had reason to believe that timber was being illegally cut and that game was being killed to fulfill contract obligations. He demanded that such actions be immediately stopped.[10] Teller at once notified Conger that the regulations heretofore in force regarding the Park were amended so as to "prohibit absolutely the killing, wounding, or capturing at any time" of game animals within the Park; fishing was henceforth to be done by hook and line only. No longer was it legal to hunt or trap within the Park "for purposes of procuring food for visitors or actual residents."[11] The Secretary's statement and the revised rule were published in the Bozeman *Avant Courier,*

February 22, 1883, by G. L. Henderson, who was then acting as Assistant Superintendent of the Park during Conger's absence, and Senator Vest was immediately informed of the Secretary's actions.[12]

Remedial action against vandals was sought from another quarter when the United States Attorney for Wyoming Territory wrote to the Attorney General suggesting that a Grand Jury, soon to be impaneled in the Territory, be authorized to investigate the acts of vandalism "said to be common" in the Park. At the same time the Governor of Wyoming Territory implored the Secretary of the Interior to make some provision whereby the Judge of the Third Judicial District of Wyoming Territory would be allowed to hold court "within or near the Park in Uinta County" since the usual sessions of the Court were so far removed from the scene of violation that "by the time the officers get there the parties and witnesses have left the country."[13] No action was taken on either of these requests.

Realizing that he could hardly make an investigative body out of the Senate Committee on Territories, Vest presented a resolution of February 17, 1883, for the appointment of a special committee of five Senators who would:

. . . examine and report to the Senate . . . what is the present condition of the Yellowstone National Park and what action has been taken by the Department of the Interior in regard to the management of said Park. . . . Also what legislation . . . is necessary to protect the timber, game or objects of curiosity . . . and to establish a system of police and to secure the proper administration of justice therein. . . .

He further requested that the Secretary of the Interior "take immediate action for the protection" of the Park, and to that end "he is requested to call upon the proper military authorities for such force as may be necessary to accomplish such purposes." The Senator maintained that Park Superintendent Conger was not to blame for the deplorable conditions in the Park; the trouble was that neither sufficient money nor men were available to rectify the situation.[14] The resolution was debated, but no further action was taken.[15]

Though Senator Vest failed to form an investigative committee, he had directed Congressional attention toward the West and the Yellowstone Park. When the House Committee on Appropriations reported the sundry civil bill, with the usual $15,000 appropriation for the Park, the bill included a new clause which would prevent the Secretary of the Interior from allowing any "exclusive privileges or monopoly" to any person or corporation. Congressman Anson C. McCook of New York offered an amendment to prohibit the Secretary from making *any* leases within the Park, voided leases already made, and directed the Secretary of War "to make necessary details of troops to prevent trespassers or intruders entering the park with the objects of destroying the game therein or for any other purpose prohibited by law." McCook called attention to Sheridan's proposals of the previous November and observed that, while men engaged in the "indiscriminate slaughter of game" paid but scant attention to civil authorities, "they have a profound respect for the power of the General Government as represented by the officers and men of the Army." Congressman John A. Reagan of Texas stated, in support of McCook's amendment, that whenever leases were let for "hotels, for gardens, or for grazing lands," jobbery was sure to occur.[16]

When discussion of the McCook amendment resumed, Congressman James H. Blount of Georgia rose in support and stated that he did not believe McCook meant the Park to remain permanently under the control of the War Department; it was his understanding that the measure was but a temporary expedient. The only way Blount could see to prevent the establishment of a monopoly and stop the depredations was to put the Park "in the hands of the War Department." Congressman Frank Hiscock from New York, the only member of the House to oppose the amendment, withdrew his objection and the McCook amendment was accepted.[17]

The amended sundry civil bill came before the Senate on March 1, 1883, and the Yellowstone Park appropriation was increased from $15,000 to $40,000. Senator Vest proposed another amendment providing that $2,000 of the appropriation would be paid annually to a Superintendent and $900 to be paid to each of ten Assistant Superintendents, "all of whom shall be appointed by the Secretary of the Interior, and reside continuously in the park." The Vest amendment, after brief debate, was accepted. After the payment of the stipulated salaries, the remainder of the $40,000 appropriation was to be expended on the construction of roads and bridges under the supervision of an Army engineer appointed by the Secretary of War. The McCook amendment was stricken and a paragraph was inserted in its place authorizing the Secretary of the Interior to lease small plots of ground "not exceeding ten acres in extent" for a period not exceeding ten years. Such leases were not to be granted within one-quarter of a mile of any of the geysers or of the Yellowstone Falls, and all previous leases were declared invalid.

The lease provisions of the amended bill brought forth sharp criticism. Senator Preston B. Plumb of Kansas thought the visitors to the Park should be made to "rough it" and wanted to abolish that part of the bill providing for hotel leases. In the opinion of Senator John J. Ingalls, also of Kansas, the Park was getting to be "a good deal of an incubus"; he thought it would be best for all concerned if the government were to survey and sell the entire area. The Senator deplored the fact that moneys had already been spent laying out "roads that nobody uses," and could not understand why the government had entered "into the show business" in the first place. While these two Senators were in a minority at that time, their type of protest might later have grown into majority opinion except for the provident inclusion of another amendment.

This addition, indeed was to save not only the Yellowstone National Park but the whole future national park system of the United States. This amendment provided that:

> The Secretary of War, upon the request of the Secretary of the Interior, is hereby authorized and directed to make the necessary details of troops to prevent trespassers or intruders from entering the park for the purpose of destroying the game or objects of curiosity therein, or for any other purpose prohibited by law, and to remove such persons from the park if found therein.

The bill, thus amended, passed the Senate and was agreed to by the House.[18]

Congress had plainly set forth its intention in regard to leases by inserting the statement, "nor shall there be leased more than ten acres to any one person or corporation" into the bill. Nevertheless, only six days after its passage, Secretary Teller intentionally evaded the meaning of the law while staying within its literal bounds. On March 9, 1883, a lease totaling ten acres was granted to the Yellowstone National Park Improvement Company, the same organization that had failed three months earlier in its attempt to lease 4,400 acres of Park land. The land granted by the new lease was divided into seven parcels, of a little more than one acre in size, each located at or near one of the seven major points of interest in the Park. Since all of the choice hotel locations were now in the control of the Improvement Company, it was evident that the Company was safely entrenched as a monopoly in the Park. Secretary Teller admitted as much when he stated that it was for the best interest of the government, the Park, and the public, that the number of persons permitted "to engage in the business enterprises in the Park" be held at an absolute minimum.[19] Firmly established in the Park, the Improvement Company constructed a large hotel at Mammoth Hot Springs and rumors and charges concerning the inefficiency of the Superintendent commenced.

The ten Assistant Superintendents provided for in the appropriation bill could be hired at the beginning of the new fiscal year, but in the meantime Superintendent Conger reported that owing to the vigilance of his present assistant and his gamekeeper, "the killing of game in the Park is partially stoped [*sic*]," and discounted various reports of the slaughter of game as having been "immensely exaggerated."[20] A few weeks later, however, no less a personage than Buffalo Bill Cody, in a letter to the *New York Sun,* pleaded for the protection of the game found within the Park, adding that the indiscriminate killing of game "does not find favor in the West as it did a decade or so ago."[21]

By the end of June, 1883, ten Assistant Superintendents had been appointed by the Secretary of the Interior at the designated salary of $900 per annum; they paid for their transportation to the Park and their subsistence while on duty there. These men were, for the most part, totally unsuited to the rigorous service demanded of them, having obtained their positions through political influence. Born and brought up in the East, they had little understanding of the duties they were supposed to perform. The few who attempted to enforce the regulations and to protect the Park from vandals found their efforts "laughed at" by the trespassers, for the only penalty for violating the regulations was confiscation of the violator's "outfit," which at times was limited to his wearing apparel.[22]

Superintendent Conger had requested that the Secretary of the Interior furnish him and his assistants with a quantity of circulars containing the laws, orders, and regulations governing the Park; he planned to distribute them to tourists, so that none could "plead ignorance as an excuse for a violation of the Law."[23] Unfortunately, more than a knowledge of the Park regulations was necessary to end the destructive vandalism, for one visitor blandly told of killing ducks, badgers, birds of all descriptions, and indeed, shooting at everything that came into his sight, before casually adding, "it is against the law to shoot anything but bears in the Park." Not satisfied with violating the game regulations, the same visitor related that, when visiting Old Faithful Geyser, his party "threw a tomato can" into the famous geyser just before its eruption, left their "names with date in several places" on the geyser formations, and inscribed "Detroit Safe Co." at another place.[24]

The Superintendent's problems were not confined to apprehending tourists, however. The already unfriendly relationship between the officers of the Improvement Company and Conger were further exacerbated when Conger, contending that any person had the right to transport passengers in the Park, found himself in opposition to the company's claim that it alone held the franchise for the transportation of its hotel visitors. C. T. Hobart, General Manager of the Improvement Company, retaliated by complaining to Secretary Teller that the roads in the Park were in a sad state of disrepair, that professional hunters were plying their trade with impunity throughout the Park, and that meat illegally obtained by such men was stored in the cabins of Assistant Superintendents who had been hired to prevent such depredations. Conger retorted that these and other allegations impugning his character and efficiency were false and without foundation, but admitted that his new assistants were hampered in the performance of their duties by the lack of legislation and moneys with which to equip and house them.[25]

In an attempt to learn what was actually going on in the Park, M. L. Joslyn, Acting Secretary of the Interior, instructed W. Scott Smith, special agent of the General Land Office, to visit the Park while en route west and, without disclosing his official connection with the Department of the Interior, investigate and report upon the management of the Park. Smith's report was a scathing denouncement of Conger and his administration. The Superintendent had "either failed to comprehend the importance of the duties of his office," Smith reported, "or had intentionally disregarded the same," never having attempted "to execute some of the most important instructions of the Department." Conger and his assistants had failed to inform visitors of the regulations and had evidently shut their eyes to the fact that professional hunters were working throughout the Park to supply the Improvement Company with fresh meat. The secret investigator was surprised to find no Assistant Superintendents patrolling the geyser basins to prevent vandalism and his astonishment was further increased when he was informed by visitors that "they had purchased very fine and choice specimens" directly from some of the Superintendent's assistants. Smith declared that the assistants who were hired to protect the curiosities were responsible for "acts of vandalism . . . more outrageous than those perpetrated by visitors," and concluded his report with, "I think the interests of the Government demand a more active, energetic and competent Superintendent than the present one. Mr. Conger is well advanced in years and . . . he does not . . . combine the qualifications required to make an efficient Superintendent."[26]

When the contents of Special Agent Smith's report were made known to him, Conger vehemently denied any wrongdoing and blamed the entire report upon the malice of the Vice-President of the Improvement Company.[27] This was given some support by one of his assistants. Having noticed a reference in the *St. Paul Press,* December 17, 1883, charging Conger with incompetence, Assistant Superintendent D. E. Sawyer wrote that the whole trouble could be traced to the insidious reports of Hobart, who resented Conger's refusal to allow the Improvement Company to "monopolize the whole park." Sawyer charged the Improvement Company with killing game for their hotel tables, adding, "they claim to have permit from Sec. Teller to kill for their own use . . . we have never been advised by the Secretary what priviledge [*sic*] they have, no copy of their lease has ever been furnished us." Referring to Conger, Sawyer maintained that "no man was ever more zelous [*sic*] in seeing that every law is lived up to and carried into effect than himself," and, after noting that there existed no law whereby the Park officials could make arrests, no penalties established and no courts of justice within the Park, he asked the plaintive question, "will you tell me in the name of heven [*sic*] what more we can do?"[28]

Conger apparently thought that the existing rules and regulations were comprehensive enough to achieve the purpose for which they were designed if only the Superintendent "were supplied with the necessary legal machinery . . . to compel obedience to them." He had no legal power to arrest and detain anyone charged with a violation of the rules, nor was there any penalty attached to a conviction for such offenses. He wrote Teller that "some legislation is needed immediately to correct and remedy the existing state of things" in the Park, since, without it, an order from the Secretary or the Superintendent was "just about as effective as was the ancient Popes bull."[29]

The legislation requested by the Superintendent and obviously needed by the Park officials was refused by Congress. At the opening of the 48th Congress in December, 1883, Senator Vest introduced a bill to revise the Yellowstone Park Act. It provided for the punishment of offenses and extended the laws of the Territory of Montana over the Park. For jurisdictional purposes, the Park was declared to be a part of Gallatin County, Montana Territory. The bill conferred on the Superintendent and his assistants the powers and duties of United States Marshals. The Vest bill was brought before the Senate on March 4, 1884, and, after considerable debate, passed the following day.[30]

During the second session of the 48th Congress, the House considered the Senate bill as amended by the House Committee on Territories. The most important of these amendments were meant to reduce the size of the Park and change the judicial jurisdiction from Montana to Wyoming Territory. These amendments were agreed upon on the House floor, and the bill passed, only to die in a conference held by a joint committee.[31]

If protection was not to be afforded the Park at this time, improvements were, and the development of the Park road system was already underway. In the appropriation bill approved March 3, 1883,[32] Congress had stipulated that $29,-000 of the $40,000 appropriation would be expended, under the supervision and direction of an engineer officer detailed by the Secretary of War, in the construction and improvement of roads and bridges within the Park. Accordingly, on July 6, 1883, 1st Lieutenant Dan C. Kingman, Corps of Engineers, "in addition to other duties as Chief Engineer Officer, Department of the Platte," was ordered to the Yellowstone National Park.[33] Lieutenant Kingman's appointment brought the first systematic direction and development of improvements, the first division of authority, and the first increment of military personnel to the Park. All had an effect upon the development of the national park system. Kingman's contributions were not limited to road and bridge construction, however, for he, with others, vehemently opposed the entrance of a railroad into the Park.

A proposal for the construction of a railroad line in the Park had been presented to Congress in 1882, but no action had been taken.[34] Rumors circulated that certain parties were interested in laying track into the Park; they were given substance when the railroad financier Jay Cooke visited the Clark Fork mines on the northeast boundary of the Park and promised the miners that they would soon be connected with the main line of the Northern Pacific by a branch line that would run through the National Park. Cooke City came into existence as a result of this visit and promise.[35] An article in the *Madisonian,* a Virginia City newspaper, stated that an engineer in charge of a survey party for the Utah and Northern Railway was laying out a route through the Park. Superintendent Conger immediately protested and maintained that a railroad would prostitute the Park.[36] Lieutenant Kingman was aware of the several railroad plans and earnestly recommended that such action "be deferred for a few years at any rate," eloquently maintaining that if the Park's valleys were to be scarred by railroads, its hills pierced by tunnels, "its purity and quiet . . . destroyed and broken by the noise and smoke of the locomotive . . . it will cease to belong to the whole people and will interest only those that it helps to enrich."[37] The conflict thus begun lasted for more than ten years before the railroad interests were finally defeated, but it is to the credit of Conger and Kingman that they recognized and opposed the danger.

More material threats to the preservation of the Park were facing Conger, however, for the new Assistant Superintendents were proving to be unreliable and inefficient. They were characterized as being about as "useful in protecting game . . . as a Sioux Indian would be in charge of a locomotive,"[38] and one observer, noting that most of them were "boys under age," thought that "a prairie wolf would frighten them out of their pants."[39] A more voluble contemporary portrayed the Assistant Superintendents as being

> . . . a herd of irresponsible imbeciles . . . a lot of poor relations and hangers on of officials who have doubtless had them pensioned off in this manner with scant hope that they will some time come into conflict with a cowboy, a wild indian, or at least wander so far away as never more to be heard from. These employees are largely made up of inefficient young fellows, ignorant of the ways of the west, and utterly incompetent to perform the duties for which they are ostensibly employed. . . . A couple of cowboys could put the whole brigade to flight with blank cartridges.[40]

The Assistant Superintendents were aware of the poor esteem in which they were held by the general public and some, after spending a few months in the wild surroundings, fled back to their homes in the East, to be replaced by other inexperienced political appointees. Some remained, but a note of resignation and despair pervaded their thinking. One of the more conscientious assistants wrote that "tourists as a rule continue to test the power of the Geysers by throwing timber in them, this and the neglect of many campers to extinguish their fires gives me all I can do." Echoing the sentiment of many Senators and Congressmen, this man tersely advised his superior to "Let the Military have charge of the Park."[41] At least one assistant was not discouraged, and, writing about a man he knew to be responsible for the slaughter of game within the Park, Edmund L. Fish knew that "nothing can be done now but if we should be empowered to enforce the laws . . . I should dearly love to snatch the son of a *Bitch* bald headed."[42] What he needed, he said, was legal power "to reach them poachers and arrest them for viola-tion." He would have willingly taken "the part of a detec-tive" in order to "straighten out their crookedness," but as it was, he could "see no [illegible] in it for what could I do if I caught them in the very act." He ended his letter with a plaintive cry, stating that he was "getting very anxious for power to act like a man and not like a sneak in Park matters" and hoped that Conger could soon "send good news from Congress."[43]

Unfortunately the "good news" was not forthcoming and the Park management continued to be berated by the press for allowing depredations to continue.[44] One supporter of the harried Superintendent blamed the insidious newspaper releases condemning Conger upon the "so-called Park Im-provement Co. who desire to control the entire park for their own benefit," and maintained that Conger was a good Super-intendent, doing all that he could with a worthless group of Assistants over whom he had no control of appointment or discharge. [45] Another, speaking for "all of the old timers and frontiersmen" who were in the vicinity of the Park, thought that Conger had "done all he possibly could with the power he had."[46]

Even Secretary of the Interior Teller realized that Conger and his assistants needed further power if they were to stop vandalism and the slaughter of game, and he finally requested Congress to take some action.[47] Congress, however, refused to consider the request, and supporters of the Park were forced to look elsewhere for help. The first effort to solve the vexing problem of the absence of an enforceable legal code was made by the Territory of Wyoming, which included about 98 per cent of the Park. On March 6, 1884, its legislature passed a law that extended the laws of the Territory over that section of the Park lying within the Territorial boundaries, authorized the Governor to appoint two Justices of the Peace and two Constables upon the recommendation of the Park Superintendent, and provided penalties for the defined misdemeanors of trespass and vandalism. An appropriation of $8,000 was provided "to carry this law into effect and to assist and aid the Government of the United States in keeping and maintaining the park as a place of resort."[48] Thus supported by legal machinery, a conscientious and efficient Superintendent (like Conger), if backed by an equally efficient group of assistants, might have been able to bring law and order to the area. Such was not to be the case.

In a terse letter, dated July 12, 1884, Secretary Teller informed Conger that "In view of the unsatisfactory condition of affairs in the Park and the improbability of improvement," he was requested to tender his resignation "to take effect on the appointment and qualification" of his successor.[49] Rufus Hatch and other officers of the Improvement Company, with whom Conger had so often disagreed, were named as having "a hand in securing Conger's removal." Surprisingly, the editor who had previously castigated Conger for his alleged lack of law enforcement now came forth in his defense, expressed "deep feelings of regret at his removal," and published a letter, signed by sixty residents of the area, commending Conger for his forthright administration.[50]

Conger's short administration had not been a successful one, but this was due more to the lack of enforcement procedure and the poor calibre of his assistants than to malfeasance on his part. He had correctly and courageously opposed the powerful influence of the Improvement Company; he had taken a similar stand against the railroad interests. He can perhaps be justly criticized for ineffectiveness, but he was neither dishonest nor corrupt. Unfortunately, his successor was both.

Robert E. Carpenter was appointed Park Superintendent on August 5, 1884, and assumed his duties on September 10, when he relieved Conger.[51] His appointment was purely political,[52] and Carpenter looked upon his new office as a source of profit for himself and his friends. The only beneficial step taken by him was the forcible removal of homesteaders who had illegally "squatted" within the Park. In this he had the full backing of the Department of the Interior; the Secretary even advised him that if he found such ejection impossible with the force at hand, the Secretary would invoke the assistance of the Army.[53] This was not needed, however, as Carpenter simply burned the settlers' dwellings and thus forced their evacuation.[54] When he returned to Washington, the new Superintendent joined forces with members of the Improvement Company and lobbied Congress for the passage of a measure designed to grant vast tracts of land within the Park to private parties for commercial purposes. The Superintendent's complicity in the scheme was exposed when it was discovered that his name appeared on the claim notices and that he had selected for himself the most desirable tracts.[55] When Acting Secretary of the Interior M. L. Joslyn attempted to defend Carpenter, claiming that the charges against him were "frivolous and unworthy of consideration," the editor of the *Livingston Enterprise* gloated with "satisfaction to know that in a few weeks [when the federal administration changed hands] Mr. Joslyn will be relieved from the necessity of taking cognizance of such frivolous matters as the business of the interior department," adding that Joslyn "has always been the tool of the Park Improvement Company."[56]

With the advent of the Cleveland Administration in Washington, Henry M. Teller was superseded by L. Q. C. Lamar as Secretary of the Interior. The ever alert Senator Vest immediately recommended that Carpenter be removed from the superintendency and that a Mr. Magoffin be named in his place. Defenders of the Republic opposed the recommendation on the grounds that Magoffin had been a Confederate; Vest then requested the appointment of Colonel D. W. Wear, who had been a "Colonel of a Federal Regiment, is in the prime of life, accustomed to field sports of all kinds, and a thoroughly honest man."[57] Colonel Wear, at that time a member of the State Senate of Missouri, was notified of his appointment "vice R. E. Carpenter to be removed," on June 1, 1885, and was commissioned Superintendent on June 20, 1885.[58]

The new Superintendent immediately set about his task with enthusiasm and vigor. His first act was to suggest that the force of assistants be changed, since he found them to be "very inefficient . . . and utterly unfit for the service" and thought that "a change of the entire force would be beneficial to the proper administration" of the Park.[59] Less than two months after taking office he could report that a man hired by him at his own expense had apprehended two hunters, who were found guilty: one received a fine of $100 and six months imprisonment, the full extent of the new Wyoming law, and the other a fine of $75 and costs.[60] This marked the first prosecution for depredations in the Park. The Superintendent then asked that Edward Wilson, the man responsible for the arrests, be appointed to the position of Assistant Superintendent, along with C. J. Baronette, since he was "compelled to have experienced mountain men to enforce the laws."[61] This request for "mountain men" was renewed a month later when Colonel Wear asked that he be authorized to select those appointed to the post of Assistant Superintendent from Westerners familiar with the ways of the frontier. He thought that Westerners could be "judiciously substituted for any of the Assistants" he presently had, and added that "Whiskey" seemed to be the "besetting trouble" with most of the men then filling those positions.[62] By November he could report the apprehension and conviction of four more poachers.[63]

Members of Congress, unaware of the better protection now afforded the Park, appointed on March 4, 1885, a Special House Committee to investigate Indian education and the affairs of the Yellowstone National Park. This committee met at Omaha the following summer, and after visiting various Indian agencies and reservations, four members of the committee spent five days in the Park. In their report, the junketeering Congressmen laid down what was to become an important statement of Park policy:

> The park should so far as possible be spared the vandalism of improvement. Its great and only charms are in the display of wonderful forces of nature, the ever varying beauty of the rugged landscape, and the sublimity of the scenery. Art cannot embellish them.[64]

But the majority of the Committee were not so sure that nature needed protection from the hand of man. The Superintendent and his ten assistants were thought to be of no "special value" in the protection of game, and the committee thought it was improbable that "any of these animals will for any considerable period remain, even in imagination, an interesting feature of this Park." The Congressmen did mention, however, that a small police force would be necessary to protect the forests from destruction "either by fire or the ax." In a minority report, two members of the committee advocated the construction of more roads and the relocation and reconstruction of the old roads; while agreeing that "the most important duty of the 'superintendent and assistants in the Park is to protect the forests from fire and ax',," they believed it was also important to "protect the objects of interest from injury, especially at the hands of the relic hunter and the professional collector of specimens, and the game from injury or destruction."[65] The majority report recommended that Congress recognize the validity of the Wyoming Territorial Act of March 6, 1884, which provided legal machinery for protection of the Park. The report also recommended turning the Park over to Wyoming's jurisdiction when the Territory became a state.[66]

Before the committee filed its report, Secretary Lamar realized that his office would be severely criticized if the report declared conditions in the Park to be what the press had long claimed. He therefore appointed his own committee of one to examine into the conditions of the Park. Special Agent W. Hallet Phillips was to direct his attention particularly to existing leases, the question of need for additional hotels, and whether there were at that time any persons living illegally within the Park.[67] Phillips reached the Park on July 26 and remained there until September 6, 1885; two weeks after his return to Washington his report was in the hands of the Secretary.[68]

The question of Park government was raised once again in the Phillips report, which focused upon the somewhat arbitrary administration of justice practiced in the Park under the Wyoming Territorial statute passed the year before. Phillips thought it strange that Congress should have neglected to provide any government for the Park. After carefully reviewing legal precedents, he concluded that a Territorial legislature had no authority to enforce its enactments within the Park. The Wyoming law had never received the assent of Congress. In his opinion, some provisions of the Wyoming law were "highly ridiculous" and other sections were

"Draconian legislation." Phillips seemed to be particularly incensed over the fact that some "prominent citizens of Philadelphia" had been arrested and fined for collecting specimens, and that other visitors of "the highest respectability, ladies and gentlemen," had been fined for similar acts of vandalism. Section 1 2 of the Wyoming law provided that all fees collected by the Justices of the Peace were to be retained by them, and Section 1 7 allowed the prosecuting witness to keep one-half the fine assessed against an offender. The stimulus of such prospective rewards could lead to wholly "unjustifiable" arrests.

Agent Phillips appended to his report a column taken from the *Chicago Tribune,* August 2 2, 1 885, dateline Cinnabar, Montana. According to the newspaper report, Judge Payson, member of Congress from Illinois, had been arrested by an Assistant Superintendent for allegedly leaving a campfire smouldering. The case was heard by Justice of the Peace Hall; Payson was found guilty, fined $60 and ordered to pay $1 2.8o costs. Refusing to be fined by what he considered to be no more than a "kangaroo court," the indignant Congressman posted a $1,ooo bond and announced his intention to appeal the judgement to the United States District Court in Wyoming. Here the proceedings took on the aspect of high comedy. Judge Hall, a former woodchopper, called upon the defendant, a former judge, for legal advice and asked him whether he, as Justice of the Peace, had the authority to "remit the fine, or costs, or either." He was advised by the defendant that he indeed had the legal power to remit the fine and "at least so much of the costs as were illegal and excessive." Hall then offered to accept $1 o for the fine and to reduce the costs from $1 2.8o to $4. Payson refused; Hall then offered to take $1 for the fine and whatever the defendant considered "right for the costs." Payson refused to pay any fine, but offered to pay a small sum "for the trouble that the alleged constable has been put to." In such a manner was justice carried out under the Wyoming statute.[69]

Phillips commended Superintendent Wear and thought he was thoroughly efficient and "desirous of promoting the interests of the Park," but also thought that the Superintendent was handicapped by having too few assistants. He opposed the granting of a right-of-way through the Park to the railroad interests, or segregation of any portion of the Park for railroad purposes, and suggested several rule changes and more stringent enforcement of the existing ones, particularly the one prohibiting the sale of intoxicating liquors. Phillips also urged that two United States Commissioners be appointed with jurisdiction to try all offenses not above misdemeanors, with Congress providing "the pains and penalties for a violation of the laws or regulations." He ended his pleas for proper legal machinery with the statement, "in a national park, the national laws and regulations should be enforced by a national tribunal." Nine years passed before this recommendation was converted into law, but the Phillips report did serve to bring about a more immediate change in the Park administration. On March 10, 1886, the Governor of Wyoming approved the repeal of the Territorial Park law, and the Park was once again left without any form of effective legal government.[70]

Superintendent Wear had been so persistent in his demands that he be allowed to dismiss assistants who were unfit for duty and replace them with men of his own choosing that by April, 1886, he had achieved a complete turnover of the ten Assistant Superintendents. The inept political appointees were gone, and in their place stood the "stalwart mountaineers" so praised by Wear and Senator Vest. Given time, sufficient appropriations, and additional men as travel to the Park increased, Wear might have been able to provide adequate protection to the Park. But the scandals of his predecessor, the ineffectiveness and later the repeal of the Wyoming Territorial statutes, the penurious nature of Congress, the avowed hostility on the part of some Congressmen toward the Park, the ill repute into which the government of the Park had fallen, and recollection of the several suggestions that troops alone could offer the needed protection for the Park, frustrated Wear's attempts to vindicate civilian administration of the Yellowstone National Park.

When the 49th Congress began its first session in December, 1885, Senator Vest introduced Senate Bill 101, to revise the Yellowstone Park Act and provide the necessary legal machinery for continued civil protection, but he was unable to garner enough support to get the bill up for consideration. He was successful in opposing a bill introduced by Senator Samuel J. R. McMillan of Minnesota to grant a railroad right-of-way through the northern end of the Park, but in so doing he alienated a group of Senators whose support he needed for his own bill.

The Senate received Special Agent W. Hallet Phillips' report on February 1, 1886, and two weeks later the Holman Select Committee reported to the House their findings on the situation in Yellowstone.[71] Both reports served to aid the opponents of Senator Vest, but it was in the House that the civilian administration was most vociferously attacked and finally ended.

The annual appropriation for the Park was included in the sundry civil appropriation bill for the fiscal year ending June 30, 1887, and, as reported by the House Committee on Appropriations, the bill called for $40,000 to be expended in the same manner as had been done in previous years. The House reduced the appropriation for the Park by $20,000 and stipulated that the money be used for road construction only, deleting the provision for the salaries of the Superintendent and his assistants. The purpose of the deletion was to end civil control of the Park and force the Secretary of the Interior to call upon the Secretary of War as provided in the act of March 3, 1883.[72] When apprised of the situation, Secretary Lamar immediately wrote to the chairmen of both the Senate and House Committees on Appropriations suggesting that "the control of the Park . . . be transferred

. . . to the War Department" since that Department would have control of the only appropriation available for the Park.[73] Lamar's letter was too late to have any effect on the bill, but in the Senate the original $40,000 appropriation was restored, as was the provision providing for compensation for a Superintendent and assistants. After brief debate the bill was passed by the Senate on July 24, 1886.[74] But the House refused to accept the restored appropriation,[75] and the conference committee's efforts to reconcile the House and Senate positions ended in a deadlock.[76]

Returned to the floor of the Senate, the bill was debated at length. Senator Vest, supporting the original appropriation, stated that "It was never intended [in the 1883 law] that the Secretary of War should put a cordon of troops around the park." In his opinion, soldiers "would be more than useless" for Park protection. He admitted that he had previously endorsed the use of troops but he was now convinced that the change would benefit only speculators who had been unable to control and direct the present Superintendent. He sincerely believed that if the civil administration were replaced by the War Department, it would mean "virtually an end of the Yellowstone National Park."[77]

Senator James B. Beck of Kentucky supported the Vest argument. Senator Preston B. Plumb of Kansas, claiming that a monopoly existed within the Park, thought the entire Park should be "lopped off," later adding that perhaps some of the curiosities should be saved, with the remainder of the area being returned to the public domain.[78] Vest, supported by Senators Dawes and Teller, asserted that while there may have been monopolistic control of the Park in previous years, this was no longer true. Teller, while defending the purpose of the Park and its government under his administration, thought that military control would serve only to "destroy the park," but agreed with Plumb by stating that the government should abandon control over the Park, retaining only "the small points where these large geysers and other things are."[79]

Senator John R. McPherson of New Jersey, supporting the House provision, contended that a military force drawn from the "five thousand soldiers" then in the vicinity of the Park, and who were serving "no purpose in the world," would afford excellent protection to the Park. Vest retorted that the character of the men in the Regular Army was such that any hope for protection would be precluded if the Park were handed over to them, and he claimed that the "government of the park today is in better condition than it ever has been." He then castigated the advocates of military rule as being stooges for the proponents of a railroad right-of-way through the Park, maintaining that he had been told time and time again that unless he withdrew his opposition to the various railroad bills "the park would be broken up." The ending of civil administration would be but the first step in a maneuver to "break it up and destroy it forever." In conclusion, Vest asserted that the present Superintendent was an honest man, that game was increasing while lawlessness was decreasing, and if the House conferees were allowed to have their way, it would be tantamount to repealing the act which created the Park itself. Vest's motion to uphold the Senate's amendment carried and another conference with the House was requested.[80]

The House debate on the Yellowstone question was as extended and intense as that in the Senate. Representative D. B. Henderson of Iowa[81] spoke for those who desired to turn control of the Park over to the War Department. Superintendent Wear's two predecessors had been from Iowa, while he was from Missouri. Thus the House debate soon degenerated into a partisan duel between the leaders from those two states. Henderson charged Senator Vest with desiring to keep the Park under civil government only in order to maintain Wear in the superintendency, and ridiculed the "mountaineers" employed by Wear, who, he said, had originated in Illinois and Missouri and "did not know a bear from a jackal or a jack rabbit from a jackass." Wear was wrongfully charged with having an interest in a coal mine near the Park line and lobbying to have that section of the Park segregated, leaving him with title to the mineral land. He was also excoriated for having an interest in the Yellowstone Park Association and for aiding that company to gain a monopoly of the hotel business in the Park. Representative John J. O'Neill of Missouri, replying to Henderson's false charges, claimed that Wear was blameless but that Conger and Carpenter, who were from Iowa and had preceded Wear as Superintendent, were the ones responsible for scandal and corruption in the Park.

Wear subsequently refuted all charges made against him and was strongly supported by the one man who could claim an element of objectivity in the affair. In a personal letter to the Secretary of the Interior, W. Hallet Phillips maintained that Wear was "a man who has done great credit to himself in the administration of the park," and described him as "honest, sober, scrupulously conscientious." He denied the charges made against Wear in the House and believed that the Superintendent "had done more for the park than all those who preceded him." But Congressmen seldom aspire to objectivity and the facts were largely ignored.[82]

The future of the Yellowstone, and with it the future of the National Park system as a whole, came near to repudiation when Representative John A. Reagan of Texas suggested that all the laws setting the territory apart as a park be repealed, all of the men engaged in taking care of it be discharged and the whole area be placed in private hands. He did not think it was the duty of the government to enter "show business" or to provide "imperial parks for the few wealthy persons," and he for one would be happy when the entire enterprise was abandoned. Representative William S. Holman of Indiana, recalling that Mackinac Island had been transferred to Michigan[83] and that Yosemite had been ceded to California, thought that the Yellowstone should be turned over to Wyoming. The debate ended with the House instructing its conferees to insist upon its provision ending the civilian administration.[84]

The appropriations bill was again referred to the conference committee. The House conferees were instructed to limit the appropriation to $20,000 for roads and bridges only, while the Senate conferees were told to withhold consent to abolition of the civilian administration of the Park. The end of the Congressional session was but two days off, 325 men were eager to leave a hot and humid Washington to take care of their political fortunes, and only one point of contention remained between the two branches of the national legislature. Senator William B. Allison of Iowa, reporting for the Senate conferees, stated that "The House of Representatives refused to agree to the Senate amendment, and I believe the very last thing we did before finally separating was to surrender the amendment put on by the Senate in reference to the Yellowstone Park." The civilian administration of the Yellowstone was facing legislative destruction.[85]

Senator Vest was disgusted, but not disheartened. He announced that in the next session of Congress he would introduce a bill to restore the Park to civil government. [86]

The Act of August 4, 1886,[87] did not prevent the Secretary of the Interior from retaining the present force of civilian employees, but it denied him money to pay them. Therefore, on August 6, 1886, the Secretary of the Interior called the attention of the Secretary of War to the act of March 3, 1883,[88] which provided that:

> The Secretary of War, upon the request of the Secretary of the Interior, is hereby authorized and directed to make the necessary details of troops to prevent trespassers or intruders from entering the park for the purpose of destroying the game or objects of curiosity therein, or for any other purpose prohibited by law, and to remove such persons from the park if found therein.

The Secretary requested that "a Captain, two Lieutenants and twenty selected mounted men from the Army be detailed for service in the park" for the purposes contemplated in the act, and to perform such other duties in connection with the management and superintendency of the Park as might be required by him. He remarked that since his Department had no funds for such purposes, the War Department would have to furnish subsistence, forage, and transportation for the requested troops.[89]

Secretary Lamar's letter was referred by the Secretary of War to Lieutenant-General P. H. Sheridan, who recommended that "Troop 'M', 1st United States Cavalry, Captain Moses Harris commanding—station Fort Custer, M. T. —be ordered . . . to perform the duties in the Yellowstone National Park that recently devolved upon the Sup-rintendent of the Park and his assistants."[90] Accordingly, Captain Harris and his troop were ordered to proceed at once to the Park, there to take station and report to the Secretary of the Interior.[91] On August 20, 1886, Captain Moses Harris relieved Superintendent Wear of his duties and the era of civilian park administration came to an end.

Looking backward, it appears that Congress acted somewhat precipitately and without full knowledge of the improved conditions brought about by Superintendent Wear and his handful of assistants when it acted to replace the civilian administration with that of the military. Given legislative and financial support, civilian administrators might well have been able to bring success to the nation's first large-scale attempt at conservation and preservation. It is equally possible, however, that the political venality that marked the late nineteenth century might have so transcended the best efforts of a conscientious civilian administrator as to produce complete failure in the Yellowstone venture; a failure that would probably have brought an end to the incipient movement toward a national park system.

V

The Saving of a Park

and a System:

1886-1889

MILITARY PROTECTION of the Yellowstone National Park was thought to be only a temporary expedient, and temporary it was, but the troops remained in the Park for thirty-two years. The administrative problems faced by the civilian Superintendents were, to a certain degree, still present under the military administration. No well-defined policy of protection had been promulgated; no judicial machinery had been provided. The average cavalryman had no previous training in protecting nature from man and some vandalism occurred under the very eyes of the new military guardians. The arrival of the military, however, did serve to remove the administration of the Park from the political arena; and under the direction of energetic and conscientious military officers the rules and regulations governing the Park were revised and enforced, various threats to the very existence of the Park were met and overcome, policy was determined, a precedent was established for a national park system, and punitive legislation was finally obtained from a reluctant Congress.

Notwithstanding the earnest efforts of the last civilian Superintendent, the military administration of the Yellowstone Park did, in a very real sense, save the Yellowstone Park from physical and legislative destruction. Congress had in effect ended the civil administration of the Park. Joseph K. Toole, delegate to Congress from Montana, was quoted as saying that the leading men of both Houses "felt as if there was a sort of ring there [in Yellowstone] that ought to be broken up. They therefore went to the opinions of Generals Sherman and Sheridan, and concluded to turn over the park to the War Department." Delegate Toole thought that "the change will work well."[1] The change in administration did work well, but the first troops assigned to duty in the Yellowstone found that they had inherited all of the charges of negligence and ineptitude that had previously been directed toward the hapless civilian administrators.

When Captain Moses Harris arrived with his command, Troop "M," First United States Cavalry, at Mammoth Hot Springs, late in the evening of August 17, 1886, he found the Park practically deserted by its staff. When word was received that Congress had failed to appropriate funds to continue their salaries, several Assistant Superintendents simply quit their posts and left the Park in the hands of the tourists and hunters. Superintendent Wear, finding that he no longer had a protective force, frantically wired the Secretary of the Interior that "lawlessness in [the] park has rapidly increased," and that his few remaining assistants were "anxious about their pay," but that he would do all that he could to preserve and protect the Park. A second telegram to the Secretary stated: "Three large fires raging in the Park beyond my control."[2]

The arrival of the military was immediately reported to the Secretary of the Interior,[3] who telegraphed that Captain Harris was to assume the duties "heretofore performed by the Superintendent." More definite instructions were to follow by letter, but the transfer of the responsibility for protection and administration of the Park became effective as of August 20, 1886.[4] Harris, accompanied by Wear, at once set out upon a tour of the Park and stationed detachments of his troop at the six stations previously occupied by the Assistant Superintendents. Harris and his remaining troopers then undertook to extinguish the many forest fires then raging uncontrolled throughout the Park; Wear asserted that they had been started maliciously by some of his personal enemies. Harris, admitting that there might be some truth in this statement, believed that most of the fires were caused by careless camping parties. Those fires which appeared to have been started intentionally he attributed to "unscrupulous hunters," who, having been prevented from hunting in the Park, resorted to this method of driving the game beyond the Park limits. "The Park," he asserted, was "surrounded by a class of old frontiersmen, hunters and trappers, and squawmen" who had no respect whatever for the rules and regulations established by the Secretary of the Interior. These men, in addition to the destructive seasonal tourists, were to be his adversaries, and Captain Harris immediately set about establishing the ground rules for the expected conflict.[5]

Camp Sheridan, Wyoming,[6] was established at Mammoth Hot Springs, and the following orders set forth the regulations to be enforced by the members of Harris' command:

I. (1) The cutting of green timber, or the removal or displacement of any mineral deposits or natural curiosities, is forbidden.

(2) Hunting or trapping and the discharge of firearms within the limits of the Park is prohibited. Fishing is forbidden except with hook and line, and the sale of fish so taken is also disallowed.

(3) Wagon tires on all wagons used for freighting purposes on roads . . . are required to be at least four inches in width.

(4) Camping parties will only build fires when actually necessary.

(5) The sale of intoxicating liquors, except by hotel proprietors to their guests, for their own use, is strictly prohibited.

(6) Trespassers within the Park for illicit purposes, or persons wantonly violating the foregoing rules, will be summarily removed from the Park.

(7) No stock will be allowed to run loose in the vicinity of the various points of interest within the Park frequented by visitors.

(8) No rocks, sticks, or other obstructions must be thrown into any of the springs or geysers within the Park.

It is enjoined upon all soldiers . . . to be vigilant and attentive in the enforcement of the foregoing regulations, and to see that the stage drivers and other employees of the hotels do not use abusive language to, or otherwise maltreat, the visitors to the Park . . . They will in the enforcement of their orders conduct themselves in a courteous and polite, but firm and decided, manner. They will not hesitate to make arrests when necessary, reporting at once . . . to the Commanding Officer.

II. All loose stock found in the vicinity . . . will be driven into corral . . . and held until proper guaranty is given that they will not again be turned loose.[7]

Even though the new military administrator considered "it beyond his province to originate any new policy," yet by the issuance of these orders and regulations, he in fact instigated new elements of policy.[8] Henceforth, alcoholic beverages could be dispensed by hotel proprietors in the Park (much to the relief of the thirsty, and much to the discomfort of the temperate guests); livestock was no longer allowed to wander over the sometimes fragile geyser formations; and "persons wantonly violating" the rules were, for the first time, made aware of the expulsion provisions of the Park regulations. Two persons were expelled by the military authorities when it was discovered that they had illegally settled within the Park, and two others were ejected for violation of regulations. Harris' Regulation Number Three, requiring four-inch wagon tires, was suspended indefinitely when it became apparent that it only produced "much inconvenience" to the visitors rather than reducing the destruction of the Park roads.[9]

Captain Harris realized that his cavalry troops lacked the proper training required for the performance of their new duties; hence he requested authority to employ three "scouts or guides" who were acquainted with the intricate trails and hunting grounds frequented by trespassers. Approval was given for the employment of one scout, with the admonition that one should be sufficient as "Capt. Harris' men must learn the country."[10] This was the first indication that the military control of the Park might be of more than temporary duration. The military commander of the troops stationed in the Park was designated "Acting Superintendent" rather than the Superintendent; and since no provision had been made for quartering the troops in the Park, Camp Sheridan was a military establishment in name only. When Harris asked whether his troops would remain in the Park during the winter, he was told that they would; the Quartermaster General, Department of Dakota, was directed to "provide such temporary shelter for the command as may be necessary for the comfort of the troops and the protection of public property."[11] When preparing the estimate of appropriations required to administer the Yellowstone Park during the fiscal year ending June 30, 1887, Harris assumed that the civil administration would be resumed, as did the Secretary of War, the Secretary of the Interior, and a majority of the Senate.[12] The military administration was indeed never made permanent by Congressional legislation but was continued year after year because Congress did not provide the appropriations necessary to support a civil administration. The historian who best chronicled the history of Yellowstone

National Park wrote in 1912: "it is not probable that public opinion will ever sanction a return to the old order [civil administration]. The administrative machinery has completely adjusted itself to the present system . . . and it is not likely to be disturbed."[13]

Recognizing the seemingly temporary nature of his assignment, and in the absence of any detailed instructions from the Secretary of the Interior, the new Acting Superintendent attempted to enforce the regulations for the protection of the Park. Since he still had no legal means to punish offenders, he wrote the Secretary of the Interior about the expulsion of trespassers from the Park, admitting that the military methods "may at times appear harsh and arbitrary," but he maintained that such procedure was "indispensable to the proper protection of life and property." Less than two months after assuming control of the Park, Harris could report that, owing to the vigilance and constant scouting on the part of the guide, Baronett, and the soldiers, "there have been no depredations of any magnitude," and confidently added, "the game has been well protected." Somewhat less confidence was exhibited when he wrote of the protection afforded the geysers and their deposits:

It is apparent from the most casual observation that the means heretofore employed for the preservation of the natural objects of wonder and beauty in the Park have been entirely inadequate. It may be said without exaggeration that not one of the notable geyser formations in the Park has escaped mutilation or defacement in some form. . . . A lead pencil mark seems to be a very harmless defacement, but names bearing the date of 1880 are still discoverable . . . names with the date of June, 1886, have been chiseled into the solid geysertie so deep that . . . many years must elapse before this mutilation will be obliterated . . . efforts are constantly being made to destroy the geysers . . . by throwing into them sticks, loggs of wood and all sorts of obstructions. . . .[14]

In his report to the Secretary of the Interior, the Acting Superintendent suggested the construction of a road system which would enable tourists to visit the principal objects of interest "without discomfort—and without passing twice over the same road." After discovering that many "irresponsible persons" were acting as guides and furnishing transportation and pack outfits to the tourists, Harris stated that in his opinion "no person should be allowed to do business of this character . . . without first obtaining permission from the Superintendent and registering their names in his office," and that tariff charges for all forms of transportation should be established on a uniform base. It was from this suggestion that the policy of "controlled monopoly" was adopted first by the Department of the Interior, and later by the National Park Service.[15]

Noting, as had his predecessors, the paucity of rules and regulations governing the Park, Harris maintained that even the few regulations in effect were no longer applicable because of the "changed conditions in the Park," and he appended a list of new rules "for the consideration of the Department."[16] He realized, however, that the mere adoption of new regulations would not save the Park from destruction and added the old plea for legal machinery:

> The enforcement of . . . rules and regulations will be difficult until some more effective penalty for their infringement is provided than expulsion from the Park. The necessity of a form of government for the Park is becoming, year by year, more urgent, as the number of visitors to the Park increases. All sorts of worthless and disreputable characters are attracted here by the impunity afforded by the absence of law and courts of justice.
>
> Evanston, the county seat of Uinta County, Wyoming, more than 250 miles distant, with a rugged and mountainous region intervening, is the nearest point at which even a justice of the peace with the necessary jurisdiction can be found.[17]

Soon after their arrival in the Park the military personnel, like their civilian predecessors, were charged with negligence and ineptitude. The Saint Paul *Pioneer Press,* September 10, 1886, published an interview with the last civilian Superintendent, D. W. Wear, in which Wear allegedly stated that "the troops in charge are not taking proper care of the Park, [they are] allowing the indiscriminate killing of game and the desecration of the formations about the mineral springs, and, unless some change is made soon, great damage will result." When Harris heard of the charge, he declared that the statement was untrue in every particular, that he had personally "made a very careful investigation as to the manner in which the . . . soldiers . . . performed their duties," and he was positive that there had "been no game killed or

New York Public Library

Yosemite Valley from Inspiration Point,
1855; lithograph from drawing by
Thomas A. Ayres

other depredations of any magnitude committed" since the troops had arrived in the Park.[18] W. Hallet Phillips, the former special investigator for the Secretary of the Interior, also condemned the military guardianship when he wrote that "the beautiful geyser cones and formations . . . were more hacked and injured while the soldiers were stationed there, than at any time since 1882–3." Captain Harris, however, impressed him as "an officer of character and determination," and the destruction was, according to Phillips, due to the fact that the soldiers' "previous training and duties were not of the category that qualified and prepared them to protect the wonders of nature."[19]

Even before the first year of military administration was up, another attack appeared in the Chicago *Evening Journal* of July 18, 1887. Captain Harris maintained that the article was filled with "untrue and malicious statements concerning the National Park" and vigorously defended the activities of the military.[20] The entire governmental policy in respect to the Yellowstone Park was branded as "curiously stupid" by a contributor to *Scribner's Monthly,* who castigated the men and officers guarding the Park, criticized the Interior Department, and even berated Congress for its "cheese-paring policy."[21] The management of the Park was obliquely questioned by the Boone and Crockett Club, which passed a resolution calling for the appointment of a committee of five "to promote useful and proper legislation toward the enlargement and better management of the Yellowstone National Park."[22] Petitions for the better protection of the Park were presented to Congress by residents of some thirty-seven states and Territories.[23]

Some heed was paid to these criticisms, for with the opening of the 50th Congress Senator Vest introduced for the second time a bill providing for the restoration of the civil administration. His bill provided for the appointment of a Park Commissioner who would have the authority to have arrested, and bind over to a federal court, any persons charged with an indictable offense. Vest's bill passed the Senate, but in the House an amendment was added to grant a right-of-way through the Park to the Cinnabar and Cooke City Railroad and no further action was taken.[24]

Despite all these trials, Harris and his command attempted to introduce an element of respect for the rules and regulations governing the Park. The reduction of tourist activity in the fall allowed Harris to direct his military force to the "important duty of affording protection to the large game." He initiated periodic boundary patrols in an attempt to keep animals in and hunters out.[25] Increased vigilance resulted in several expulsions. On April 23, 1887, William James was apprehended, his belongings were confiscated, and he was expelled from the Park "for trapping beaver." A similar fate befell Frank Chatfield "for killing an elk," and on September 10, 1888, William Moore was expelled "for repeated acts of drunkenness and disorder." Three days later Thomas Garfield was arrested and expelled from the Park "for trapping beaver on Willow Creek."[26] Expulsions from the Park did not always have the salutary effect desired. One person, expelled for poaching, wrote a friend, "As I am ordered out of the Park I am determined to go and taken up a homestead on the South Boundary line, for the purpose of being a nuisence to the Park and its Officers."[27]

Since no other form of punishment was available, however, expulsions continued. Between July 4 and July 10, 1887, Harris expelled sixteen men "of suspicious appearance, who were destitute of means of subsistence and were without employment." Of this mass expulsion, the Acting Superintendent hastened to note that no discrimination "has been or ever will be made by me for the rich and well dressed, as against the poor or working classes." He maintained that the Park was to be enjoyed by all alike and that there were many working men "out of employment" who traversed the nation's Park on foot, "with pleasure and satisfaction and with the same protection afforded to others."[28]

This effective policing and patrolling did not go unnoticed, and Professor Charles S. Sargent, an eminent dendrologist of Harvard, suggested that, because of the excellent example established in protecting the Yellowstone, the guardianship of all the nation's forests should be confined to the Army and "that forestry should be taught at West Point."[29]

If the military government seemed at times to be rather harsh and arbitrary, this applied only to those who flagrantly violated the regulations. Many careless visitors were merely admonished for their transgressions; and law and order, so far as the imperfect legal machinery would permit, were rapidly being established. For the first time since its inception, the Park was being patrolled by well-mounted and well-equipped soldiers, poachers were being arrested and expelled, and during the tourist season, points of interest within the Park were being protected against wanton vandalism. Through the activities of the military and the suggestions of the Acting Superintendent, policy, later to be adopted and transformed into National Park policy, was evolving piecemeal. The first military commander echoed earlier visiting Congressmen when he advised the Secretary of the Interior that "this 'wonderland' should for all time, be kept as near as possible in its natural and primitive condition." He believed, however, that some money was required to allow the cleaning up of rubbish, the destruction of shacks, and the painting of signs directing tourists along paths to the various attractions.[30] Another element of policy was established when, in reply to a letter offering the sale of buffalo to the government for the purpose of placing these rapidly disappearing animals in the Park, Harris stated:

> It is not the policy of the government to endeavor to make this Park attractive, by making a collection of domesticated animals, but rather to preserve the reservation in its natural condition and to protect the existing game animals so that they may breed in security.[31]

A decision that saved innumerable wild animals from slaughter and aided in the protection of game within the Park was made when Harris categorically denied permission for game killed outside of the Park, ostensibly for use of lessees of hotels within the Park, to be brought into the Park. Despite angry cries from the lessees who maintained that this was their only supply of fresh meat, the Secretary of the Interior declined "to interfere with any action" taken by the Acting Superintendent.[32]

While these measures helped establish fundamental Park policy, Harris realized that the small force of men at his disposal was inadequate to fully protect the Park during the tourist season. To cope with the ever-increasing number of visitors he requested the assignment of two additional scouts and one company of Infantry for duty in the Park during the summer months and asked for "such legislation as will define the jurisdiction of the territorial courts within the Park," as well as "a stringent law for the protection of the game."[33] The requested "stringent law" did not come forth until 1894, but his request for additional troops was answered in the summer of 1888, when the policy of augmenting the Park force in summer was inaugurated. The temporary character of the military administration was noted in this correspondence, and the Department of Dakota Commander approved the seasonal increase only because he thought the military regime in the Park would be temporary.[34]

Even with the added force at his command, Harris found his dual role of Acting Superintendent and commander of Camp Sheridan sometimes exasperating. Appropriations for the purely military activities of his troop were provided through normal allocations by the Quartermaster General's Office; appropriations for the protection and preservation of the Park should have come through the Department of the Interior, but they did not. The previous annual Congressional appropriations of $40,000 had provided for the payment of salaries to the Superintendent and his assistants, for

the normal costs of administration, and for the construction
of roads and bridges. This money had also allowed the civilian administration to provide signboards, mark the various
roads and points of interest, and clean up and remove the
debris left by camping parties. The appropriation for the
fiscal year 1887 was reduced by half and earmarked for road
and bridge work. The officer performing the duties of Superintendent was thus left with no money to expend in connection with the preservation of the Park.

The difficulty of operating without legislative appropriations was highlighted when Harris tried to obtain "a few
hundred dollars" to provide a building in which he could
transact the public business necessary to the Superintendent's
position. When he became Acting Superintendent Harris
had found that his office was located in an "old blacksmith
shop, built of rough boards full of wide cracks which admitted the wind and dust," a place of so "mean and squalid
character" that he found it "humiliating" to have to transact
business therein.[35] An appeal for money was made to the
Secretary of the Interior, who passed it on to the War Department, stating that he had no funds.[36] The sum of $500 for
an office building was eventually obtained from the Quartermaster General.[37]

When Harris learned that the appropriation bill for fiscal
1888 had been reported by the House with $20,000 for the
construction of roads and bridges only, he wrote to W. Hallet Phillips asking his assistance in securing a legislative appropriation to meet the needs of the Park administration.
Harris included the names of Congressmen and Senators
who had previously visited the Park, in the hope that these
men would "bear witness to the necessity of the small appropriation" requested by him.[38] This effort failed, however.
Harris and the Park had to wait for several years before
Congress came forth with the desired appropriation for administrative and protective purposes.[39]

Harris was also hindered, like his predecessors and immediate successors, by the increasingly noticeable lack of laws necessary to punish violators of the Park regulations. Unlike his predecessors, however, Harris energetically made use of that provision of the Act of Dedication that provided for the expulsion of violators from the Park. In addition to expulsion, moreover, violators often had their equipment confiscated and the Department of the Interior soon found itself the owner of assorted equipment, rifles, horses, and animal pelts. Unfortunately this process worked little hardship upon the professional poachers, who did not much mind the loss of a little equipment, which was easily replaced. Nevertheless, the policy of expulsion did affect the occasional poacher who lived near the Park, for many of them depended on summer employment in the Park as packers, guides, teamsters, or laborers. A man once expelled for violating a regulation could be ejected again and again. This process was extralegal, but it was the only form of punishment available until Congress could be persuaded to establish laws, legal machinery, and well-defined punishments for the violation of those laws.[40]

In the absence of laws and well-defined Park policy, it was fortunate for the future of the Yellowstone National Park that the first military Acting Superintendent was a man of Harris' caliber. A man of less character might have devoted himself wholly to military matters and have performed his Park duties of Acting Superintendent in a perfunctory manner. Harris, however, according to one of his successors, was "austere, correct, unyielding," and a "terror to evil doers." He was often disagreeable (as indeed is any man who is always right), and Harris was "always *sure* that he was right before he acted, and then no fear of consequences deterred him."[41] The protection of the game within the Park had never seriously been attempted before Harris' arrival, but in the three years that he was Acting Superintendent he inaugurated and set in motion most of the protective measures utilized by his successors.

VI

The Development of a Policy:

1889-1894

THE ADMINISTRATION of Captain Moses Harris proved rather tranquil, in the absence of partisan politics, and was marked by close cooperation between the Acting Superintendent and the Secretary of the Interior. That of the second military superintendent was almost the opposite. Conflict between the Secretary of the Interior and the Acting Superintendent scarred the administration of Harris' successor, politics were introduced into administrative affairs, and unprincipled men, prompted only by motives of monetary profit, attempted ingress into the Park. Despite these disruptive influences, the new Acting Superintendent was able to continue the policies begun by his predecessor and to introduce new programs and policies designed to better protect and preserve the Yellowstone Park.

Captain Gustavus C. Doane, the officer who had provided military escort for the Washburn-Langford-Doane Expedition of 1870, had tried to be named the first military superintendent of the Park. He was, indeed, the logical man for the job. He was thoroughly acquainted with the Park area and it was due, in part, to his lucid report of the 1870 Expedition that Congress had established the Park in 1872. When Congress provided for military management, Doane was in the Southwest campaigning against Geronimo and was not considered for the Park detail, although he had previously requested the assignment. In 1889 Doane, now a Captain assigned to the Presidio, San Francisco, began his intensive letter-writing campaign. Recommendations from generals and politicians, in addition to numerous petitions from private citizens, poured into the Interior office.[1] These efforts were in vain, however, and Troop "K," 1st Cavalry, Captain F. A. Boutelle commanding, was relieved of duty at Fort Custer, Montana Territory, and ordered to march to Camp Sheridan, Wyoming to relieve Troop "M" and Captain Harris.[2]

Captain Boutelle assumed the duties of Acting Superintendent on June 2, 1889, and almost immediately entered into small disputes with the Secretary of the Interior. He found that lack of proper equipment hindered the extinguishment of the many fires started by careless campers, and he requested, by telegraph, funds for the purchase of "twenty axes and twenty rubber buckets." Three letters followed the telegram, but none were acknowledged by the Secretary's office.[3] Boutelle had earlier requested advice about the proper disposal of property confiscated from trespassers; this request, too, was unanswered. Authorization for the installation of a telephone in the Superintendent's office had been delayed a month, and in the interim Boutelle had been forced to "run a half mile distant" to a telephone in the hotel. Perhaps this unnecessary exercise, or the fact that he had been "personally fighting forest fires for some days and nights," made Boutelle write a hurried note to the Secretary of the Interior:

> If you do not think it proper to give me such things as I ask for, I certainly am entitled to recognition. I take the liberty of

enclosing this letter under personal cover, in order that I may feel sure that it reaches you in person and wish . . . that in the future I shall not be ignored. In the Department in which I have served for twenty-eight years I have been accustomed to have some respectful actions taken on my papers.[4]

Action was taken on this letter, but it was less than respectful. The Secretary suggested that perhaps the Acting Superintendent was disposed to be "troublesome" and was altogether too "quick to attribute delinquencies to others." Boutelle indignantly retorted that he had "waited for days" for a reply to his telegram and letters informing the Secretary that fires were raging in the Park, and that the requested "rubber buckets were indispensable." This was so apparent that a "Mr. Lesvis of Pennsylvania" had donated, "from his pocket," forty dollars for the purchase of buckets. Boutelle maintained that he was working every hour and that he thought that he was entitled to "fair recognition."[5] With this statement the water bucket episode was dropped, but it reappeared a year later.

The next conflict between Boutelle and the Secretary of the Interior culminated in an apparent victory for Boutelle —a victory that, while establishing a precedent for later Park policy, was partially responsible for his transfer from the position of Acting Superintendent. Sensing the possibilities of profit, D. B. May of Billings, Montana, in March, 1889, applied to the Secretary of the Interior for permission to erect an elevator at the lower falls of the Yellowstone River, "to enable tourists to descend to the bottom of the Canyon, thereby getting a much more favorable view of the Falls." May agreed to construct the proposed elevator under the supervision of the Superintendent, whose selection of the site would be final and conclusive.[6] The Secretary of the Interior requested that Professor Arnold Hague, United States Geologist, then in the Yellowstone Park, join with Captain Boutelle in examining the May application and report upon the feasibility of the project.[7] Boutelle subsequently reported, after a careful examination made by Hague and himself, that the "scheme is believed to be perfectly practicable" and that an elevator so constructed would be entirely out of view and "in no way objectionable." It was his considered opinion that the construction of an elevator would "add materially to the pleasure of a visit to the canyon."[8] This favorable report was forwarded to the Secretary in October, 1889; a contract to construct the proposed elevator was granted to D. B. May by the Secretary on May 17,1890.[9]

When the contents of the elevator contract were made known to Boutelle, he regretted that approval had been given before he had had the opportunity to examine it, for it provided for the construction of the elevator in a place different from the one suggested by Hague and himself. Reversing his earlier position, he was now convinced that the "whole matter has been a mistake" and was "mortified that at any time, in any way, I approved of it." It was now his opinion that no matter how carefully the elevator was constructed, it would "destroy the wild view from the head of the great falls, one of the grandest in the Park," and advised the Secretary that, "if not too late . . . the lease should be cancelled."[10] Secretary Noble reminded the Captain that he had originally approved the scheme, that the elevator could be constructed so as to not be in general view, and that the construction of a shelter at the elevator's base "could scarcely appear as a blot on the scene" because of the great distance from which it would be viewed from the top of the canyon. Boutelle was directed to inform May that the elevator track should be constructed so as to not mar the view or "deface the canyon to any appreciable extent."[11]

In his annual report to the Secretary of the Interior Boutelle again protested the elevator lease, maintaining that if it were allowed, a policy of "commercialization" would result, and the original purpose of the Park would be prostituted. The fire bucket episode was recalled in an attempt to display the handicaps under which any Acting Superintendent was forced to operate. His sharply critical report was immediately returned "for reconsideration" by the Secretary, who thought that Boutelle had done the Department and himself a "great injustice" by including in the report statements concerning the purchase of buckets and his revised opinion on the elevator. Boutelle agreed to revise the report and admitted his error in relation to the elevator lease, an error which he considered the "greatest mistake in the past two years of my life except perhaps my entering upon this duty without an effort to avoid it."

> I was selected for it without being consulted and came here against my wish. My selection may have been unfortunate but being here I take great interest in my work, and, as has been the rule of my life, do as well as I can. It is not the first time I have paid the penalty of efficiency . . . While my interest in the Park is great and I have here an importance which I should not enjoy at an ordinary frontier post . . . I shall for many reasons be glad when my relief comes. I should be glad to remain and see some of the work I have inaugurated carried to a successful termination, but at a military post I am able to please my Commanding Officer while here I have the world to consider and appear to be about as successful as the old man with the ass in the fable.[12]

Captain Boutelle's stubborn objection to the "commercialization" of any element in the Park had a lasting effect. On October 15, 1890, the permission granted to May to erect an elevator was revoked, and another element of national park policy was established.[13]

While Boutelle's administration was short and stormy, other innovations were introduced under it that ultimately became recognized as national park policy. When the Acting Superintendent discovered that the fish of the Yellowstone Lake were infected with parasitic worms, he notified the United States Fish Commissioner and requested information concerning a remedy. The remedy came eventually from Boutelle himself, who suggested that the barren streams of the Park be stocked with healthy trout as a replacement for the infected fish; on September 25, 1889, he reported "young trout all planted in perfect order."[14] Subsequent stocking of the Park's waters was carried on by the United States Fish Commission under the direction of Boutelle's successors and the Yellowstone National Park ultimately became known as a Mecca for trout fishermen.

During the summers of 1889 and 1890 Boutelle's troops were mainly engaged in fighting and extinguishing fires started by careless campers. In an attempt to prevent this, he established regular campgrounds and limited campers to those places designated. The system of specifically designated campgrounds, subsequently established in all national parks, was thus inaugurated.[15]

The policy of patrolling the isolated areas of the Park during the winter months by small detachments of soldiers mounted on "Norwegian skiis," in an attempt to prevent the poaching of game, had been initiated by Acting Superintendent Harris. These detachments were forced to live as did their quarry, carrying provisions on their backs and constructing temporary shelters when they stopped for the night. In order to alleviate its worst hardships and systematize this winter scouting, Boutelle requested authority and funds to construct "five or six log cabins" spaced throughout the Park "for shelter of snow shoe parties scouting the Park in winter." Authorization for the construction of six cabins "not to exceed $100 each," complete with tin boxes for the preservation of provision, was eventually received from the Secretary of the Interior.[16] This system of utilizing patrol cabins, termed, then and now, "showshoe cabins," was adopted by the rangers of the National Park Service and continues to the present day.

The farsighted Boutelle also opposed both the granting of a railroad right-of-way into the Park and the alternate proposal of eliminating the northern portion of the Park to allow a rail access to Cooke City. When a proposal was made in Congress to extend the southern boundary of the Park, Boutelle informed the Secretary of the Interior that he thought "it would be well to go a little further south" than had been suggested, so as to include within the Park "Jackson's lake country and the Teton peaks." Had this suggestion been followed, the government would have avoided much of the later litigation and expense concurrent with the formation of Grand Teton National Park. Realizing that the few remaining bison were rapidly nearing extinction, Boutelle implored the Governor of Wyoming and the Secretary of the Territory of Idaho to work for the passage of laws that would protect the animal from continued slaughter. He continued to request from Congress legislation that would provide punishment for persons who wilfully violated the regulations of the Park.[17]

Boutelle also demonstrated his awareness of his duties as Acting Superintendent by the character of expulsions from the Park during his term of office. A Mr. Imes of Bozeman was expelled for his "unsufferable insolence to a Non-Commissioned Officer"; a butcher in the employ of the Yellowstone Park Association was expelled for "wantonly killing a bear." A similar fate befell a woman from Utah who "persisted in throwing stones into a Geyser after repeated remonstrances," and "every tramp who found his way inside Park limits" was also ejected.[18] E. E. VanDyke, a notorious poacher, had been expelled for killing game within the boundaries of the Park, and when he requested readmittance to accept a job in the Park, Boutelle informed him that he was "an infernal rascal" or a "damned fool," and in either case, "not a proper person to be employed in the Park." Readmittance was refused.[19]

Military guardianship of the Park was not, however, above reproach. On two occasions Boutelle recommended that "the carnivorous animals of the Park be destroyed" in order to protect the game animals but this unfortunate policy was not inaugurated until Theodore Roosevelt's day.[20] In addition to charges of "harsh and arbitrary rule" voiced by miscreants who had been expelled for violation of the rules, the *Omaha World* stated that the soldiers guarding the Park had established a system of "espionage" and were "levying blackmail" upon visiting tourists. The anonymous correspondent maintained that the tourists were "annoyed by the boys in blue" until they were given money, and that if no money was handed over the tourist was arrested on a "trumped up charge." Boutelle maintained that he cared "nothing for . . . untruthful vaporings . . . and would not take the trouble to reply" to some charges made in the Omaha paper, but he did take steps to disprove the accusation of extortion. He was sure that the charges were false, and solicited statements from various visitors to the Park to support

National Park Service

Soldiers and others at post Exchange,
Mammoth (Fort Yellowstone)

his belief. One Judge S. T. Corns stated that "we received from them [soldiers] only courtesy and kindness throughout our journey"; E. Hofer wrote that he had never "heard one disparaging word against the soldiers," and maintained that they "had always been polite and gentlemanly in the discharge of their duties"; F. B. Riley found that he could "honestly state . . . that the soldiers conduct themselves well and are deserving of commendation"; W. W. Wylie, a man who conducted camping parties through the Park, had "yet to learn of a single instance whereby the boys in any manner insisted on being recompensed," and he had never "seen any ill treatment or want of courtesy by any of the troops."[21] Nevertheless it is probable that some of the soldiers were not always "polite and gentlemanly" to tourists. Many disliked the duty thrust upon them, and failed to recognize the sublimity of the mighty wonders of nature. It is only natural that some would vent their dislike of army life upon the sometimes exasperating tourist with his endless questions and propensity to destroy what the soldier was charged with protecting.

The activities of a group of unhappy and self-deluded Indians finally extricated both the Secretary of the Interior and the Acting Superintendent from their increasingly difficult relationship. The Teton Sioux of South Dakota, displeased with their life on the reservation, forsook all labor and began practicing a religion preached by "Wovoka," a Paiute messiah who promised the disconsolate Indians that the white man could be made to disappear and their ancestral lands returned to them, if they would but perform certain rites, dances, and ceremonies. Eager to achieve what they had been unable to win by fighting, a large number of the suffering Sioux began dancing; the whites became apprehensive, and a call for military troops went out. Troop "K," 1st Cavalry, Captain F. A. Boutelle commanding, was ordered to the field to take part in the "Sioux Campaign of 1890–1891." A detachment of nine men was left at Camp Sheridan to protect the Park and its government property. The Secretary of the Interior immediately requested that the Secretary of War detail "another officer with a company of the same number as Captain Boutelle had, for duty in the Park."[22]

Captain Gustavus C. Doane, now stationed at Fort Bowie, Arizona Territory, again began a campaign to be appointed Superintendent of the Yellowstone Park. He devised a plan of overland marches that would obviate transportation expense and called upon his friends to intercede on his behalf. Identical letters were written to the Secretary of War by Senator W. F. Sanders of Montana and General William E. Strong recommending the appointment of Doane, and both received identical replies: "The Department does not deem it advisable to order him [Doane] on this duty." The Secretary of War then informed the two men that the Sixth Regiment of Cavalry was then serving in a section of the country nearer to the Park than Fort Bowie, and that Captain George S. Anderson of that regiment, then on duty at Fort Meyer, Virginia, had been selected as Acting Superintendent. In explanation, the Secretary added, "the selection of this officer [Anderson] involves no expense other than his transportation from this city to Pine Ridge Agency where the troop to which he has been assigned is now stationed."[23]

Obviously the decision not to appoint Doane to the position was based upon more than the somewhat specious explanation given by the Secretary. Doane had planned his march from Arizona to the Park so that no expense would be entailed, and the weakness of the Secretary's explanation was illustrated by Major General Nelson A. Miles, Commanding General, Division of the Missouri, who objected to the transfer of Anderson and Troop "I" to duty in the Park. The troop chosen had been in the field nearly two months, and the distance from Pine Ridge to Camp Sheridan was 630 miles, "which to march in midwinter would cause great suffering," while the distance by rail was 1,662 miles. Furthermore, according to Miles, there were "other good reasons" why Troop "I" should not be detailed for the Park duty.[24] Notwithstanding these protestations, Captain George S. Anderson, Sixth Cavalry, was appointed Acting Superintendent of the Yellowstone Park and assumed his duties on February 15, 1891.[25]

The new Acting Superintendent was ideally suited for his position. He had many friends in Washington, was extremely interested in the preservation and protection of the Park, and was responsible for the formulation of many new policies and programs that were later adopted by the National Park Service. During his six-and-a-half-year administration, the present road system was completed, the Park was saved from the threat of commercialization and dismemberment, the last serious threat of railway ingress was thwarted, and legislation providing for legal machinery within the Park was passed by Congress.

When Captain Anderson and his troop of cavalry arrived in the Park, the troops were still being quartered in the "temporary" shelters constructed some five years before and designated as Camp Sheridan. Captain Boutelle had recommended that a permanent military post be constructed in the Park, and this recommendation was accepted. Land necessary for the establishment of a permanent post was granted by the Department of the Interior to the United States Army. On February 27, 1891, the Fort Yellowstone military reservation was established. The first buildings, constructed of quarried stone and designed to accommodate one company of cavalry, were completed and occupied in the autumn of 1891. These, and buildings later constructed for military purposes, form the nucleus of the present Yellowstone National Park headquarters.[26]

The problems of protection and police were becoming more complicated and difficult as towns grew up around the borders of the Park, vandals and poachers increased in number, and the construction of hotels and roads enabled the increasing number of visitors to spread over a greater area.

In 1890 Company hotel visitors numbered 3,800; in 1895, the first year records were kept, 5,348 persons visited the Park. Congress still refused to pass legislation necessary to enforce the rules. Confiscation of trespassers' property was ruled illegal by the Attorney General,[27] and the military authorities were forced to fall back upon their own ingenuity. Not surprisingly, sometimes illegal procedures were invoked. Captain Anderson found the main problems were the "propensities of women to gather 'specimens,' and of men to advertise their folly by writing their names on everything beautiful within their reach." He placed small squads of soldiers on guard at every main geyser basin and instructed them to arrest and threaten with expulsion anyone found breaking off material, gathering specimens, or writing names. Any arrested person was escorted to the Acting Superintendent, who administered a tongue lashing as only a seasoned cavalry officer could, and then released with the warning that a second arrest would be followed by expulsion from the Park.

This method proved to be unsuccessful, for Anderson still found that the "names of the vain glared at one from every bit of formation, and from every place where the ingenuity of vanity could place them." He then instituted a process whereby every person found guilty of carving his or her name in one of the geyser formations was ordered back to the scene of his crime, where, amid the taunts and gibes of his fellow tourists, and under the watchful eyes of an armed escort, he was forced to "obliterate the supposed imperishable monument to his folly" with the aid of soap and brush.[28] This method had some effect according to one observer from Missoula, Montana, who wrote Anderson that he had seen a bride and groom busily writing their names wherever they could find a smooth place on one particular formation. The observer informed the youthful couple that "as their names were on the hotel register they would be known and the soldiers would take them in charge and march them out of the Park." Upon hearing this, the "bride nearly fainted" and begged the groom to wipe their names off, which he did, but the Montanan thought "it was as good as a circus to see him on his knees rubbing away at the writing for dear life."[29]

Yet the military commander found that despite the sharpest watch, new names were constantly being added and it became increasingly difficult to distinguish these new signatures from the old ones. Finally, in the early part of the 1892 season, all of the inscriptions were removed from the various formations with the aid of hammer and chisel and the Park and its protectors "started even with the world." Writing in 1894, Anderson could claim that his remedy was "heroic and successful," for the geyser basins were then "practically free from this disfigurement."[30]

As the popularity of the Park increased, the problem of fire prevention grew in proportion to the increased number of Park visitors, and Anderson found that ever-increasing vigilance on the part of fire patrols was necessary to protect the forests from destruction. He insisted upon rigorous enforcement of the regulation requiring expulsion from the Park of any campers who left their fires unextinguished. Anderson found that "one or two expulsions each year served as healthy warnings," and that these, reinforced by a system of numerous patrols by the soldiers, had "brought about the particularly good results of which we can boast."[31]

An even more serious problem was the protection of wildlife. When Captain Anderson assumed control of the Park there was still no law under which poachers could be punished, and consequently they plied their trade with increasing intensity. The last remnants of the great wild bison herds that had previously wandered the plains now found refuge in the Park; beaver, relatively scarce in other portions of the West, were fairly common in the Park, and great numbers of deer and elk were still to be found there. An enterprising poacher could make a good living preying upon these animals, and if he were apprehended, expulsion usually meant little more than a slight inconvenience. With the virtual disappearance of the great bison herds, the meat and hide hunting of the previous decade was no longer possible, but the head of the shaggy animal was still valuable. Mounted bison heads, Anderson was told by one taxidermist, were "worth $1500.00 in the market," but if one could find a "rich and anxious customer, they might bring a good deal more." Taxidermists from Livingston, Billings, or Helena would pay $500 and up for an unmounted average head.[32]

For these and other reasons Anderson recommended that Fort Yellowstone be enlarged to accommodate two troops of cavalry on a year-round basis, and that the troop customarily detailed for service in the Park during the summer months be assigned there permanently. Military orders were issued making the requested change.[33] Aided by a civilian scout who knew both the topography of the Park and the most notorious poachers living in the surrounding communities, Anderson was now ready to wage war upon the transgressors.

During the winter months the majority of the two troops of cavalry were necessarily billeted at Fort Yellowstone, but at least five outposts were garrisoned during the entire year. In addition, scouting parties were sent out patrolling the entire Park and, traveling on skis, were instructed "not to follow the regular trails, but to go to the most unfrequented places," so that they "might happen on a malicious person." The "snowshoe cabins" constructed during Boutelle's administration were utilized for shelter, and "dressed in fur caps, California blanket coats, leggings, and moccasins,"[34] these strangely uniformed cavalrymen soon became a nemesis to the poacher slipping into the Park in search of beaver or bison.

During the summer months these back-country patrols were increased in both number and scope, and four additional outposts were garrisoned. One observer, who accompanied a cavalry patrol over fallen timber and through "frightening morasses," found this "typical manner" of policing the Park, "monotonous, toilsome, and uneventful work"; but it was useful because it left the track of the cavalry horseshoe in the most remote parts of the preserve, where the poacher or interloper could see it and become apprehensive. It was this person's opinion that "two regiments could not entirely prevent poaching in the mountain wastes of the great reservation," but he thought that the two troops were "successful enough at the task."[35]

In his attempt to end poaching, Anderson was hindered by the resentment of the American pioneer toward game laws and game preservation. The settlers surrounding the Park refused to recognize the fact that the protection of game within the Park would profit them as the surplus of animals thus protected spilled over into the surrounding areas. A greater hindrance, however, was the continued failure of Congress to provide legal machinery. Anderson was advised by the Secretary of the Interior that trespassers could be punished only by expulsion, there being "no legal jurisdiction . . . by which their property can be confiscated." The Secretary also informed him that if an offender returned to the Park after expulsion, he could then "take possession of all means of transportation and equipment reporting the same for disposition," but admitted that such a process "may be a fine point to decide" and one that would necessarily be left to the military commander's "sound discretion."[36] Faced with the choice of adhering closely to the law and simply expelling offenders, or of going beyond the law and devising extralegal punishment, the Acting Superintendent chose the latter course.

One especially pernicious poacher was apprehended while illegally trapping, his property was confiscated, and, contrary to all rules of law, he was confined in the guard house at Fort Yellowstone pending advice from the Secretary of the Interior, advice which for some reason was very slow in arriving. Ultimately his release was ordered, but in Anderson's opinion "this imprisonment for a month" had done more to break up trapping and poaching "than all the other arrests made since the park was established." He realized that he had no authority to imprison the poacher but he thought that his actions were justified since "simple removal had absolutely no effect on such characters." The property confiscated from this poacher was not returned to him in spite of his repeated requests. Two years after his arrest and release from confinement the man wrote, "Now don't you think I hav bin a very good boy ever saince you gave me your lesson at the Springs—now as I have quit hunting and gon to ranching—I will ask you to please send my field glass up to me—as it comes very handy to hunt horses and cattle with [*sic*]." A year later the man wrote again, explaining that he was no longer in the vicinity of the Park and asked that Anderson "give my field glass and six shooter up to me."[37] Another hunter was found "with two buffalo calves" which he claimed had been captured outside of the Park, an explanation that Anderson refused to believe. His equipment, too, was confiscated and he was imprisoned in the guard house. The Secretary of the Interior was not informed of the situation until a month had passed and he then immediately telegraphed orders for the prisoner's release.[38]

Individuals with a known propensity to enter the Park to pursue game animals were closely watched, cooperation was obtained from law enforcement officers of the neighboring states, private detectives were hired to gather information about planned poaching expeditions, and letters of private individuals were intercepted. One piece of correspondence opened by the military authorities contained the instruction: "You had better get a bottle of strychnine and poison some of those cross and silver grey fox at the Canyon this winter their hides can be sent by mail."[39] All of this served to reduce poaching, but did not prevent it. Congressional legislation was still needed.

In an attempt to bring law and order to this area neglected by the lawmakers, Anderson determined to make expulsion as unpleasant as possible. When a transgressor was apprehended in the southern part of the Park, he was marched on foot, accompanied by a mounted escort, to the extreme northern entrance to the Park and there "expelled." The process was reversed if apprehension occurred in the northern portion of the Park. Usually the culprit's belongings, if not confiscated, were deposited at the opposite boundary. The process was admittedly extralegal, but it was effective. In one case, when notified that one Max Caufman, staying at the Lake Hotel, had attempted assault upon a chambermaid, Anderson sent an order to the officer in charge there to have the alleged offender "marched out of the Park." In reporting the incident to the Secretary of the Interior, Anderson stated, "He was brought as far as Norris yesterday, arriving near midnight, nearly exhausted. He was allowed to ride a saddle horse to this point [Headquarters, Mammoth Hot Springs] today, and was marched on to Gardiner, where he was set at liberty."[40]

Revision of the rules was often found necessary. Suggestions for revision originated with either the Acting Superintendent or the Secretary of the Interior. All suggested changes from the Secretary were passed down to the Acting Superintendent for approval before being promulgated, and it was only through the efforts of Captain Anderson that Rule Number 9 ("No drinking saloon or bar room will be permitted within the limits of the Park") was not revised to completely prohibit the sale of alcoholic beverages within the Park proper. His continual insistence that such beverages were necessary, from the medicinal standpoint, finally overcame the complaints of temperance advocates and the predilection of the Secretary of the Interior. Anderson emphasized the injurious effect of the altitude upon travelers and related the story of "a distinguished surgeon" who was traveling with him. The surgeon "came into my room at 2 *a.m.* saying, 'I'm dying, for God's sake get me some whiskey,' and quite probably the immediate production of it saved his life." Continuing his medical defense of alcoholic stimulants, the Captain stated that "most of the waters of the Park affect the bowels of many tourists and the most temperate need brandy medicinally. I think they should be able to get it." On another occasion he maintained that "stimulants are held by high medical authority to be often necessary and the bar rooms . . . are intended to supply this want."[41] Whatever the validity of his arguments, the Captain won the battle, and "spiritous liquors" were dispensed to hotel guests until national prohibition terminated the practice.

Anderson's motives were probably not altogether unselfish. John W. Meldrum, the first United States Commissioner appointed with jurisdiction over the Park, remarked that when he was introduced to Anderson the Acting Superintendent replied, "right off the bat: 'Good to see you, let's have a drink.' " When describing his first residence in Yellowstone, Meldrum stated that "on the other side of the hall was the bar room. There was music every night until midnight . . . the chief trumpeter in there would always be Captain Anderson."[42] A strong defender of the imbiber, Anderson was an enemy of the gambler, and it was he who established the rule that "under no circumstances will a gambling establishment of any kind be permitted within the park."[43]

Anderson also stipulated an element of later National Park policy when he determined that it was not "necessary or advisable, to limit the season of fishing." He continued the process of fish planting begun by his predecessor and obtained permission to "prohibit fishing for two years in any waters newly stocked."[44] During his administration, also, live trapping of animals in the Park for shipment first to the Smithsonian Institution in Washington and later to zoos throughout the United States was begun.[45]

VII

The Development of

a Legal Structure

WHILE THE ARMY was protecting the natural features and wildlife of the Park, others were working for legislation to aid in that protection. The battle for legal machinery was a long and difficult one, extending from 1882 to 1894. On one side were arrayed the forces advocating protection and conservation; on the other side were those who sought to exploit and disrupt the Park. The conservationists had as their spokesman Senator George C. Vest of Missouri; their opponents included several Senators and Congressmen who heeded the influence of a powerful lobby known as "The Railroad Gang." Vest, backed by Senator C. F. Manderson of Nebraska, enlisted the aid of George Bird Grinnell, editor of *Forest and Stream*, Arnold Hague, William Hallet Phillips, and all of the Acting Superintendents of the Park, and focused his campaign on one target: the passage of a bill providing legal machinery to punish violators of Park rules. Their opponents, the mining interests and real estate speculators in Cooke City and the surrounding territory, directed their attack on two fronts, both designed to frustrate the purpose of the National Park. One was termed "segregation," designed to reduce the area of the Park; the other was designed to gain a right-of-way for a railroad through the Park. Ultimately the proponents of protection and preservation won the battle, with the passage of the Lacey Act in 1894.

On December 12, 1882 Vest secured adoption by the Senate of a Resolution calling upon the Committee on Territories to review possible legislation to protect the wildlife, forests, and natural wonders of the Yellowstone National Park. In response to this Resolution, he, as chairman of the Committee on Territories, reported a bill to amend the Yellowstone Park Act of 1872. Vest proposed to extend the area of the Park, place it within the criminal jurisdiction of the Montana Territorial courts for offenses against life or property, and create within the Park a police jurisdiction for the arrest, examination, and punishment of those who violated the rules made by the Secretary of the Interior. Unfortunately, no action was taken on this or a similar bill introduced in the House; but the groundwork was established for an eleven-year struggle, culminating in 1894 with the passage of similar legislation.[1]

Six times, between 1883 and 1893, Senator Vest maneuvered his bill through the Senate; six times his bill was reported favorably in the House, but each time it emerged with a crippling amendment granting a railroad right-of-way through the Park. The proponents of the right-of-way assumed that those who wanted to protect the Park would rather have a bill providing protection and carrying the railroad rider than no bill at all. The advocates of Park protection, however, feared that not only would the construction of a railroad destroy natural features of the Park, but that it would also establish a precedent making the exclusion of other railroads impossible. These men chose to bide their time, backing every "Vest Bill" in its course through the

Senate, opposing the amended bill as it was reported out of the House.[2]

Blocked in other directions,[3] proponents of the railroad began agitation for a boundary readjustment that would restore the northern part of the Park to the public domain and thus allow access to the Cooke City mines without going through the Park. The Northern Pacific Railway Company had previously extended a branch line to the northern entrance of the Park, thus connecting Gardiner and Livingston, Montana. The residents of Livingston were the most vocal supporters of the various segregation bills, fearing that if a line were not run into the mining area from the West, the trade of Cooke City would be drained eastward. The various bills proposed to accomplish this dismemberment were collectively known as "segregation bills" and were vigorously opposed by friends of the Park, who maintained that the proposed boundary change would exclude from the Park one of its most attractive portions, in addition to destroying the winter range of the elk, antelope, and mountain sheep, which would in turn "lead to the destruction of half the game in the Park."[4]

The pressure applied by the railroad lobby to segregate a portion of the Park was so intense, however, that even those Senators who had long been stalwart defenders of the Park trembled and tottered. A bill introduced by Senator Francis E. Warren of Wyoming, designed to return to the public domain the northern portion of the Park desired by the railroad promoters, was placed before the Senate on February 26, 1892.[5] When it came up for debate on May 10, Senator Vest, the man who had repeatedly fought off all attempts at encroachment, confessed "with considerable humiliation" that he had finally been defeated. Noting that Idaho, Montana, and Wyoming had recently become states, he claimed that, out of senatorial courtesy, he would henceforth bow to the wishes of the Senators from those new states. In a frank admission of senatorial impotence, Vest admitted that "a persistent and unscrupulous lobby are able to do almost what they please with the public domain" and that "the fact remains that no legislation can be had for the park until the demands of these people are conceded." When questioned as to why the Senate of the United States must concede to the wishes of a mere lobbying group, Vest replied that the railroad lobby was "exactly like a compact military organization working for one object alone. They are persistent, aggressive, sleepless, untiring, and they are determined to own a charter into this reservation." Because of this constant pressure, he, for one, was submitting to the segregation legislation "because I can not help myself, not because my judgement approves it." Explaining his apparent capitulation to the railroad power, Vest maintained that, if all railroad companies were allowed to construct roads on the land segregated from the Park, the attempts by one company to form a monopoly would be frustrated and the sole object of the railroad lobby would be defeated. "I do not believe," he said, "they [the railroad lobby] will permit—and I use that language with its full significance—this bill to go through the House of Representatives."[6]

With the foremost defender of the Park seemingly rendered helpless, opposition to the segregation bill was confined to Senator William B. Bates of Tennessee. Senator Bates thought that the very existence of a powerful lobby operating in the halls of Congress was reason enough to vote against the bill, and although he had never visited the Park, his speech on its behalf illustrated an exact understanding of its purpose:

> . . . the Yellowstone National Park is a reservation set apart by the Government for the people in common. . . . I do not desire to see it diverted from the original intention. . . . I look upon it as I do upon the reservation of Yosemite Valley and of the big trees in Mariposa Grove. If some one thinks he can

make a fortune out of the big trees of Mariposa, shall we allow him to go there and cut down those wonderful . . . natural objects and destroy that magnificent scenery . . . ? . . . shall we give away the principle that this park [Yellowstone] was to be kept sacred and held apart for the people of this country . . . and that strangers from all parts of the world who come hither to see the beauty and grandeur of our country may look upon it with admiration . . . ? . . . I want to preserve that park in its entirety, and I do not wish to see the object for which it was originally set apart changed and diverted into other channels.[7]

In rebuttal to this eloquent plea, Senator James H. Berry of Arkansas, representing the materialistic attitudes of the age, stated that he did not believe that the "Government ought to engage in the raising of wild animals," that it was not a "profitable industry" for the government, and that he would, if given the opportunity, vote to abolish the Park entirely, breaking it up into 160 acre lots, allowing settlement and cultivation, and if that process were not practicable, he would "sell it to the highest bidder and place the money in the Treasury."[8]

Senators Henry M. Teller of Colorado, Francis E. Warren of Wyoming, Wilbur F. Sanders of Montana, and Orville H. Platt of Connecticut all rose in defense of the segregation bill, while a somewhat feeble opposition was voiced by Senators Henry L. Dawes of Massachusetts, Arthur P. Gorman of Maryland, and John M. Palmer of Illinois. On roll call vote, the bill passed the Senate by a vote of 32 to 18. In the House, the Senate version was favorably reported out of the Committee on Public Lands, but fortunately for the integrity of the Park, no further action was taken.[9]

The passage of this bill through the Senate marked the apogee of the railroad group's effort to gain control of a portion of the Park. While the senatorial supporters were weakening, other proponents of the Park idea were forming themselves into an articulate and persuasive lobby group.

George Bird Grinnell filled the columns of *Forest and Stream* with editorials and articles denouncing those who advocated the reduction of the Park, and in 1892 he distributed throughout the country a pamphlet entitled, "A Standing Menace; Cooke City vs. the National Park." Acting Superintendent Anderson bombarded the Secretary of the Interior with letters opposing the entrance of a railroad line into the Park and maintained that if any of the segregation bills were passed or a railroad franchise given, the results would be "the ruin of the Park and its complete destruction as a forest or a game preserve." He further stated that if "any public good would be subserved" by such a procedure, he would not oppose it, but in his opinion, the proposed legislation was "purely in the interest of private greed, and that too of not a very high order." Anderson traveled to Washington, and there appeared before a House committee in opposition to the boundary change and railroad permit.[10] A United States Civil Service Commissioner, Theodore Roosevelt, thought that "so far from having this Park cut down it should be extended, and legislation adopted which would enable the military authorities . . . to punish in the most rigorous way people who trespass upon it";[11] residents of Wyoming, Idaho, and Utah signed petitions of protest against the granting of a railroad right-of-way through the Park and presented them to Congress;[12] President T. F. Oakes of the Northern Pacific Railway stated that his company had thoroughly examined the mines at Cooke City and the various proposed routes to them, and that under no circumstances would his company build a road to them.[13]

When the 53rd Congress was called into special session by President Cleveland, primarily in order to repeal the Sherman Silver Purchasing Act, the railroad lobby again became active, but they were now fighting a losing battle. Bills were introduced into both Houses of Congress designed to authorize the construction and operation of an "electric railroad in the Yellowstone National Park," but the immediate response by Captain Anderson, who labeled the bills as "unneeded, unadvisable and vicious," had salutary effect and both bills were reported adversely from committees.[14] Senator Vest again introduced his bill providing for legal machinery and punishment of violations in the Park, but no action was taken on it. If the supporters of the Park were disheartened by Congressional refusal to pass the Vest bill, they had cause to rejoice when Congress also refused to provide legislation favoring the railroad interests. Segregation bills were introduced by Senator Joseph M. Carey of Wyoming and Congressman Charles S. Hartman of Montana; Representative Coffeen of Wyoming proposed a bill that would have granted Park lands to a railroad company. The Secretary of the Interior and the Acting Superintendent of the Park opposed these measures and supporters of the Park in the Senate and the House managed to kill the bills.

Thus ended the last serious attempt to segregate Park lands and force a railroad through the Yellowstone Park. Much bitterness was engendered in this fight, and the very existence of the Park was threatened. One man reported: "I heard some men talking today about the failure of the Government to grant the right of way through the National Park . . . they said that at a certain time fires would be started in the Park and all of the Park timber burned." A local editor reported rumors of arson and commented that, "Everyone concedes that the destruction of the Park by fire would be a public, a national calamity." He thought that the only way to avert such an impending danger would be for Congress to grant the "reasonable request of the people of the West and pass the segregation bill." As late as 1913 segregation was still contemplated by some, and on May 1 of that year Senator Meyers of Montana introduced a bill providing for the return of the public domain of "that area of the park lying north of the Yellowstone River," including the same area previously desired by the railroad interests. The bill was not reported out of committee and appears to have been the last attempt to remove that portion of the Park.[15]

With the defeat of the railroad lobbyists, the advocates of

conservation and preservation were now able to direct their energies to the long-standing campaign of achieving legal protection for the Park and its wildlife. Every civilian Super-intendent and every military Acting Superintendent had constantly urged the adoption of such necessary legislation, but the general public, then as now, was generally apathetic. Until public opinion could be marshaled by the defenders of the Park, it appeared that Congress would continue to ignore the pleas for legal machinery. The lamentable situation in the Park was publicized in the columns of *Forest and Stream* and its editor, George Bird Grinnell, utilized every capture and

National Park Service

Soda Butte Soldier Station, Yellowstone, 1905

subsequent release of poachers in the Park as a cause for editorials, news releases to newspapers throughout the country, and the printing of circulars, all of which were thrust upon Senators and Congressmen every time one of the Vest bills was before committee in hearing. Influential persons visiting the Park were told of the deplorable situation by Captain Anderson, and others were requested to write their Congressmen and join the ranks of those already enlisted in the campaign to preserve the Park. Still no action was forthcoming from Congress. The 53rd Congress refused to pass Vest's bill (S. 43); Senator Joseph M. Carey of Wyoming introduced a similar one (S. 166), reported it from the Senate Committee on Territories, only to see it meet the fate of the previous Vest bills.[16] Fortunately, one adventitious event finally prodded a reluctant Congress into action.

Edgar Howell, a resident of Cooke City, was arrested on March 13, 1894, in the Yellowstone Park and charged with the wanton killing of buffalo. This was considered by Captain Anderson to be the "most important arrest and capture ever made in the Park," and was replete with all of the suspense and surprise of a popular novel. In reporting the capture to the Secretary of the Interior, Captain Anderson wrote:

Some time since one of my snowshoe [ski] parties got on the trail of a man with a sled, on Astringent Creek, near Pelican. The trail was old when discovered, and in consequence it was not followed. About the same time a man ascertained to be one Ed. Howell of Cooke City, passed my station of Soda Butte in the night—and went on into Cooke. I knew that . . . he was not carrying out any trophies so I determined to make further search on the Pelican. . . . On the 6th inst. I started out a party consisting of Captain Scott, Lt. Forsyth, Burgess [Felix] the scout, two sergts. and Haynes [F. Jay], the park photographer . . . on the 12th inst. in a terrific storm, Burgess and the Sergt. started across to the Pelican country and camped. . . . Next A.M. he found, near his camp, a cache of 6 buffalo scalps and skulls, 3 *good* skins and 3 more that the hair had been partially taken off. . . . The trail was there,—but dim—of the poacher and it was soon lost. However Burgess kept on and about noon of that day he ran into a fresh trail which he followed to a lodge, erected near the mouth of Astringent Creek. While there he heard several shots & soon saw the culprit down in the middle of the Pelican Valley. Here he performed an act of bravery that deserves especial mention and recognition. The poacher was undoubtedly armed with a repeating rifle; it was equally certain that he was a desperate character & would resist arrest even to the point of taking life. The only arms Burgess and the Sergt. carried was a single Army revolver. Notwithstanding the serious risk, they boldly started forward over the 400 yards of open valley. The poacher was so occupied in skinning his buffalo that he did not see Burgess until he was within 15 or 20 feet of him. He then started for his rifle, but on order from Burgess stopped and surrendered. Near him were the bodies of 5 buffalo, freshly killed.[17]

Howell was confined in the guard house at Fort Yellowstone pending instructions from the Secretary of the Interior; his bedding, tepee, and toboggan were destroyed, and the scalps of the slaughtered bison were preserved with the intention of presenting them, mounted, to several select military and government officials. Anderson immediately sensed that the event could be capitalized on and recommended to the Secretary that it "be made the occasion for a *direct* appeal to Congress for the passage of an act making it an offense . . . for any one to kill, capture or injure any wild animal in the Park," and that the punishment "should be graded between a small fine only and a long term of imprisonment."[18]

Two things set the arrest of Howell apart from the previous arrests of poachers. This was the first time a poacher had been apprehended in the very act of killing and skinning game and his guilt undeniably established by the presence of still warm bodies. Also, by a happy coincidence, a team of reporters was in the Park, sent by George Bird Grinnell to collect material for *Forest and Stream.* Through the reportorial skill of Emerson Hough and the photographs of F. J. Haynes, the facts of the case were immediately made known to Grinnell, and he, together with influential friends, at once set out for Washington hoping that this flagrant case of bison killing would convince a still skeptical Congress that legislation was necessary to protect the game animals in the Park. In less than two weeks the desired legislation was introduced in the House by Congressman John F. Lacey of Iowa.[19]

Lacey's bill included the main features of the bill so often introduced in the Senate by Vest. It was reported from committee on April 4, 1894, slightly amended, and passed the House without debate on April 6, 1894.[20] This rapid process in a House that had previously crippled all attempts to provide a legal framework for the Park was due in part to the active role assumed by the bill's advocates. Grinnell had filled every issue of *Forest and Stream* with articles by Hough about the Howell case, together with editorials demanding Congressional action. Suggesting that "every reader who is interested in the Park . . . should write to his Senator and Representative," Grinnell advised his readers that the last remnants of the once numerous bison would surely be slaughtered if some action was not taken immediately.[21] When his cry was picked up by the national press, Congress was inundated with petitions and letters from an indignant public finally made aware that no law existed whereby poachers could be punished. Theodore Roosevelt planned to appear before the Senate Committee on Territories and stated that he would "use the recent unfortunate slaughter of buffaloes for all it was worth for trying to get legislation through." He thought that Howell should be "sent up for half a dozen years," and talked with every Congressman he could find in an attempt to hurry the protection bill through Congress.[22] Another friend of the Park, W. Hallett Phillips, convinced members of the Senate Committee on Territories that the bill before it was "a pretty poor one, too weak to do any good," and was responsible for the addition of penalties more severe than those provided in the House bill. He informed the Park Superintendent that "Roosevelt says you made the greatest mistake of your life in not accidentally having that scoundrel [Howell] killed and he speaks as if he would have shot him on the spot." Phillips said merely that "the killing of the buffalo has excited people very much and may stir Congress up to do something."[23]

It did. The bill, reported from the House Committee on Public Lands by Representative Lacey, was passed by the House and went over to the Senate, where it was immediately referred to the Committee on Territories. Senator Vest, as a member of this committee, secured the substitution of his bill for the House measure and his substitute was favorably reported out on April 14. When this substitute bill was debated on the Senate floor on April 21 and 23, Vest was able to obtain several amendments that increased fines and provided an annual salary for a United States Commissioner with jurisdiction over the Yellowstone Park. Thus amended, the bill passed the Senate and a conference committee was appointed. This committee agreed to some thirty amendments that dealt with unimportant changes in wording; the committee report was agreed to by the House on May 1, and by the Senate the following day.

In the Senate, the bill was questioned only by Senator Charles F. Manderson of Nebraska, who had to be assured that the bill did not in any way change the boundaries of the Park, and that the bill included "nothing looking to any entrance by any railroad." Vest assured him on these two points and reminded the Senate that "all that could be done . . . with a criminal the other day who killed a number of buffalo . . . was to take his old gun and a pair of blankets and put him outside the park." He thought that the bill before the Senate was "a good measure as far as it goes," admitted that it did not go so far as some of the bills previously introduced by him, but thought that "it is as far as Congress can go now under existing conditions." Senator Joseph M. Carey of Wyoming stated that "it is a bill that should be placed upon the statute book quickly, as it is said that during the last month one party of men, or as we call them in the West an 'outfit,' killed game to the value of more than $10,000, and they remarked when they were arrested and finally turned loose . . . that they would have made two or three thousand dollars in their two months' work if they had not been apprehended." Government for the Yellowstone National Park became a reality when President Grover Cleveland signed the Act on May 7, 1894.[24]

Surpassed only by the Act that established the Yellowstone Párk, the Act of May 7, 1894, stands as a great landmark in Park legislation and a monument to those unselfish individuals whose efforts and continued interest brought it about. By this Act the Park was placed under the sole and exclusive jurisdiction of the United States and constituted as a part of the United States judicial district of Wyoming. The laws of the state of Wyoming were made applicable in cases where an offense was not prohibited or punishable by federal law or regulations laid down by the Secretary of the Interior. All hunting, killing, wounding, or capturing of any bird or wild animal, "except dangerous animals, when it is necessary to prevent them from destroying human life or inflicting an injury" was prohibited. The Secretary of the Interior was directed to make "such rules and regulations as he may deem necessary and proper for the management and care of the park and for the protection of property therein . . . and for the protection of animals and birds in the park . . . and for governing the taking of fish." Possession within the Park of dead bodies of any wild bird or animal was to be *prima facie* evidence of violation of the Act. It made it a misdemeanor for any "persons, or stage or express company or railway company" to transport animals, birds, or fish taken in the Park, such transportation being punishable by a fine not exceeding $300. The heart of the Act was embodied in the following paragraph:

> Any person found guilty of violating any of the provisions of this Act or any rule or regulation that may be promulgated by the Secretary of the Interior with reference to the management and care of the Park, or for the protection of the property therein, for the preservation from injury or spoliation of timber, mineral deposits, natural curiosities or wonderful objects within said park, shall be deemed guilty of a misdemeanor, and shall be subjected to a fine of not more than one thousand dollars or imprisonment not exceeding two years, or both, and be adjudged to pay all costs of the proceedings.

The practice of confiscating the offender's equipment and vehicles was legalized and made mandatory.[25]

Legal administration was provided for the Park by a United States Commissioner and provision was made for the appointment of one or more deputy marshals, all of whom were to reside permanently in the Park. The Commissioner was given jurisdiction to hear and act upon all complaints of violations of the Act and of violations of regulations made by the Secretary of the Interior. He was empowered to issue process in the name of the United States for the arrest of any person charged with violations, and to hear evidence in the case of a person accused of having committed a felony, binding the accused over to the United States District Court of Wyoming. The Commissioner was to receive, in addition to the fees allowed by law, an annual salary of one thousand dollars and the use of an office to be constructed near the Park headquarters. Although a significant and necessary part of the legal process provided by the Lacey Act, the Commissioner has historically been little more than a legal functionary, performing the duties usually associated with a justice of the peace. John A. Meldrum was appointed the first Commissioner of the Park on June 20, 1894. He held that position until June 30, 1935, resigning at the age of 91 years.[26]

The enactment of this law should have pleased the advocates of Park protection but there were some who wanted more. Theodore Roosevelt thought that the law was "by no means as good" as he would like, but admitted that it was "a good deal better than the present systems and . . . it at least gives us a groundwork on which to go."[27] Edward A. Bowens, Commissioner of the General Land Office, attempted to have the bill amended so that the deputy marshals would be appointed by the Acting Superintendent, and in this way remove the "danger of some of the outlying poachers and that sort of cattle getting the appointments . . . as political favors." While the law would have been better with the inclusion of amendments proposed by W. Hallett Phillips and himself, he thought that "on the whole it is pretty good."[28] Phillips advised Anderson that, as the law stood, "it is very doubtful whether the Commissioner can exercise jurisdiction over offenses committed within that portion of the Park, which lies within the boundaries of Montana and Idaho," since when those states were admitted into the Union they did not relinquish jurisdiction over those portions of the Park. He pointed out, however, that "this point . . . is not generally known, and if I were you I would not mention it to any one but go on and enforce the Act over the whole Park."[29] Anderson regretted that the Act did not provide for the appointment of additional scouts, but Phillips said this complaint surprised him as he (Phillips) had "labored very hard" to have the Park bill amended to enable the Acting Superintendent to get as many scouts as he wanted under the "guise of Deputy Marshals."[30] Notwithstanding these shortcomings, the law was effective and has served as the cornerstone for all subsequent Park legislation.

Ironically, the first man to be arrested and tried under the new law was Edgar Howell, whose original arrest had led to passage of the Act. Howell had been illegally confined in the guard house at Fort Yellowstone until his release was ordered by the Secretary of the Interior. He was then escorted to the Park boundary, expelled, and ordered never to return. But he did return, and when apprehended in the Park the following summer he was arrested, charged with violating the order of expulsion, found guilty by the newly appointed Commissioner, fined fifty dollars and sentenced to thirty days in jail under the provisions of the Lacey Act. Howell appealed his conviction to the United States District Court and was subsequently released. Gibson Clark, United States Attorney for the United States District Court of Wyoming, stated that Howell could not be prosecuted criminally upon the charge of returning to the Park after having been removed because such an act did not "constitute a criminal offense under any statute of the United States." Nor could Howell be tried for the killing of the buffalo in March, because "there was no statute in force at that time." An act of the Wyoming Legislature making the killing of buffalo an offense was not applicable because the Act of Congress admitting Wyoming into the Union provided that "exclusive jurisdiction and control over all the Territory embraced in the Yellowstone National Park was reserved to the United States." Faced with this legal frustration, Gibson could only state, "If I could see any way by which this man could be prosecuted criminally, I should most gladly exhaust the power of the court in bringing him to justice for his outrageous wanton acts."[31]

Howell's relationship to the Park and its guardians in later years was changing and contradictory. In 1896 he was refused permission to make a trip through the Park, but a year later he was employed by the Acting Superintendent as a scout with the sole duty of apprehending poachers—a case of "using a thief to catch a thief."[32]

The provisions of the Act of May 7, 1894 marked a major turning point in the military administration of the Park. No longer would the military commanders be forced to utilize extralegal methods to punish violators of the rules; no longer would profit-minded poachers prey upon the Park's wildlife without fear of retribution. Poaching did not completely cease with the passage of the Act, but it was substantially reduced. Vigilance was still maintained, patrols continued to search the back country, and an occasional hunter or trapper was apprehended.

The first eight years of military control had been successful ones. The Park had been protected, the forests and wildlife preserved, and major elements of policy had been determined. During these years, the rules and regulations governing the Park had been constantly revised and enforced; the very real threats of segregation, commercialization, and railroad ingress had been met and defeated; and a definite policy, in reference to lessees, of "controlled monopoly," had evolved. A permanent military post had been established, the Yellowstone garrison doubled, fish planted, snowshoe cabins constructed, and Congress had been persuaded to pass legislation providing legal machinery and laws for the Park.

The successful military administration of the Yellowstone National Park prompted the establishment of the same type of administration in the National Parks in California. Yosemite, General Grant, and Sequoia had been established as "public parks" or "forest reservations" in 1890 and placed under the jurisdiction of the Secretary of the Interior. Congress as usual failed to provide legal means for the protection and preservation of these parks. Ultimately the provisions of the Act of May 7, 1894, were extended to these and other parks later established by Congress, but until this was done, it was the responsibility of the United States Army to protect them from devastation and destruction. Operating in the California Parks from the time of their inception until 1900 without Congressional sanction, and for the duration of the military administration without the aid of law enforcement machinery, the United States Cavalry saved these parks from destruction in much the same manner that it had saved the Yellowstone.

VIII

The Extension of the System:

Yosemite, Sequoia and

General Grant National Parks

THE EXPERIMENT INITIATED IN 1865 when Congress granted to the State of California the Yosemite Valley and the Mariposa Big Tree Grove, while noble in purpose, soon proved to be ignoble in practice. The experiences of the early Superintendents in the Yellowstone were duplicated in the Yosemite Valley, where the attempts of the first administrators to preserve and protect were frustrated by apathy, lack of appropriations, and public hostility bolstered by personal greed. Realizing that state control and management had degenerated into lack of control and mismanagement, a few interested and dedicated men took up their pens, appeared before Congress, filled newspaper and magazine columns with impassioned pleas, and finally convinced Congress that some action must be taken to prevent complete destruction of the lands it had attempted to preserve. Congress replied in 1890 by establishing a forest reservation surrounding the Yosemite Valley. Portions of the public domain containing the giant trees of California were set aside as public parks, and the responsibility for the preservation and protection of these areas was placed in the hands of the Secretary of the Interior. State control and administration of the Yosemite Valley itself continued until 1906, when the Valley was re-ceded to the United States Government by the State of California and made a part of the Yosemite National Park. Using the Yellowstone experience as precedent, the Secretary of the Interior turned, in 1890, to the United States Army, and the Army responded, as it had in the Yellowstone, by providing efficient management and protection for these areas.

The Congressional Act of June 30, 1864, granting the Yosemite Valley and the Mariposa Big Tree Grove to the State of California, clearly outlined the conditions upon which the grants were made. It provided that they should "be held for public use, resort and recreation" for all time; that leases not exceeding ten years might be granted by the State for portions of the areas, providing that the revenue from such leases would be expended "in the preservation and improvement of the property, or the roads leading thereto"; and that the areas would be managed by nine commissioners, one of whom was to be the governor of the state, all of whom were to serve without compensation and to be appointed by the governor.[1]

Governor Frederick F. Low acknowledged the Congressional grant in 1865 and appointed the first board of commissioners to manage the two areas.[2] When the State legislature met the following spring it passed a law formally accepting the grant and sanctioning the board of commissioners. The act provided that the commissioners were to have full power to manage and administer the grants, including the authority to "make and adopt all rules, regulations, and by-laws for . . . the government, improvement, and preservation" of the land. A "Guardian" was to perform such duties as might be prescribed by the commissioners, and to receive compensation not exceeding $500 per year. The act further provided what the Yellowstone lacked for so many years, a definition of prohibitions and penalties:

> It shall be unlawful for any person willfully to commit any trespass whatever upon said premises, cut down or carry off any wood, underwood, tree, or timber, or girdle or otherwise injure any tree or timber, or deface or injure any natural object, or set fire to any wood or grass upon said premises, or destroy or injure any bridge or structure of any kind, or other improvement that is or may be placed thereon. Any person committing either or any of said acts, without the express permission of said Commissioners through said Guardian, shall be guilty of a misdemeanor, and on conviction thereof shall be punished by fine not exceeding five hundred dollars, or by imprisonment in the county jail not exceeding six months, or by both such fine and imprisonment.[3]

The first board of commissioners included Professor J. D. Whitney, William Ashburner, I. W. Raymond, E. S. Holden, Alexander Deering, George W. Coulter, Galen Clark, Governor Frederick F. Low, and Frederick Law Olmsted, who was made chairman. By-laws were immediately drawn up stipulating that the board was to meet twice each year, once in the Yosemite Valley and once in San Francisco. In 1866 Galen Clark, one of the original commissioners, was named as Guardian. No definite code of rules governing the activities of visitors was adopted. Writing some years later, Frederick Law Olmsted stated that he visited the Valley frequently, "established a permanent camp in it and virtually acted as its superintendent."[4]

Had Olmsted remained in California and devoted his energies to the preservation of the Yosemite Valley, it is likely that the history of its care under state supervision would have been far different. Olmsted was one of the few nineteenth-century persons whose foresight and dedication to conservation helped to preserve some elements of nature for later generations. In a report to the California Legislature in 1865, Olmsted pointed out that it had been only sixteen years since the Yosemite Valley was first discovered by white man, yet already hundreds of people were overcoming the difficulties of transportation in order to visit the area, and that "before many years . . . these hundreds will become thousands and in a century the whole number of visitors will be counted by the millions." He warned that an injury to the natural features of the Valley, however slight, would be an injury of "deplorable magnitude." Olmsted then stated what has become the fundamental precept of the National Park Service:

> The first point to be kept in mind . . . is the preservation and maintenance as exactly as is possible of the natural scenery; the restriction, that is to say, within the narrowest limits consistent with the necessary accommodation of visitors, of all artificial constructions and the prevention of all constructions markedly inharmonious with the scenery or which would unnecessarily obscure, distort or detract from the dignity of the scenery. Second: it is important that it should be remembered that in permitting the sacrifice of anything that would be of the slightest value to future visitors to the convenience, bad taste, playfulness, carelessness, or wanton destructiveness of present visitors, we probably yield in each case the interest of uncounted millions to the selfishness of a few individuals.[5]

Unfortunately, Olmsted did not remain in California to superintend the development of the Valley according to his precepts. In November, 1865, he returned to New York City and again undertook the duties of landscape architect for Central Park.[6] Faced with a variety of obstacles and deprived of Olmsted's leadership, the Board of Commissioners soon found that the activity required of them was exceedingly difficult.

One of the first obstacles to be overcome was the removal of individual settlers who had located within the boundaries of the two grants. Two such settlers proved to be exceedingly reluctant to relinquish their holdings after being invited to do so by the Commissioners, and it was only after a bitter legal battle, culminating with a United States Supreme Court decision, that the claimants reluctantly agreed to accept a monetary compensation for their property and turn it over to the Commissioners.[7]

In their attempts to improve the Yosemite Valley and to make it more easily accessible and comfortable for visitors, the Commissioners were faced with another obstacle—lack of funds. They realized that accommodations, roads, and trails within the Valley should be constructed, but, as in the later case of Yellowstone Park, the moneys were not forthcoming. An initial appropriation of $2,000 for the development of the area was made by the State Act of 1866, but this was soon expended. Succeeding legislatures had somewhat grudgingly appropriated funds for improvement of the grants, but these barely covered the salary of the Guardian. The Commissioners finally had to appeal to private individuals for the capital necessary to construct roads and to erect buildings suitable for public accommodation in the Valley. Ten-year leases were awarded to those who constructed buildings; road and trail contractors were given the exclusive right to collect tolls for a similar period of time.[8]

The letting of leases to private individuals solved the problem of improvement, but it also opened the way for charges of graft, favoritism, the development of virtual monopolies, and eventually, complete estrangement between concessioners, Commissioners, and state legislators. Between 1874 and 1878 some concessioners appealed directly to the state legislature to intervene in disputes between them and the Commissioners, and it was not uncommon for the legislature to completely overrule the Commissioners' decisions. The situation rapidly deteriorated as public and private opinion of the Board of Commissioners became more acute and vocal. By 1880 communication between the various interested groups reached an impasse, and the state legislature attempted to dissolve the original board and appoint an entirely new one.[9] There followed a bitter dispute when the members of the executive committee of the first Board of Commissioners stated that they could not legally be dismissed, and refused to vacate office or to surrender any of the property belonging to the Yosemite management. Suit was filed by the state, and the old board finally surrendered when a decision favorable to the state was rendered by the State Supreme Court.[10]

The new Board of Commissioners approached their assigned task with admirable zeal. A full report of existing conditions in the Yosemite Valley was drawn up and presented to the state legislature; the previous Commissioners were charged with gross neglect. The report stated that "most of the available land" in the Yosemite grant had been leased to private individuals for gardens and pastures, that the entire Valley was choked with underbrush, and that the lack of "good carriage roads or trails" was most noticeable. In an appended report the newly appointed Guardian James Hutchings maintained that much of the good timber on the Valley floor had been cut and that the Merced River was choked with driftwood.[11] Later, in an effort to order the chaos, the Commissioners appealed to the State Engineer to formulate a plan for administration of the grant. Drawing on ideas originally promulgated by Frederick Law Olmsted, State Engineer William H. Hall, in 1882, recommended that a definite road system be developed on the Valley floor, that all forms of transportation be confined to these roads so as to prevent the tramping out of small plant life, that the accumulated debris be cleared from the streams, and that "as few of the necessary evils of civilization as possible" be introduced into the Yosemite Valley. Realizing that much of the beauty of the Valley depended on its water supply, Hall recommended that steps be immediately taken to protect and preserve the watershed, which was even then being threatened by the activities of sheepmen, miners, and lumbermen operating to the east and southeast of the Valley.[12]

The Commissioners chose to ignore that part of Hall's report that called for the preservation of the Valley in its natural state. Instead they called attention to a part of the report that seemed to recommend enlargement of the grant to include the mountain divide surrounding the Valley. Opposition to any extension of the boundaries of the original grant, and consequent expansion of the Commissioners' authority, was immediately raised by a variety of groups and individuals. Cattlemen and sheepmen wanted continued use of the Valley's watershed for summer grazing purposes. Others claimed that both the old and the new Board of Commissioners had been so inept in protecting the Valley from destruction and disfigurement that no extension of the grant should be made, however desirable it might be in other respects. Criticism of mismanagement by the Commissioners soon caught the attention of the public press, and conditions then existing in the Yosemite Valley became a matter of concern to residents throughout the state.[13]

Criticism of the Commissioners became so intense and bitter by 1888 that it brought on an official investigation. A legislative committee was directed to examine the situation in the Yosemite Valley and to report on the advisability of abolishing the entire commission system. While charging the Commissioners with misconduct and negligence, the members of the committee stated that they were not prepared to recommend abolishment of the commission system because the Act of Congress granting the area to California had definitely prescribed that form of government, and to abolish it would only leave the Valley and the Mariposa Big Tree Grove without any ruling authority whatever.[14] The Board of Commissioners feebly maintained that it proposed "no defense, for none is necessary. The State's defense is in the bad character or despicable motive or rank antecedents of her accusers."[15]

Both the investigative report and the defense by the

Commissioners were so complicated by personal, political, and commercial considerations that they obscured the facts of the situation. The entire process was summed up by George Davidson, of the United States Coast and Geodetic Survey, who stated, "I found great discordance of views in the valley, and it was evident that strong personal feelings clouded unprofessional opinions."[16] When Governor A. W. Waterman refused to censure the Commissioners, both he and they were charged with conspiring to support the interests of transportation companies doing business in the Valley.[17] Charges and counter charges were made and refuted; editors of California newspapers chose sides, some opposing the Board of Commissioners, some supporting them. The dispute rose to such a pitch that it soon became a national concern, extending far beyond the boundaries of California.

In the midst of this public outcry there came together two men, one from the East, one from the West, both of whom were to have great impact upon the future of the Valley. John Muir was born April 21, 1838, in Dunbar, Scotland, and arrived in Yosemite for the first time in 1868. From that time until his death in 1914 he was the foremost nature explorer, writer, researcher, interpreter, and advocate of conservation in the United States. Muir, more than any other one person, was responsible for the establishment and preservation of the Yosemite National Park. Aided by other naturalists and conservationists, Muir organized the Sierra Club and was president of that organization from its inception in 1892 until his death on December 24, 1914.

During the early summer of 1889 Muir, accompanied by Robert Underwood Johnson, associate editor of *The Century* magazine, took a camping trip in the Sierras surrounding the Yosemite Valley. Here, amid the mountains he knew and loved, Muir pointed out to his companion "the barren soil fairly stippled by the feet of the countless herds of sheep" and "hoofed locusts" which had denuded the mountain meadows and destroyed all signs of grass and flowers. When the two men descended into the Yosemite Valley they found "portions of the beautiful wild undergrowth of the Valley . . . turned into hayfields . . . large piles of tin cans and other refuse in full view," a ramshackle hotel, saloon and pig-sty, and acres of tree stumps, where, but a few years before had grown a luxuriant forest. Much to their dismay, Muir and Johnson learned of plans then under way to throw colored lights upon the falls, and to "cut out the whole of the under-brush of the valley so that one could see . . . the approach of the stage."[18]

After viewing the devastation in and around the Valley, Johnson and Muir started a two-man campaign to work for a Yosemite National Park. Muir agreed to write articles for *The Century* and fired the first salvos in an article for the *San Francisco Bulletin,* where he "exposed the abuses and havoc wrought under state control" in the Valley.[19] Johnson con-tributed editorials and solicited letters from interested per-sons which were published in *The Century.* One observer offered the thinly veiled threat that if the present system of management were continued, "the complaints which are now whispered will be spoken with such force and volume as to ring in the ears of the public and literally compel the National Government to retake what it has placed as trust in the hand of the State of California."[20] Another suggested the employment of a "man eminent in the profession of land-scape gardening and artistic forestry," and the payment of commission members. These reforms would at least bring forth remedies "where the evil is not past remedy."[21] The Guardian of the Valley was reported to have said:

> There is no plan for the improvement or care of the valley; each guardian has his own idea, each board of commission has some idea, ill defined, that something ought to be done, and often individual members of the commission have their own ideas in regard . . . to trimming, cutting, etc. New Commission-ers appoint new guardians, and each guardian follows in the

footsteps of his predecessor by doing as his own judgment dictates.[22]

Johnson maintained in an editorial of January, 1890, that what was needed, after the development of a definite plan for preservation of the Valley and its environs, was a "fitness of qualification and permanence of tenure in its administrators." He asserted that "a large sentiment in California would support a bill for the recession to the United States with an assurance of as capable administration in government as now characterizes the Yellowstone Park."[23] Muir admitted that he would "rather see the Valley in the hands of the Federal Government," but thought that the State of California might be reluctant to allow the transfer, adding, "A man may not appreciate his wife, but let her daddie try to take her back."[24]

The proposed extension of the Yosemite grant was supported by the editors of *The Nation,* who suggested that the entire grant be taken over by the Interior Department, since, in their opinion, California had "forfeited its title" by regarding the preservation as an "endowment, not a trust."[25]

The complaints aired during the winter and spring of 1890 were only a prelude to the denunciation launched by John Muir the following summer. In an article published by *The Century* in August, Muir described the natural wonders of the Valley and surrounding areas, and then with infinite detail described the destruction then being wrought by lumbermen who cut, blasted, and sawed the giant sequoias, and then set fire to the woods to clear the ground of limbs and refuse, thus destroying seedlings, saplings, and many "unmanageable giants." Left in the wake of these rapacious men were "black, charred monuments"—mute testimony to man's greed and folly. The ravages of lumbermen, however, were small when compared with the comprehensive destruction caused by sheepmen and their all-devouring "hoofed locusts," according to Muir. He charged that the beauties of the Valley were rapidly being destroyed under state administration, and he backed up his charges by photographs. Pictures of stumps standing two to four feet high, all that remained of once luxurious groves of young pine trees, and pictures of wildflower fields plowed up to plant hay, accompanied the article.[26]

The difficulties of re-ceding the Yosemite grant from the State of California to the Federal Government decided the proponents of preservation to turn their energies toward forming a National Park to surround the Yosemite Valley. In his second article for *The Century* in September, 1890, Muir warned that the formation of such a park could not come too quickly since the entire region was even then being "gnawed and trampled into a desert condition." When the area had been stripped of its forests, he said, "the ruin will be complete." In a spirit of urgency, the naturalist maintained that "ax and plow, hogs and horses, have long been and are still busy in Yosemite's gardens and groves. All that is accessible and destructible is being rapidly destroyed." There was no defense for such destruction, since most of it was "of a kind that can claim no right relationship with that which necessarily follows use."[27]

The activities and statements of the members of the Board of Commissioners furnished additional ammunition for the park advocates. Since 1885, in their biennial reports, the Commissioners had recommended that all the available land on the floor of the Yosemite Valley be seeded in grass and cultivated for hay for the "augmentation of the revenues of the State."[28] In June, 1889, they announced a plan to uproot and destroy all undergrowth, brush, and trees that had grown "in the last forty years" in an attempt to reduce the chances of conflagration. *Century* editor Robert Underwood Johnson blasted the Commissioners for not heeding the advice given by Frederick Law Olmsted some years before and charged that the "natural pleasure grounds" had been "ignorantly hewed and hacked, sordidly plowed and fenced, and otherwise treated on principles of forestry which would disgrace a picnic ground." In reply to this, a member of the commission was quoted as having said that he "would rather have the advice of a Yosemite road-maker in the improvement of the valley than that of Mr. Frederick Law Olmsted."[29] Professor J. D. Whitney, formerly a chairman of the executive committee of the Yosemite commission, opposed any extension of the grant under California authority and stated, "If the Yosemite could be taken from the State and made a national reservation I should have some hope that some good might be accomplished."[30]

The controversy over the alleged mismanagement of the California grant reached such proportions that Congress adopted a resolution directing the Secretary of the Interior to inquire and report to the Senate, "whether the lands granted to the State of California . . . have been spoliated or otherwise diverted . . . from public use contemplated by the grant . . ."[31] Although Congress acted to prevent destruction of that area surrounding the Yosemite Valley before receiving the requested report, the Secretary did gather information that substantiated the charges previously made.

Aided by correspondence, photographs, and the report of a special agent who made an investigation, the Secretary of the Interior reported to Congress on January 30, 1891 that:

(1) There has been a very general and indiscriminate destruction of timber . . . from mere wantonness. A former guardian of the park (Mr. Hutchings), writing in 1888, states that "within three years not less than 5,000 trees have been cut down."

(2) A large portion of the valley . . . has been fenced in and put to grass or grain. The fencing is largely done with barbed wire . . . and the inclosures . . . confine travel to narrow limits. . . . There seems to be very little room left for paths for pedestrians in the Valley.

(3) The valley has been pastured to such an extent as to destroy a great many rare plants which formerly grew there luxuriantly. Formerly there were over 400 species of plants . . . nearly all of these have been destroyed if not exterminated by herding and the plow. . . .

(4) The management seems to have fallen into the hands of a monopoly. . . .

Referring to that portion of the Yosemite grant lying outside of the Valley, the Secretary reported:

This seems to have been abandoned to sheep-herders and their flocks. The rare grasses and herbage have been eaten to the bare dirt. The magnificent flora . . . has been destroyed . . . These acts of spoliation and trespass have been permitted for a number of years and seem to have become a part of the settled policy of the management. . . . For the purpose of realizing the largest possible revenue obtainable from the valley there has, it is claimed, been permitted a largely indiscriminate devastation of the magnificent forest growth and luxuriant grasses that many years alone can repair.[32]

Certain residents of California had long been interested in the preservation of those groves of giant trees that had escaped destruction at the hand of the lumberman. As early as 1879 the editor of the Visalia, California, *Weekly Delta* had recommended that a particularly fine stand of trees, known as the Fresno-Tulare Grove, be made a national park. Though unsuccessful in this attempt, the editor and his friends did succeed in having the area containing the big trees suspended from entry. In 1881 the residents of Visalia convinced John F. Miller, candidate for the United States Senate, that some action should be taken to provide permanent protection for the trees, and in December, 1881, Miller, having been elected, introduced into the Senate a bill providing for the establishment of a national park encompassing the "whole west flank of the Sierra Nevada." The tremendous size of the proposed park called forth great opposition and the bill was not reported from committee.[33] The undaunted supporters of such a plan continued to fill the *Weekly Delta* with editorials and articles concerning forest fires, timber trespasses, the need for preserving the big trees and for conservation procedures, and mailed copies of these issues to the Secretary of the Interior. Amid rumors that the entry suspension was to be lifted, the local conservationists "thought of the Yellowstone National Park and read the act creating it and decided that only a national park would insure permanent preservation" of the big tree groves.[34] The matter was taken up with the Congressional Representative from their district, William Vandever, and on July 28, 1890, he introduced a bill into Congress providing for the dedication and setting apart "as a public park, or pleasure ground, for the benefit and enjoyment of the people," a tract of land containing the Fresno-Tulare Grove in California. The bill was favorably reported by the House Committee on Public Lands, amended to enlarge the area so set aside, and passed the House without debate on August 23.[35] Similar action on the bill was taken by the Senate, which passed the Vandever bill by unanimous consent, again without debate, on September 8, 1890. The Sequoia National Park became a fact when the Act of Congress was signed by President Benjamin Harrison, September 25, 1890.[36]

Earlier, on March 18, 1890, Congressman Vandever had introduced another bill designed to establish a forest reservation in the area surrounding the Yosemite grant to California. It was hoped that this might stem the destruction in the Valley. The bill was referred to the Committee on Public Buildings and Grounds as H. R. 8350 and not reported out of that committee. On September 30, 1890, five days after the Sequoia bill had been signed into law, Congressman Lewis E. Payson of Illinois, the same "Judge Payson" who, in 1885, had run afoul of the "kangaroo courts" established in the Yellowstone National Park, introduced a substitute bill for H. R. 8350, designed to "establish the Yosemite National Park." Payson's bill, besides incorporating everything in the original Vandever bill, provided for the setting aside of that area soon to be known as the General Grant National Park, though this name was not stipulated in the bill.[37] Congressman Charles E. Hooker of Mississippi stated that the bill "is going to excite controversy, debate, and discussion that can not fail to take time." The bill did create controversy, debate, and discussion, but not in either house of Congress. The bill passed the House without debate.[38]

Payson's substitute House bill (H. R. 12187) was introduced into the Senate by Senator Preston B. Plumb of Kansas, on the same day it passed the House. The bill passed the Senate without debate or discussion. The bill establishing Yosemite and General Grant National Parks was signed by the President on October 1, 1890.[39]

The ease and facility with which the Yosemite bill was rushed through Congress attests to the fine groundwork established by its advocates. Realizing that considerable opposition would be raised by some Californians if the bill proposed to take back the Yosemite Valley, which Congress had granted to the State in 1864, they inserted the clause that nothing in the proposed act "shall be construed as in anywise affecting the grant of lands made to the State of California." Settlers on the land set aside by the Act were disarmed by the addition of the statement that nothing in the act "shall be construed as in anywise . . . affecting any bona fide entry." John Muir had advised the proponent of the bill, Robert Underwood Johnson, that "taking back the Valley on the part of the Government would probably be a troublesome job," since California was at that time "about evenly divided between Republicans and Democrats," and "both parties in Congress would be afraid to defend her." Muir also advised his friend to "stand up for the Vandever Bill and on no account let the extension be under state control if it can possibly be avoided."[40]

In establishing these three national parks in California, Congress had again failed to provide any laws or legal machinery for enforcement of rules and regulations promulgated by the Secretary of the Interior, just as it had done some eighteen years before in establishing the Yellowstone Park. All three national park acts (the original Yellowstone Act, the Sequoia Act, and the Yosemite and General Grant Act) provided that the Parks should be under the exclusive control of the Secretary of the Interior, who was directed to make rules and regulations for their care and management. Such regulations were to "provide for the preservation from injury of all timber, mineral deposits, natural curiosities, or wonders, . . . and their retention in their natural condition." The Secretary was authorized to grant leases within the parks and was to "provide against the wanton destruction of the fish and game" found therein. In all three Acts, the only penalty for trespassing or otherwise violating the rules established by the Secretary was removal of the trespasser or violator from the Parks.[41] This omission by Congress was to frustrate the administrators of the California parks just as it had the administrators of the Yellowstone.

In neither of the Acts establishing the California parks is the term "national park" used. Sequoia was called "a public park, or pleasure ground," and both Yosemite and General Grant were set apart as "reserved forest lands." That they were considered by Congress to be national parks is evident by the language of the two bills, identical to that of the Yellowstone Act of 1872.[42] The Sequoia National Park was so named by Secretary of the Interior Noble immediately after its creation. The reason for choosing the name was "more weighty than that it is the name of the trees," he reported, for the trees themselves had been "called Sequoia by Endlicher in honor of a most distinguished Indian of the half breed, the inventor of the Cherokee alphabet"; thus "appropriate honor" was bestowed upon the "Cadmus of America," Sequoyah. Yosemite National Park was so named, according to the Secretary, because "this reservation surrounds the Yosemite Valley." The name "General Grant

National Park'' was chosen because ''this name had become, by common consent, that of the largest tree there . . . and the park could not consistently be called aught else, unless it were 'The Union'.''[43]

By following too closely the wording of the Yellowstone enabling Act, Congress failed also to provide any appropriation for upkeep and management of the Parks. A month later the Secretary of the Interior noted this omission and remarked that ''whether the parks shall be put under charge of civil custodians or a military cavalry guard shall be sent to each is a subject now being considered and investigated.''[44] The Act of March 3, 1883, authorizing the Secretary of War to make troops available for the protection of the Yellowstone National Park was not applicable to the parks later established by Congress, and hence there existed no legal basis for the use of troops in the Yosemite, Sequoia, and General Grant National Parks.

Nevertheless, aware that the new Parks demanded protection, the Secretary of the Interior also looked to the Yellowstone for precedent and, on October 21, 1890, requested that the Secretary of War detail two troops of cavalry for use in the California Parks, adding that possibly the labor requested would ''not prove onerous to some of the very intelligent gentlemen who are in that section of the country.'' Finding some resistance from the Secretary of War, the Secretary of the Interior then appealed directly to the President, recommending that a troop of cavalry, with a commanding officer of the rank of Captain, be stationed in the Yosemite Park with instructions ''not only to look after the treatment that the State of California may give to the park still within its control,'' but to also send out scouting parties throughout the park ''to prevent timber cutting, sheep herding, trespassing, or spoliation in particular.'' A second request was approved by the Secretary of War on January 13, 1891, and on April 6, 1891, Troops ''I'' and ''K,'' 4th Cavalry, stationed at the Presidio of San Francisco and com-

manded by Captains A. E. Wood and John Dorst, were selected for duty in the Yosemite, Sequoia, and General Grant
National Parks.[45]

From 1891 to 1912 it was customary to detail troops only
during the summer months, relying on the heavy winter
snows to protect the Parks during the winter. Two troops of
cavalry were usually dispatched for duty in the three Parks,
departing from the Presidio of San Francisco in early May
and arriving in the Parks some two weeks later after an
overland march of 250 miles. One troop remained in the
Yosemite, and one was sent southward to patrol the Sequoia
and General Grant Parks. The officer in charge of the southern detachment was named Acting Superintendent of the
Sequoia National Park and administered the General Grant
Park also; his brother officer to the north operated under the
title Acting Superintendent of the Yosemite National Park.
Each officer submitted to the Secretary of the Interior an
annual report, and with the exception of the annual movement to and from the Parks, each operated as a separate
detachment. No permanent military post was established in
any of the California Parks; the Yosemite troops established
a temporary summer headquarters on the extreme southern
boundary of the Park near the town of Wawona, and from
this point sent mounted patrols throughout the Park. The
logical place for the establishment of a headquarters was in
the Yosemite Valley, situated in the center of the National
Park. It was not available for military use, however, since it
remained outside the Park and under state jurisdiction.
When the Valley was re-ceded to the Government in 1906,
military headquarters were moved to this central position.
The troops dispatched to Sequoia and General Grant Parks
utilized a variety of points for a headquarters camp, often
outside the boundaries of either Park and usually on private
land, since "there was no place in the park, where so many
men and horses could camp."[46]

The very nature of the area they were detailed to guard

determined from the outset that the duties and problems of the cavalry in the California Parks would be somewhat different from those in the Yellowstone. Here there were no large number of big game animals to tempt poachers; there were no geysers or fragile geyser formations to be destroyed by the curious tourist. There were forests, however, and there could be game if only it were protected. The boundaries of the Parks were not marked; roads and trails into and through the Parks were practically nonexistent; cattlemen and sheepherders grazed their stock on Park lands in violation of the Acts establishing the Parks, and, unlike the Yellowstone, there were countless acres of patented lands lying within the areas set aside by Congress. Eventually the boundaries were marked, trails blazed, and roads constructed, but the evils of stock grazing and the existence of privately owned lands within the Parks proved to be a continual obstacle to efficient administration.

In an attempt to begin what he termed a "square deal" with the cattle and sheep owners who utilized the Park lands for grazing purposes, Captain A. E. Wood, the first Acting Superintendent of Yosemite, sent letters to every stockholder "in middle and southern California" advising them to keep their stock away from the Park boundaries. He firmly declared:

> This Yosemite Park is to be a Park throughout all time—it is not a temporary arrangement. The time will be when the United States will be possessed of the title to all the lands within its boundaries and in the meantime it would be better if the citizens living near the Park would make arrangements to conform to the new conditions of things, thus avoiding the consequence of a violation of the law.[47]

Wood found that most of the cattle owners "generally tried to observe the law" and thereby presented only minor difficulties. The sheepherders, however, most of whom were "foreigners—Portuguese . . . Chilians, French, and Mexicans," ignored his warnings and proceeded to push their destructive flocks over the ill-defined boundaries. Of course, there was no legal penalty beyond ejection from the Park, but realizing that the sheepmen were not aware of this, the enterprising Captain attempted a bluff that would make him "master of the situation." Trespassing herders were arrested, escorted to the military camp near Wawona, and informed that they would have to stand trial in San Francisco. Unfortunately, the United States District Attorney for the northern district of California had published in the San Francisco newspapers "a long opinion on the subject of trespass, in which . . . he declared that no criminal action could lie under the law," and the Captain's bluff failed.[48]

The following year Captain Wood approached the problem of sheep trespass from a more effective direction. Following the Yellowstone precedent, he inaugurated the practice of arresting sheepherders, marching them to the boundary of the Park furthest from their herds, "a march consuming four or five days," ejecting them, and scattering their herds outside the opposite boundary. By the time that the herders and herds were reunited, the herds had usually been decreased considerably through the activities of forest predators. This was perhaps an extralegal process, but it was effectively used by subsequent military commanders; it proved to be a more severe punishment than could have been expected from a court of law.[49]

Such punitive expulsions made the sheepmen and herders aware that the Parks were being patrolled and that the regulations were more than mere words issued from far-off Washington. Although they were described as men of "the lowest order of intelligence," the herders soon devised methods to frustrate the cavalrymen. In the Sequoia Park, herders would drive their sheep into the Park with one or two men to watch them, while they left their riding and pack animals with all of their supplies just outside the Park boundary. To drive the sheep to the other side of the Park for expulsion would be "playing into the herders' hands, for the sheep would eat everything on the way" and the direction of travel would be the one desired by the herders, who would have stationed other men on the opposite side of the Park to gather the sheep as they were expelled. Also the herders soon combined forces and hired scouts who were stationed on commanding points to watch the movements of the military patrols. When the troops approached the area where the sheep were grazing, a warning was given and the herds immediately moved just outside the Park boundaries.[50] Faced with such frustrating maneuvers, the military guardians at times resorted to arbitrary force. In 1905 the French Chargé d'Affaires forwarded to the Secretary of State a complaint lodged at the French Consulate at San Francisco by a Mr. F. Nicolas, "a French national citizen, engaged in the sheep trade, against Second Lt. W. S. Martin, 4th Cavalry." Nicolas claimed that he had entered the Yosemite Park, with no sheep, was met by 2nd Lt. Martin, "who . . . ordered him with his revolver pointed at him, to lead the way to the place where his flock was grazing . . . The officer struck him on the head with the butt of his revolver, kicked him in the abdomen and driving him before him compelled him to walk a distance of about four miles to the place where his horse was. . . . Thence . . . to Camp Wood some 50 miles distant . . . My fellow countryman was held two days by the Lieutenant."[51] Unfortunately, Lieutenant Martin suffered no reprimand for his capricious action.

The seasonal nature of the military occupation allowed the sheepmen to await the departure of the troops in the autumn and then move their flocks into the unprotected Park areas, taking advantage of the grasses that had been protected during the summer. When they returned in the spring, the military commanders could do nothing but survey the damage and send forth repeated pleas for legal machinery that would allow "just one trial and conviction," believing that such a process "would have more effect on these law breakers than all the proclamations which could be issued in a lifetime."[52] Also the practice of rotating the detachments assigned to the Parks made for fluctuating and inconsistent policies toward trespassers; some commanders were strict, others merely attempted to expel trespassers with the least inconvenience to both the troopers and the herders. The newly assigned officers, unfamiliar with the habits of the sheepmen and knowing little of the Park terrain, were often outwitted; the underpaid troopers were sometimes bribed to close their eyes to the obvious trespassing of sheep and herders.[53]

The imperfect protection afforded by the military was far better than none, however, and the naturalist John Muir, returning from a trip through the Yosemite Park, happily reported: "For three years the soldiers have kept the sheepmen and sheep out of the park, and the grasses and blue gentians . . . are again blooming in all their wild glory." Several years later he maintained that "The best service in forest protection—almost the only efficient service—is that rendered by the military." Referring to the military guardians of both the Yellowstone and Yosemite, he wrote, "They found it a desert as far as underbrush, grass and flowers were concerned," but with effective policing, "the skin of the mountains is healthy again."[54] Robert Underwood Johnson thought that the "increased and steady flow of the waterfalls in the Valley" was due to the military protection of the watershed, and quoted a Forestry Bureau ranger who told him that "one could follow the boundary of the park by the line to which the sheep had nibbled." Another observer of the transformation in Yosemite Park thought that the very process of passing from the trampled meadows outside the Park into the "protected meadows of the National Park was a lesson in patriotism," and strongly advocated the extension of military administration over "all the national domain."[55]

In an attempt to achieve some consistency as regards the trespassing herders, a standing order was issued by the Acting Superintendent of Yosemite in 1904, and, while never incorporated into the rules and regulations of the three Parks, it was faithfully followed by his successors:

> When sheep are caught trespassing on the reservation, and are accompanied by herders, the sheep will be expelled in one direction, the herders in another, and their outfits in another. . . . Ordinarily the sheep will be driven out of the park on its east side, the herders and outfits if practicable, on the northern and southern side.[56]

By closely adhering to this practice, the threat of spoliation by herds of sheep was lessened, and, while subsequent Acting Superintendents still requested the passage of laws providing punishment for trespassers, they also reported that sheep trespass had practically ended.

Attempts of cattlemen to use the protected park areas for grazing produced the same problems, but the cattlemen, treated with expulsion like the sheepmen, soon learned to respect the boundaries of the parks. No real problem arose from the prospector and miner simply because no large deposits of minerals were discovered. Two men were ejected from the Yosemite Park after they were discovered placer-mining, but, according to the Acting Superintendent, "they seemed glad of a good excuse to quit" since their average findings were but "40 cents per day each."[57]

While the military superintendents gradually overcame the nuisance and evil of stock trespass, a greater hindrance to efficient administration and protection of the California Parks persisted—that of patented lands existing within the Park boundaries. The privately owned lands scattered throughout the government Parks in small, detached holdings formed a variety of independent units in what should have been a homogeneous whole, and frustrated the efforts of the military units to preserve and conserve the Parks. Each successive military commander noted the existence of these lands, and each in turn requested that these private holdings be eliminated. Some suggested outright purchase by the government of private lands, others that the boundaries of the Parks be realigned so as to exclude those portions most heavily claimed by individuals. The first military superintendent of the Yosemite Park recommended that the Park be reduced to its "natural boundaries," stating that such a reduction would exclude most of the agricultural and assumed mining land from the Park, while still including "the only portion of the country that furnishes a reason for a national park."[58] Subsequent commanders opposed the reduction of the Park area by any method and advocated the purchase of private lands, maintaining that it was but "good policy to preserve the timber in those forests and keep the forests themselves in a state as near that of nature as possible, for the benefit of those who come after us." One Acting Superintendent, urging the Government to acquire all private lands within the Parks, cited a statement of John Muir's, made in relation to settlers:

> The smallest reserve, and the first ever heard of, was in the Garden of Eden, and though its boundaries were drawn by the Lord, and embraced only one tree, yet the rules were violated by the only two settlers that were permitted on suffrage to live in it.[59]

A 1903 survey of patented lands within the Park resulted in a list of over 370 separate entries, the majority having been patented in 1889 and 1890, and most of them comprising tracts of 160 acres each. Private landholdings existed within the boundaries of the Sequoia National Park also. A bitter battle between a "Bellamy type communal cooperative," the Kaweah Cooperative Commonwealth Colony, organized in 1886, and the Secretary of the Interior occurred in 1890 when the Sequoia Park was established. The Kaweah colonists had filed upon government land, constructed homes, a sawmill, and a road into their settlement, all within that area dedicated as a public park. It was finally determined that the land entries were fraudulent and the Kaweah Cooperative was dissolved, but not until after the fight had been carried to the floor of Congress and an exhaustive study of the land laws, filing procedures, and legal processes had been made.[60]

While these conflicting suggestions were annually being forwarded to Washington, stock and timber owners, military administrative officials, mountaineering clubs, and local newspapers drifted into two opposing camps, and once again a struggle developed between those who wished to preserve the mountain fastness for the public and posterity and those who wished to use the land for personally remunerative purposes. The question of boundary realignment or purchase of patented lands might have continued indefinitely had not the actions of the Yosemite Lumber Company emphasized the necessity of taking some action. This company had, through purchase from private individuals, acquired extensive holdings in the southern and western parts of Yosemite Park and in 1903 it began logging operations. The resulting barren strips cut through the forested land prompted the Secretary of the Interior to take action. A commission was appointed to examine the condition of the Park and to ascertain whether portions of it could be eliminated. Meeting in June, 1904, this commission recommended that in view of the many scattered patented lands and the resultant obstacles to effective administration, it would be best to eliminate those areas with the greatest density of private landholdings. These included timberlands in the southwest and the west, and the mineral lands of the Chowchilla range. The crest of the Sierras was recommended as the natural boundary to the east—this eliminated a vast area on that side of the park. The committee further recommended that the area remaining after the boundary changes had been accomplished be officially known as the Yosemite National Park. All of these recommendations were incorporated in the Congressional Act of February 7, 1905.[61] This Act reduced, but did not eliminate, one of the major problems facing the military administrators.

As in the Yellowstone, the lack of laws complicated administration in the California Parks. The first Acting Superintendent requested that Congress pass a law "making it a misdemeanor for the violation of Rules . . . with the maximum fine fixed at $1,000, and the maximum imprisonment fixed at 6 months, or both, at the will of the court of competent jurisdiction."[62] Referring to similar requests by the Acting Superintendents of both the Yosemite and the Yellowstone Park, the first military commander in charge of Sequoia, after recommending the passage of laws providing penalties for all infractions of the regulations, hinted that if such laws were not forthcoming the military would be forced to resort to illegal methods. He maintained that if an Acting Superintendent "commences to quibble about the propriety of every action that seems necessary," and to debate with himself whether such action "is technically legal or illegal, he will accomplish nothing."[63]

After Congress provided a legal structure for the Yellowstone Park in 1894, pleas for similar legislation for the new Parks became more incessant. The military superintendents, finding that without penalties the rules were "virtually a dead letter," asked that their Parks be placed on the same footing as Yellowstone.[64] Some of the Acting Superintendents suggested that they be given the powers of United States Commissioners, others recommended that the Parks be made a separate United States Court District with a resident commissioner; all requested the passage of legislation defining what was prohibited and fixing a penalty for the violation of the same. The Secretary of the Interior included these requests in his annual reports to Congress, but Congress remained apathetic and there was no Howell case to attract publicity. Finally, after fifteen years, Congress made a feeble move in the direction desired by the military commanders. In 1905 an act was passed authorizing "all persons employed in the

forest reserve and national park service of the United States"
to make arrests for violation of the rules and regulations
pertaining to the forest reserves and parks, and provided that
persons so arrested be taken before the "nearest United
States Commissioner . . . for trial." This was of no effect in
practice, as the only penalty for violation of the rules was
expulsion; the nearest United States Commissioner was some
100 miles distant from the Parks, and the very process of
taking a violator before a Commissioner would have
achieved the expulsion prescribed by law; the Commissioner
would be unable to levy further penalty or punishment.
Legal machinery and laws fixing penalties for violation
of the park regulations were still needed in the California
Parks.[65]

Out of sheer desperation the Acting Superintendents
snatched at anything that might provide them with legal
sanction and legal penalties. Beginning in 1910 they appended to the published rules and regulations of the three
Parks an excerpt from an act entitled "An Act to Provide for
Determining the Heirs of Deceased Indians . . ." This Act
provided a fine and imprisonment for any person cutting
trees or leaving a fire burning upon land that had "been
reserved . . . by the United States for any public use." The
act had been designed to protect Indian reservations and
allotments, but it provided threat of punishment in the Parks,
and was the only piece of punitive legislation available during the entire military administration of the California
Parks.[66]

The absence of legal penalties in the California Parks
would have presented an even greater administrative problem had there existed the all-pervading evil of poaching that
encumbered the Yellowstone administration. Poaching was
not a major problem in the Yosemite and Sequoia Parks,
because of the absence of any large number of game animals.
Acting Superintendent A. E. Wood reported in 1891 that the
principal game to be found in the Yosemite consisted of

bear, deer, grouse, and quail, but added that "neither [*sic*] variety is very plentiful." He thought that the prevention of sheep grazing would enable the game to increase, and the Acting Superintendent of Sequoia recommended the extension of that Park's boundaries to achieve the same purpose, adding, however, that the paucity of game was due to its being frightened by "the proximity of sheep herders and having had its feed destroyed by bands of domestic sheep."[67] The expulsion of the herds of sheep did not immediately bring an increase in the number of game animals, however. The Acting Superintendent in Sequoia reported in 1894 that "the game, particularly the deer, are decreasing in numbers," blaming this upon the still present "all-devouring and all-destroying sheep" which were "making the country uninhabitable for man or beast."[68]

After the sheep problem was abated, the military commanders faced the problem of the all-devouring and all-destroying human being. The few game animals in the Parks were somewhat protected during the summer months when the military patrols were present, but after their departure in the fall, market hunters and trappers entered the park areas and plied their destructive trade with impunity. Unable to prevent the killing of game in the winter, the military commanders devised methods to better protect that game during the summer. In 1895 they began to confiscate all firearms of persons entering the parks and return them when they left. The salutary effect was soon noted and subsequent administrators reported that game was increasing in number and that the animals exhibited less fear of humans than in previous years. When charges were made that the soldiers assigned to protect the Parks were actually killing game themselves, the troops were stripped of their carbines and henceforth armed with revolvers only.[69] Many tourists going through the Parks requested permission to carry rifles and shotguns for "protection," but such requests were usually denied by the military commanders. It was customary, however, to allow men to carry revolvers "when they were accompanied by women, but in no other cases . . ."[70]

Finding the streams and lakes of the Parks as lacking in fish as the forests had been of game, the military superintendents immediately took steps to rectify the situation. Receiving no reply from the United States Fish Commission to a request for young trout to stock the barren park waters, the Acting Superintendents turned to sportsmen's clubs and the State of California for assistance. During the second year of military administration some 55,000 trout were planted in the streams of the Yosemite and Sequoia Parks, and with yearly additions, the streams were soon "teeming with fish." One military commander was able to state that "the parks are becoming probably the finest fishing grounds in the world."[71]

Separated into detachments in the manner originally adopted in the Yellowstone Park, the troops in the California parks expelled trespassers, extinguished fires, constructed trails, and, to the extent that their seasonal patrolling allowed, protected the game. While no permanent military posts were constructed, this idea was suggested several times, as was the stationing of troops in the Parks for the entire year rather than just the summer months. The activities of the military guardians were lauded by conservation-minded Californians and it was assumed that the annual dispatching of troops to the Parks was to be a permanent process.

The illegal aspects of the use of the United States Army in the Parks were not considered until 1896. In that year the Secretary of the Interior's now routine request for the military detail was questioned by the Secretary of War, who doubted his authority, "without some sanction of law such as exists in the case of the Yellowstone National Park," to assign military officers and men to what was actually "civil duty." He requested that the Secretary of the Interior furnish him with information which would afford him the authority for which he had not at that time "been able to find satisfactory warrant." In reply, the Secretary of the Interior stated that while there existed "no law specifically authorizing" the Secretary of War to assign Army units to the Parks, they had to be protected and his Department was without the means to provide that protection. He thought, moreover, that the precedent of five years was sufficient "authority" for such procedure. The Secretary of War evidently accepted this reasoning and troops were accordingly assigned to all three of the California Parks in the spring of 1896 and again in 1897.[72]

During the United States' "splendid little war" with Spain in 1898, the annual assignment of troops to the California Parks was suspended for the duration, leaving the Parks unprotected, save for the nominal supervision and protection offered by a civilian, J. W. Zevely, a special inspector for the Department of the Interior who was named Acting Superintendent in the absence of the military. Zevely was relieved of his duties in September by a detachment of the First Utah Volunteer Cavalry under the command of Captain Joseph E. Caine, and the Volunteers remained in the Parks until October. Upon his arrival in the Yosemite Park, Captain Caine found numerous forests fires raging, an estimated 200,000 sheep roaming "at will over the national reserve," and hunters frequenting the parks "with impunity."[73] Local residents of California were aware of the depredations being committed in the Parks, and the Deputy Sheriff of Merced County suggested that he be authorized to station his company of volunteers (which had been raised for "home defense") in the Parks to provide protection against spoliation. The Secretary of War respectfully declined this proffered assistance.[74] This brief experience reinforced the idea that the Parks could best be protected by the military, and in 1899 troops were once more dispatched from Presidio of San Francisco for guard duty in the Parks. Opposition, however, to this now customary but extralegal process of using military units for civil duty was beginning to develop.

One of the main arguments for military guardianship of the nation's parks was that the use of the military required little or no additional appropriation of money over what was normally required to sustain the troops. In an attempt to disprove this allegation, Congressman J. C. Needham of California requested from the Secretary of War figures showing the exact cost to the Government of sending troops to the California Parks in excess of the cost of maintaining the troops in garrison. A reply from the Adjutant General's Office estimated the average additional cost per year at $7,557.22, a figure much less than that required to substitute an equal civilian protection force. Representative Needham was silenced, but the propriety of continued military management had been questioned.[75] A complete review of the situation was requested by the Secretary of War, and the resulting memorandum included the statement:

National Park Service

Theodore Roosevelt and Colonel Pitcher,
Park Superintendent, Yellowstone, 1903

The law does not provide in any way for the employment or use of troops in the Sequoia, Yosemite and General Grant parks or reservations, but these parks are placed by law under the exclusive control of the Secretary of the Interior. The officers in command of the troops report to and receive their instructions from the Secretary of the Interior.[76]

Because the use of troops in the Parks seemed illegal, the Secretary of War in 1900 showed some reluctance to comply with the annual request to send troops to the Parks. There was, he said a "constant demand for troops for purposes of a military character," and the employment of troops to guard the Parks could scarcely be regarded as military. He suggested that it might be practicable for the Department of the Interior to furnish its own force. Ignoring this suggestion, the Secretary of the Interior again requested the troops "as a matter of favor" and said he would recommend to Congress legislative sanction for this practice, as in Yellowstone. Congress accordingly included in the sundry civil act approved June 6, 1900, the clause:

The Secretary of War, upon request of the Secretary of the Interior, is hereafter authorized and directed to make the necessary detail of troops to prevent trespassers or intruders from entering the Sequoia National Park, the Yosemite National Park and the General Grant National Park, respectively, in California, for the purpose of destroying the game or objects of curiosity therein, or for any other purpose prohibited by law or regulation for the government of said reservations, and to remove such persons from said parks if found therein.[77]

Thus the presence of troops in the California Parks was, after a delay of nine years, finally legalized. In 1906, after a long and bitter struggle between the California Board of Commissioners for the Yosemite Valley and the conservation interests, California re-ceded to the United States the two grants made in 1864, and the Yosemite National Park was made an integral whole.[78] Military headquarters were moved to a central position in the Yosemite Valley, and the military protection previously confined to the area surrounding the Valley was extended to the Valley itself.

The United States Army continued to detail troops to the Sequoia and Yosemite National Parks until 1914, when they were withdrawn and replaced by a force of civilian rangers. The withdrawal of the troops was finally accomplished at the insistence of the military commanders assigned to the Park duty, who maintained that conditions in and around the Parks had been materially altered since the troops were first called upon for protection.[79] In the earlier days the Parks had been surrounded by a hostile population, accustomed to free use of the land for grazing, hunting, and woodcutting, which resented the curtailment of these privileges and tried in every way to circumvent the authorities. With no war threatening, the Army was regarded more as a public utility than as a combatant force; this had made it seem reasonable to use troops to prevent depredations on the public domain. Toward the end of the military administration of the three Parks in California, the Acting Superintendents found that there were few attempts to graze sheep or cattle in the Parks, and even though the game had increased, there was comparatively little poaching. Instead of arduous patrolling over rough and broken country, the soldiers' duties consisted of supervising construction of roads and trails, gate-keeping, and advising visitors. Outposts were still maintained throughout the Parks, but their only purpose was to report the varieties of game seen, look for fires, seal firearms, and register tourists. The surrounding population had gradually changed its attitude from antagonism to friendly helpfulness, and those who had previously attempted to destroy the Parks had become actively interested in their preservation. The presence of cavalry in the Parks was a survival of earlier days and different conditions.

The major activities of the troops assigned to the Parks

were, strictly speaking, without legal sanction. The law providing for the assignment of troops prescribed their duties as preventing "trespassers or intruders from entering" the Parks and the removal of such trespassers. All other duties performed by the troops were technically illegal. Also illegal were orders from the Secretary of the Interior to the Acting Superintendents directing them to utilize their troops in checking automobiles, collecting tolls, guiding tourists, patrolling for and fighting forest fires, registering tourists, searching for lost parties, driving sheep and cattle across the park as a punitive measure, reading stream gauges for the Department of Agriculture, providing pack trains for transporting Interior Department supplies, and planting fish. These duties were illegal, but they were not necessarily onerous. Writing in 1913, the last military commander assigned to the Sequoia National Park, 1st Lieutenant Hugh S. Johnson (later head of the New Deal N.R.A.) noted that the annual detail of troops to the Parks "furnishes a very pleasant and desirable detail to any troop of cavalry and one upon which all its members are eager to enter. For the officers it provides an independent command, a change from the routine army duties, a pleasant summer's outing with fishing and the coolness and enjoyment of a mountain summer. For the men, there is, in addition to most of these things, a surcease from army discipline, drill, and restraint."[80] Nevertheless, the military, acting without benefit of well-defined legal stipulations, and hampered by the absence of punitive legislation, did save the Yosemite, Sequoia, and General Grant National Parks in the same manner that they had saved the Yellowstone National Park. Without the protective presence of the United States Cavalry, much of what exists today as a part of the National Park system could well have become, like other nonprotected areas, scarred, disfigured, and destroyed. Park visitors, who today view the glaciated splendor of Yosemite, or find a bit of solitude among the giant trees of Sequoia, owe these forgotten men a debt of gratitude.

IX

The Culmination of an Idea

TWENTY-TWO YEARS ELAPSED between the passage of legislation providing legal machinery in 1894 and the formation of the National Park Service in 1916. Meanwhile the military commanders in the Parks continued the policies established by their predecessors and developed new elements of management that were later adopted by the civilian administrators who succeeded them. Changing conditions in and around the Parks terminated some of the older problems and gave rise to new ones. Game animals, once so ruthlessly hunted by poachers, were so well protected that new policies had to be developed to handle adequately the resulting surplus. A program to interpret Park wonders to the public was originally suggested by the military commanders and scientific data were collected by them. Cooperation of individuals who lived near the Parks was achieved by the impartial and effective policing of the Park areas, and many earlier administrative problems were thus negated. The road and trail systems used by modern tourists were planned and constructed by Army engineers using Army labor. Fort Yellowstone, built of quarried stone, stands today as the central unit of the National Park Headquarters in the Yellowstone. In the California Parks, seedling sequoias planted by Army personnel remain as testimony to the labor and foresight of the earlier military guardianship.

The advisability of eventual transfer of the National Parks to civil authority had been foreseen by several military commanders and their suggestions and plans enabled the transfer of authority to be made with some facility. Many of the military personnel who had served in the Parks accepted discharges from the Army and formed a cadre around which was constructed the first civilian ranger service.

One of the larger legacies resulting from the military administration is the fact that the National Parks are game refuges. In the Yellowstone, the administrators could have easily and naturally provided protection for the thermal features only; in the California Parks, the major administrative problems would have been eliminated had protection been confined only to the big trees and Yosemite Valley. Fortunately, the early policy makers looked beyond the obvious and extended protection to include most life within the parks.[1] One beneficent result of this policy was the preservation and restoration of the American bison, an animal that was rapidly nearing extinction in the 1890's.

Estimates place the original number of bison at sixty million; by 1830 the once vast herds had been pushed west of the Mississippi River and their numbers reduced to an estimated fifteen million. The slaughter of these remaining animals was so rapid that by 1886 the chief taxidermist of the National Museum in Washington was able to locate only 541 of the beasts, and most of these were found in the Yellowstone National Park. By 1894 the animals in the Yellowstone were the only bison still living in a wild state in the United States. Poachers, old age, accident, and disease reduced the Yellowstone herd to an estimated fifty animals in 1900.[2]

The continual decline in the Park herd forced the military

commanders to re-examine the policy, originally inaugurated by Captain Moses Harris, of not introducing "domesticated animals" into the Park, and as early as 1893 Captain George S. Anderson suggested the infusion, through purchase, of outside blood into the dwindling wild herd. No action was taken on this suggestion at the time, but when the number of bison in the Park dropped to twenty-two and the danger of inbreeding and eventual sterility became apparent, Major John Pitcher, Acting Superintendent of the Yellowstone, again suggested the purchase of outside animals in order to start a new herd and to diffuse new blood into the original wild herd. Through the efforts of Congressman John F. Lacey of Iowa an appropriation of $15,000 was obtained; fourteen cows were purchased from the Pablo-Allard herd in Montana, and three bulls from the Goodnight herd in Texas. Several calves were captured from the wild herd and all were placed in a large fenced enclosure, with the idea of setting them free after they had been confined long enough to assure that they would remain in the vicinity of the Park.[3]

The natural increase in the new herd developed from the three separate strains was so great that in 1907 a "buffalo ranch" was established in the Lamar Valley, an area somewhat removed from tourist travel. The ranch was placed under the direction of a salaried "Buffalo Keeper," who requisitioned supplies and reported directly to the Acting Superintendent. Though nonprofit, the ranch was operated in the same way as a domestic cattle ranch. Corrals, chutes, shelter sheds, barns, and fences were constructed; red top and timothy hay were sowed, irrigated, and harvested, and in the first year of operation, 200 tons were cut and stacked for winter feed. All of the animals were branded with a "U.S." on the left hip, some of the bulls were made into steers, and births of young bison were carefully noted. The total number of bison in captivity was placed at sixty-one in 1907.[4]

With the infusion of new blood into the wild herd by the

periodic release of bulls from the tame herd, it too began to increase and in 1916 seventy-two wild bison were counted. These animals were the descendants of that small number that had escaped capture and killing, and thus represented the only true line of bison to have continuously lived in a wild state in all of the United States. By 1916 the domestic herd had increased to 273 animals and it had become possible to transfer some buffalo to other game refuges and municipal parks throughout the country. The American bison had been saved from total extinction and the military commanders of the Yellowstone National Park had played an important role in its preservation.[5]

The story of the elk is quite different. The wapiti or American elk had, like the bison, been forced into smaller and smaller areas of wilderness as civilization continued to envelop the West. Historically these animals had lived and grazed in the mountains during the warmer months of the year, but as winter approached they formed into herds and migrated to the open valleys and plains in search of food. As the American settler pushed into these lowland regions, fenced the land and pre-empted the grass for his domestic stock, this migratory pattern was destroyed. Meat hunters took their toll of these animals and, just as the bison had been killed for their tongues, many elk were slaughtered for their canine teeth, which sold for as high as ten dollars a pair and were used as unofficial badge of membership in the Benevolent and Protective Order of Elks.

Large numbers of elk found refuge in the Yellowstone National Park and these were, during the winter months, diverted into two separate groups, the Northern and the Southern herd. Protected from illegal hunters, these herds increased tremendously at a time when their customary winter feeding grounds outside the Park were being reduced by settlement. The Northern herd had traditionally migrated northward outside the Park during the winter, but now this was endangered by armed hunters who formed a firing line in anticipation of the annual migration. The Southern herd faced the same danger as it migrated into the Jackson Hole country to the south. As these animals moved southward they became wards of the State of Wyoming, and had to be fed by the State in order to prevent starvation due to the shrinking grazing area and the concomitant increase in the number of animals. Some animosity was thereby aroused and the Governor of Wyoming said: "When the elk are fat and sleek they belong to the government of the United States. When they are starving they belong to the people of Wyoming."[6]

When it was suggested in 1911 that the Park authorities institute a winter feeding program to reduce the number of animals that annually died from starvation, the Acting Superintendent of the Park protested that such a procedure would only increase the number of animals, and thus produce a problem of ever-increasing magnitude. He maintained that not only would winter feeding be very expensive, but that once started it would have to be continued since the animals would very soon develop a dependence upon this unnatural assistance. The original problem would increase each year until some other process was devised to reduce the herds to the number determined by their summer grazing ranges. His suggested solution was to accelerate the program begun in 1892, of capturing the excess animals and shipping them to areas in the United States where they had become extinct. He was confident that the capture of a thousand of these animals a year would not be detrimental to the balance of the herds that would remain, and would be less expensive than any feeding program.[7]

The transshipment of surplus elk was accelerated, but unfortunately so was the winter feeding of the animals in the Park. The latter process produced more animals than could be drained off by transshipping and the problem of annual elk reduction remains to this day one of the most controversial subjects faced by the Yellowstone administrators. Elk are no longer fed and live trapping procedures begun under military rule are still utilized, but the elk problem persists. Today, excess numbers of elk are killed by the Park Ranger force, and while practical and realistic, this judicious slaughter has produced, in addition to much emotion, an unsatisfactory answer to the dilemma raised by a realistic wildlife management program on the one hand and the maintenance of National Park policies of preservation and protection on the other.[8]

Although the military authorities were unable to solve the problem of an overabundance of game animals, they were successful in establishing the rudimentary beginnings of the National Park interpretive program. Admittedly, the average soldier was not equipped to answer all the inquiries of the curious tourist, and it was not uncommon for him to rely upon the fantastic in order to cover his lack of scientific knowledge. Troopers detailed to patrol the natural curiosities in the Parks were instructed to give what information they could, in a courteous manner, when requested to do so. The information produced by these men was probably far different from that given today by the "ranger naturalist" who is trained in botany, geology, zoology, and other branches of natural history, but a step had been taken toward what eventually evolved into the naturalist program later developed by the National Park service.

In the Yellowstone particularly, surrounded as they were with strange natural phenomena, the early military commanders attempted to maintain a close watch on the freaks of nature; geyser eruptions were charted and any change in activity was closely noted. Constant observation of the various geysers made it possible to predict their time of eruption with sufficient accuracy to inform tourists of impending geyser activity, and it was discovered that there was a close connection between the temperature of the water in a geyser and the time of its eruption. Newly formed geysers were examined and measured, temperature readings were taken, and their locations were duly reported to the Acting Superintendent. One civilian observer stated that the Park's military guardian "had a pronounced weakness for geysers . . . stopping at every little steamjet to examine it." He supposed that the Acting Superintendent felt "a personal responsibility in having them [geysers] go regularly."[9]

Definite steps were taken toward the development of an interpretive program in the Yosemite National Park when the Acting Superintendent requested the Secretary of Agriculture to send him books and publications treating the natural history, sylva, flora, and fauna of the Park. He then proceeded to construct an arboretum and botanical garden in the Park. An area comprising some 100 acres was selected, paths were opened, trees trimmed, debris and deadwood cleared, and signs designating the scientific and common nomenclature of the local trees and plants were erected. Trees and plants found in other parts of the Park were transplanted to the selected area and seats provided for the tourists. The originator of the arboretum hoped that it would "some day be supplemented by a building serving the purpose of a museum and library." This same farsighted individual suggested that the entire park be developed and preserved as a "great museum of nature for the general public free of cost." Unfortunately the location selected for the arboretum was on patented land within the Park. When the boundaries were relocated in 1905, that portion was excluded from the Yosemite Park.[10]

With the advent of the National Park Service a definite interpretive program was developed, guide folders were printed, and conducted nature tours and lectures were made available in some of the Parks. Later, museums were established and experiments in visual education were inaugurated, largely through the cooperation of the American Association of Museums and the Smithsonian Institution, augmented by funds from the Rockefeller Foundation. As early as 1908, however, the Acting Superintendent of the Yellowstone had requested that books on natural history be

furnished his office for the "better education and information" of the protectors of the Park. The entire museum and
interpretive program later developed by the National Park
Service was suggested in 1913, when Acting Superintendent
Lieutenant Colonel L. M. Brett of the Yellowstone called the
attention of the Secretary of the Interior to the "necessity for
an administration building, housing all that is interesting in
historical data and specimens of natural curiosities, etc." He
suggested that "small branches of the administration building in the shape of bungalows might be erected at Norris,
Upper Basin, and the Canyon, containing like data and specimens, and presided over by one able to give intelligent information." The same suggestion was made later by M. P.
Skinner, who was destined to become the first National Park
naturalist. But Skinner, after talking with the Secretary of the
Interior, said that "the consensus of opinion seems to be that
the project is a little too advanced for the present. The museum feature in connection with the administration building
they are not ready to handle yet."[11]

The military commanders also suggested what has only
recently been adopted by the National Park Service, namely,
inducing Park visitors to remove themselves from the heavily
traveled portions of the Parks and to visit the less frequented
and wilderness areas. The Acting Superintendent of the
Sequoia Park in 1899 lamented the fact that there existed no
guidebooks or hotels to "advertise the highest and roughest
mountains" in the Park; as a consequence "those travelers
who are content to stumble over the discarded baskets of the
last camping party" missed the finer pleasures of Park travel.
This perspicacious individual maintained that:

> If one is to know the real beauties of the Sierra country, he
> must penetrate many places which are most difficult of access,
> must reach the summits of the highest mountains and explore
> the gorges of the deepest canyons. Rough and broken, steep
> and high as the Sierras are, they can still be traveled, and will

be by enthusiasts, too, if the Government will take the initiative and introduce them to its people.[12]

While almost all of the procedures inaugurated and suggested by the military commanders have been adopted by the National Park Service, many of them spread far beyond the Parks themselves. The Acting Superintendents were frequently requested to give advice on proper game protection, fire fighting methods, administrative policy and methods, financial procedures, and indeed, any and all information concerning the establishment and management of parks. Information forwarded to Japan was considered by the Japanese to have been of "no small service" to them in their "preparations for the scheme of [their] National Park"; information supplied to the museum director in Stuttgardt, Germany, permitted him to greatly expand the perspective of the Museum für Länder und Volkerkunde. The military management of the Yellowstone became the model for game control in the Game Preserve on Grand Island, Michigan; the Commissioners of the Palisades Interstate Park in New York requested and received information concerning rules and regulations. Information concerning fire-fighting methods was forwarded to the State Forester of New Jersey upon request, and a state senator of North Carolina, faced with the imminent question of establishing a National Park in his state (Appalachian National Park), requested from the Acting Superintendent of Yellowstone all of the information at his command on administrative procedures. The advice and suggestions made by the military commanders thus became a part of the world-wide conservation movement.[13]

Fortunately, the military administrators were able to avoid the pressures that occasionally overwhelm present-day Park superintendents. Operating on the wise assumption that nature cannot be improved upon, they resisted the temptation to introduce into the Parks every modern convenience and innovation. When tourists complained about the lack of improvements in the Yellowstone, for example, Acting Superintendent Brett replied:

> To make the Yellowstone National Park resemble Atlantic City is unthinkable. . . . To put a rustic dress on each geyser, chain in every hot pool, and erect pagodas over the paint pots, would certainly complete the grotesque picture . . . this wonderland is Nature's entertainment for mortals, and every touch of the human hand is a desecration.

The Army Corps of Engineers laid out roads so that they did not interfere with natural conditions and restricted them to the smallest area consistent with access to the principal objects of interest. Hiram M. Chittenden, one of the most prominent of the engineers, believed that Government policy was to maintain the Parks "as nearly as possible in their natural condition, unchanged by the hand of man." Some modern Park administrators appear to think that nature *can* be improved upon and go about building unsightly roads, housing developments, and tourist lodgings and committing other acts of official vandalism.[14]

Gradually the military superintendents were able to convince a skeptical public that preservation of the Parks was in the public interest and not an unwelcome invasion of private rights. The initial hostility on the part of residents of the area was in time overcome. This was a major contribution. For a while, as game became rarer in other parts of the country, but increased within the areas protected by the cavalry, the feeling of enmity toward the government Parks was intensified. But the military commanders were able to convince the settlers around the Parks that the benefits of keeping the Parks intact and the game protected would eventually outweigh any immediate gain they might realize by sabotaging Park operations. Legislators of the surrounding states were aided in drafting realistic game laws and close cooperation was obtained from game wardens and other state officials. Citizens' protective clubs were organized in the surrounding communities by the military commanders, and men who had once been enemies and poachers now became friends and protectors of the Parks. President Theodore Roosevelt recognized the significance of citizen support when he wrote, "Eastern people, and especially eastern sportsmen, need to keep steadily in mind the fact that the westerners who live in the neighborhood of the forest preserves are the men who, in the last resort, will determine whether or not those preserves are to be permanent. They cannot . . . be kept . . . game reservations unless the settlers roundabout believe in them and heartily support them."[15]

With the passage of the Lacey Act in 1894, the military commanders of the Yellowstone Park found their duties materially lightened. The existence of legal machinery, coupled with an occasional but well-publicized conviction, provided an effective deterrent to vandalism and poaching. One major fault remained in the law, however. A violation of the Lacey Act was meant to be a misdemeanor, but the inclusion of the phrase stipulating "imprisonment not exceeding two years" automatically elevated any violation of the law to the status of a felony. Felonies were legally treated as crimes under the Constitution and any person so accused must be indicted, prosecuted, and tried by a court. This legal technicality vitiated the jurisdiction of the resident United States Commissioner, and all cases arising under the law had to be tried before the District Court at Cheyenne, Wyoming. This fault was not discovered until 1913, however, and the Acting Superintendent immediately recommended that the Lacey Act be amended to remove the difficulty. Four separate bills were introduced into Congress, all designed to lessen the penalty provided for in the original act, making the offenses against Park law misdemeanors rather than felonies. On June 28, 1916, Congress approved legislation providing for a maximum penalty of $500 or six months' imprisonment rather than the $1,000 fine and two-year imprisonment provided for in the original act. The change greatly simplified enforcement proceedings and substantially reduced the time and expense of criminal proceedings.[16]

The purely military activities of the cavalry units assigned to the Parks were necessarily few, for the troops were usually dispersed in small detachments varying from two to six men. This arrangement was not conducive to formal military training, but discipline was maintained, and the constant mounted work required of the soldiers on detached service taught them how to ride and care for their horses and gave them a certain self-reliance which they were not liable to gain in ordinary garrison duty. They became, if not good parade ground soldiers, good field soldiers. Troop activities were not confined to the pursuit and capture of poachers, however. In the Yellowstone, the usual garrison duties were attended to, military inspections were held, a lyceum was established to teach signaling and hippology, and weekly drills were held. The troops annually assigned to the California Parks returned to garrison every year, and the summer assignment provided six months of intensive field training, including the overland march to and from the Presidio of San Francisco.

Yet the isolation of the Park commands and the hard work in an uncomfortable winter climate convinced many troopers that $13 per month, plus food and clothing, was not sufficient recompense for the hardships of military service, and many deserted. Others found that guard posts were frequently usurped by hungry bears or marauding moose, and discovered that they, as protectors of the game animals, faced much more severe penalties for killing game than did the civilian poacher. For officers, park service presented the opportunity of more autonomy and greater freedom in command. Many officers realized, however, that the duties required of them were not precisely those for which they had been trained and suggested that a civilian service be designed to relieve the military of its civil duties. In 1907 a retired Army officer was named Acting Superintendent of the Yellowstone Park with instructions from the President to devise a plan for a civil guard to replace the military in the Park.[17]

The scheme proposed by Lieutenant General S. B. M. Young to establish a Yellowstone National Park Guard included an estimated $50,000 annual appropriation. The Park was to be divided into four districts; a chief inspector, four assistant inspectors, and twenty civilian guards were to form the entire protective force. During the heaviest part of the tourist season the guard force was to be enlarged. The estimated $50,000 included neither the salary of a superintendent nor funds for the maintenance of park roads; the construction and maintenance of roads supposedly would be left under the direction of the Army Engineers. According to the general's estimates, the annual cost of military administration was over $150,000; his proposed civilian guard could be established at one-third this cost and its members could be recruited from among discharged soldiers who had served in the parks.[18]

The plan thus proposed was remarkably similar to that eventually utilized in the formation of the National Park Service some ten years later. By the time the plan had been drawn up and presented to the Secretary of the Interior, the President had changed his mind and the Secretary of the Interior was not willing at that time to request an increased appropriation. Admitting that the administration of the parks was developing into a sort of three-headed monster—with the roads under the direction of the Army Engineers, the cavalry under control of the Secretary of War, and the Acting Superintendents serving both the Department of the Army and the Department of the Interior—the Secretary still thought that the moral effect and the saving of expense were enough to justify the continuation of military control.[19]

The Secretary of War, however, was beginning to think otherwise. The system was obviously unjust to the Army. Appropriations charged to the War Department were being spent on duties that were the responsibility of the Department of the Interior. Although the soldiers assigned to the Parks were gaining valuable field experience, some military men thought that such duty was detrimental to military discipline and training. Several years passed before the dilemma was resolved by events beyond the borders of the United States.

Revolution in Mexico in 1910–11, followed by counter-revolution in 1913 and the presidency of Victoriano Huerta, led many Americans to believe that military intervention into Mexico was not improbable. The Secretary of War suggested that the squadron of troops then on duty in the Yellowstone be immediately reduced to a detachment of selected cavalrymen having a natural taste and aptitude for Park duty. Thus, should the necessity arise, these men could be discharged from the Army and taken over by the Secretary of the Interior as civilian rangers. The Secretary of War further suggested that the military detail in the Yosemite Park be reduced to one troop of cavalry and that no troops be detailed for service in the Sequoia and General Grant Parks. These suggestions were acceptable to the Secretary of the Interior and organization of the Yellowstone Park Detachment was initiated.[20]

The Acting Superintendent of the Yellowstone was instructed to recommend the names of those soldiers who preferred transfer to the newly formed organization. A force of 200 men was drawn from nine regiments. According to the original plans, this Detachment would exist as a military unit for only a short time, and form the transition from military to civil control. Complete civil take-over did not occur until 1918, however, and in the interim, the military commanders lobbied incessantly for an end to the military administration of the Yellowstone.[21]

Military management of the Yellowstone would have ended several years earlier had it not been for the resistance of some members of Congress. Congressman J. J. Fitzgerald of New York, Chairman of the House Committee on Appro-

priations, held that a civil guard would be far more expensive
than continued use of the military. Fitzgerald maintained that
Congress had placed the Yellowstone under the protective
arm of the military and he believed that Congress intended
for it to remain there.[22] The military commanders fell back
upon arguments previously used: that conditions in and
around the Yellowstone had changed considerably, that the
surrounding states had provided protective laws over the
adjoining lands and had also legislated excellent game laws.
While poachers formerly had to be guarded against by constant vigilance, they were now a threat only a few months out
of each year when game seasons were closed in the surrounding states. The military lobbyists claimed that the sentiment
of the communities around the Park was now overwhelm-
ingly in favor of strict compliance with the regulations.[23] It
was suggested that the use of soldiers to work on roads and
telephone lines, to check automobiles, stock streams with
fish, fight forest fires, register tourists, and indeed, to perform any duties other than those specified in the Act of
March 3, 1883, was strictly illegal. If the law were to be
followed, the soldiers could only eject trespassers, leaving
other tasks to be performed by a large civilian force.

All these arguments had previously been cited in reference to the California Parks, but now there was a new argument: the President had stated that the United States Regular
Army was not large enough for the military demands of the
country in times of peace; hence it could not afford to detach
troops for use in the Parks, it was claimed. The cost to the
government for the military guardianship of the Yellowstone
for fiscal 1915 was placed at $194,193.59 and it was alleged
that a civilian force could be formed for less than half that
sum. When Newton D. Baker was named Secretary of War
in the spring of 1916, the opposition to continued use of the
cavalry in the Yellowstone increased. All the previous arguments were repeated, and strengthened by an opinion from
the Judge Advocate General stating that the troops could be

used only to prevent trespassers from entering the Park, and to remove those who did gain entrance.

Comprehensive plans for the development of a civil guard to replace the cavalry in the Yellowstone had been developed by the military superintendents as early as 1907. Subsequent military commanders advocated the formation of a separate government bureau that would have the responsibility of guarding and administering all of the National Parks. In 1911 the first of several conferences between Department of Interior officials, Acting Superintendents, and other interested persons was held in the Yellowstone National Park. A second conference was held in the Yosemite National Park the following year, and a third was convened in Berkeley, California, in 1915. Out of these conferences there developed an increasing awareness that conditions in and around the various parks had changed and military protection was no longer necessary. Several bills were introduced into Congress, all designed to establish a separate bureau within the Department of the Interior to supervise, manage, and control the National Parks and monuments under that Department's jurisdiction. The continual opposition to the use of cavalry units as Park guardians finally proved effective and on August 25, 1916, President Woodrow Wilson signed an Act establishing the National Park Service. The newly formed bureau did not begin functioning until after funds providing for its formation were approved in the deficiency appropriation act of April 17, 1917.[24]

Members of the Yellowstone Park Detachment who desired to remain in the Park were discharged from the Army and appointed as rangers in the Park Service. The military force then guarding the Park was withdrawn, Fort Yellowstone was abandoned as a post, and the guardianship of the Park was transferred to the Department of the Interior, effective October 1, 1916. No attempt was made to establish the valuation of improvements made by the Army, and all buildings were transferred to the Department of the

Interior without cost. The men who desired to remain in military service were reassigned to their original units and, accompanied by the last military Acting Superintendent, departed from the Park on October 26, 1916. For the first time since 1886, no cavalry troops were stationed in any of the nation's Parks.[25]

The abandonment of military establishments has always been accompanied by a furor of protests by residents of towns situated near those establishments, and the abandonment of Fort Yellowstone was no exception. Opposition came from residents who looked upon the maneuver from a purely commercial standpoint. Petitions opposing the withdrawal of troops were forwarded to the Secretary of War and, since 1916 was an election year, the politicians were drawn into the fray. Senators Thomas H. Walsh and H. L. Meyers of Montana were attending the Democratic National Convention in Chicago when they learned that orders had been given ending the military guardianship of the Yellowstone. Walsh immediately telephoned the Secretary of the Interior and demanded that the troops not be recalled from the Park until January 1; telegrams were sent by both him and Meyers demanding that they be heard before any further action was taken. When informed that the orders had already been given, the two Senators pleaded that the order be at least postponed until after the election. Apprehensive over the effect the withdrawal of troops might have upon their constituents, the two Senators placed their case before the President of the United States, claiming they had received only evasive replies from the Secretary of War. President Wilson, in the midst of a campaign for re-election, stated that he was very much disturbed and requested that the Secretary of the Interior confer fully with the Montana Senators before executing the order. But this was too late to have any effect, for the troops were even then departing from the Yellowstone.[26]

Unable to obtain what they wanted by telegrams and

letters, the Senators from Montana turned to Congress for relief. By exerting pressure upon their colleagues in the House of Representatives, they were able to have included in the sundry civil bill for fiscal 1918, the provision that no part of the appropriation for the Yellowstone Park be used for payment of salaries for a civilian protective force, and that protection of the Park be performed by a detail of troops. The Secretary of War protested these provisions and claimed that the war with Germany necessitated the employment of every soldier in the wartime army then being constructed. However, since the appropriation bill included the two noxious provisions, the Secretary of the Interior faced the dilemma of either requesting a detail of troops, or closing the Park to visitors. Either alternative involved the discharge of the previously selected ranger force. A request for troops was made, a squadron of the Seventh Cavalry was detailed to Fort Yellowstone to police the Park, and upon its arrival on June 26, 1917, the ranger force was dismissed from service. The civilian Supervisor remained at his post, and no administrative duties were assigned to the military commander.[27]

The immediate results were chaos and confusion. The Department of the Interior, through its civilian Supervisor, controlled the concessionnaires, authorized the rate charges, and supervised the admission of automobiles and the care of the wild animals; the water, electric and telephone systems were under the control of the Interior Department also, but its authority went no further. All road and trail construction was done by Army Engineer Corps, and the actual protection of the Park was entrusted to the cavalry. This three-headed administrative animal was less than docile and conflict soon erupted between its separate parts. Owing to the exigencies of war, the Army officers were changed several times within a matter of months; general dissatisfaction among the soldiers assigned to the Park resulted in gross inefficiency; tourists complained about the soldiers' arrogance and sometimes drunkenness and were curious as to why troops were patrolling the Park when their sons and brothers were being drafted to fight a war. The civilian Supervisor found that it was not safe to leave any personal belongings unguarded, lest they disappear, and complained that the War Department was utilizing the Park command as a transient station for unassigned officers and men, that the troopers never learned their duties and cared nothing for the welfare of the Park. One seasoned cavalryman assigned to the Yellowstone questioned the advisability of using 450 men trained in the art of combat to replace fifty rangers for peaceful patrol work, and claimed that if he did not have a mother and sisters he would "pull out" and enlist in the Canadian Army.

Congress was finally convinced of its folly, the clause providing for the non-use of funds for administrative and protection work was deleted from the sundry civil bill in 1918, and in that year the United States Army was finally and completely withdrawn from the Yellowstone National Park.[28]

Epilogue

THE WITHDRAWAL of the military units from the
National Parks marked a major turning point in the development of the National Park idea. Henceforth the direction of
the Parks would be in civilian hands and future development
would be civilian development. Admitting that, in principle,
military control and administration of any civil matters may
be undesirable in a democratic society, it was fortunate for
the future of conservation in the United States that the Army
was given the duty of protecting the first Parks. The Yellowstone Park, itself an experiment, was formed during a time
of notorious political corruption; it could well have become
a political plaything and in the process might have been
destroyed. If it had been manipulated by unscrupulous politicians, it is doubtful whether the constant threat of dismemberment, spoliation, and destruction could have been
thwarted. Writing at the turn of the century, the country's
foremost naturalist and park propagandist, John Muir, noted
this: "In pleasing contrast to the noisy, ever-changing management or mismanagement, of blustering, blundering,

plundering, money-making vote-sellers who receive their places from boss politicians as purchased goods, the soldiers do their duty so quietly that the traveler is scarcely aware of their presence."[1]

From the Act establishing the Yellowstone National Park has grown a national park system comprising some 264 units including parks, battlefields, cemeteries, seashores, parkways, and historic sites. A national forest system protects more than 185 million acres of timbered land and some 370 state forests exist under varying degrees of protection. Municipalities and individuals have set aside large areas for recreation and scientific purposes; thousands of wildlife refuges dot the land. Credit for these protective systems obviously belongs to many nonmilitary men and processes. However, the United States Cavalry did protect the beginnings of the National Park system at a time when no other protection was feasible. By 1916 military control and administration of the nation's parks were anachronistic. The embryonic park system had fulfilled, by that time, the expectations of its founders, and the mere presence of protected bits of wilderness justified the wisdom of establishing other parks. The idea of conservation was becoming an established part of the nation's thinking and National Parks were considered by an increasing number of people to be worth preserving. Many individuals, politicians, and corporate interests resisted the idea, but then they still do.

Then and now the major conflict concerning natural resources was between those who would exploit and those who would preserve for posterity. Present, too, were the conflicting views of the Easterners—who viewed the Parks from afar —and the Westerners—who viewed the Parks as a violation of their economic destiny. These conflicts were exhibited in the debates over bills providing for a railroad through the northern portion of the Yellowstone. In one instance, Representative Joseph K. Toole of Montana urged passage of a railroad bill and maintained that "the privileges of citizenship, the vast accumulation of property, and the demands of commerce" should not yield to the "mere caprice of a few sportsmen bent only on the protection of a few buffalo in the National Park." This economic argument was seconded by Lewis E. Payson of Illinois, who found that he could not understand the "sentiment" which favored the "retention of a few buffaloes" over the proposed railroad, which would lead to the development of mining interests amounting to millions of dollars, giving profitable employment to perhaps thousands of men."

The rebuttal to these utilitarian arguments, calling forth the imagery of Thoreau and Bryant, was quick and harsh. New York's Representative S. S. Cox stated that the railroad measure was inspired by "corporate greed and natural selfishness against national pride and natural beauty." He thought it was not a question for "Montana nor other Territory or locality," but rather should be considered a "question for the United States, and for all that gives elevation and grace to our human nature." Supporting Cox, William McAdoo of New Jersey asked his fellow Representatives to "prefer the beautiful and the sublime and the interests of millions to heartless mammon and the greed of capital." In this case the aesthetic arguments prevailed, but the same conflict remains, even in the present age of intense environmental awareness.[2]

One of the main tenets of the Yellowstone organic Act, a clause consequently applied to the other Park Acts, is embodied in the article requiring the "preservation, from injury or spoliation, of all timber, mineral deposits, natural curiosities or wonders within said park and their retention in their natural condition." Today, in the name of progress, several National Parks and monuments are threatened by proposals that completely ignore the very purpose of the Park system. The planned Bridge Canyon Reservoir would back water through the Grand Canyon National Monument with the water reaching Havasu Creek in the Grand Canyon National

Park. An opposite effect is being brought about by the draining of portions of the Everglades National Park, resulting in the slow destruction of its unique plant and animal life. Officials of the State of Arizona have stated their desire to "enhance the beauty and recreational value" of the Grand Canyon by constructing four reservoirs within the canyon. The people of San Francisco, after having once assaulted the Yosemite National Park, now desire to compound the crime by enlarging the Hetch Hetchy Reservoir to include the entire Grand Canyon of the Tuolumne, thus inundating a large area of the Yosemite. Acadia National Park is threatened by the introduction of heavy oil tankers into the Gulf of Maine and the Bay of Fundy. The "Save the Redwoods League" was recently reactivated in order to preserve several groves of the ancient giants threatened by man-made superhighways and lumbermen. The history of almost every National Park is filled with attempts by acquisitive individuals to introduce railroads, dams, power generating machinery, reservoirs, tramways, mineral and timber claims, and sundry other schemes that, if allowed consideration, would violate the still not too sacred boundaries of the National Parks.

In the past, threats to the integrity of National Parks have come from interests outside the Parks; today, the Parks are threatened from both without and within. In the second revision of his chronicle of the Yellowstone National Park, made shortly before his death in 1917, Hiram M. Chittenden stated: *"If official ambition for innovation and the mercenary ambition for private gain are held under adequate restraint,* there is no reason why it [Yellowstone] may not continue to the latest generation a genuine example of original nature . . ."[3] Today, official ambition for innovation appears to be threatening, if not the existence, the stated purpose of our National Parks. At present, professional Park personnel too often view the nation's Parks as belonging to them and not to the public. This is due, in part, to the evolution of the responsibility of the Park ranger from one of protecting parks *for* the public, to one of protecting parks *from* the public. Given the destructive propensities of the visiting tourist, this stance is understandable and perhaps admirable, since employees of the National Park Service are directed by law to provide protection for the Parks "so that they remain unimpaired for future generations." The same law also stipulates that the Parks be managed in such a manner as to provide for the public use of those parks. Since even restricted use of the Parks by the public impairs to some extent protection of their natural state, compromises leaning in one direction or the other are necessary if the conflicting demands of an idealistic law and a demanding public are to be satisfied.[4]

Today the persistent and increasing press of population demands more and more use of the Parks. Park superintendents, as if to justify their efficiency and existence, gleefully report every increase in Park visitation, without noting that increases in visitation and utilization necessarily connote a decrease in protection and a consequent impairment of the assumed enjoyment of future generations. The dilemma is real, and at present, the fluctuating attempts to follow a middle ground between the attitude of the user on the one hand and that of the preserver on the other have been singularly unsuccessful, and have produced a considerable amount of controversy, misunderstanding, and distrust.[5]

Continuing studies and constant re-examination of fundamental Park policies may produce acceptable answers. Some Parks may, of necessity, become "pleasuring grounds" in their entirety; others may be preserved in a pristine wilderness state. Congress attempted to placate both the preservationist and the user when it created the nation's newest Park in the State of Washington. The North Cascades National Park, established October 2, 1968, is part of a larger complex encompassing two national recreation areas, a new national forest wilderness, and an enlarged forest wilderness area. The new Park is bisected by a National Recreation corridor in which most human activity will presumably occur, thus allowing more intensive protection of the natural habitat within the Park. This experiment in use and preservation, if successful, may serve as an example for administrators of the older Parks. The mere presence of man denotes some use of a given area; the differentiation between use and preservation is simply one of degrees of use. A solitary hiker traversing a wilderness is using that area, just as two million people motoring through Yellowstone are using that area. The differences in impact, however, are considerable. The combination of recreation and formal wilderness in the North Cascades resulted from compromises formulated by representatives of the Bureau of Outdoor Recreation, the Park Service, the Forest Service, and a number of conservationists.[6]

Over sixty years ago, a President of the United States remarked that almost no one was opposed to conservation. The same holds true today. Yet the future of conservation may be in greater danger today than it was then. For now, the interested public risks being lulled into complacency by reassuring statements from the White House, the Secretary of the Interior, and major industrial concerns. The urbanization of the United States, the increasing population, innovations in transportation, the never-ending worship of progress, and the ever-present personal greed of individuals all point toward more and larger threats to the existence of an inviolate National Park system.

We have admittedly come a long way from the time when wholesale destruction of the nation's resources seemed necessary to achieve our industrial destiny. Then resources were endless and people were few. Today, when the opposite holds true, we must be ready to take advantage of new land management skills, of advanced technology and research, so that what we have left will not go the way of what we once had. If it is true that man must become civilized to appreciate or desire an uncivilized state of being, it is possible that the material society which grew from widespread exploitation of a continent may be the society that is best prepared, both materially and mentally, to appreciate and preserve those extant elements that escaped the destruction of an earlier era. As man increasingly insulates himself and his culture in concrete, steel, and glass, he may develop an increasing awareness and appreciation for the natural world that he has either taken for granted, ignored, or attempted to mold to fit his varying impulses.

Unfortunately, the poet and philosopher, George Santayana, was only partially correct when he stated, "Those who cannot remember the past are condemned to repeat it." Today we seem determined to repeat, if not all, at least some of the errors of the past. A review of conservation literature indicates that the pleas, warnings, and suggestions of today are composed of phrases spoken and words written in ages past. More than one hundred years ago George Marsh pleaded for a commensurate sense of responsibility as man's power to transform the natural world increased. Marsh wrote, "Man has too long forgotten that the earth was given to him for usufruct alone, not for prolifigate waste." His admonitions were eloquently repeated more than fifty years later by Forest Service employee Aldo Leopold, when he called for the development of an ecological conscience and the establishment of an ethic stressing man-land relations. Today, Raymond Dasmann, Fraser Darling, Stewart Udall, and William O. Douglas are repeating essentially the same pleas.

We need not, however, be ashamed of our conservation record, for it stands in remarkable contrast to that of many older—and some younger—nations. We admittedly have not yet reached the point where man is in accord with his natural surroundings, but we did change our destructive direction sufficiently to allow the preservation of some elements of our natural heritage. The fundamental significance of the Yellowstone, Sequoia, Yosemite, and General Grant National Parks lies in the fact that they represented a marked innovation in the traditional policy of governments: the government purposefully set aside portions of the public domain, and permanently excluded settlers and exploiters. The great naturalist, John Muir, recognized that the United States Cavalry aided the successful realization of this innovation when he wrote: "Blessings on Uncle Sam's soldiers. They have done the job well, and every pine tree is waving its arms for joy." Although materialistic members of society still attempt to vitiate the National Park system, bits of a once seemingly endless wilderness have been preserved; trees and mountains have been saved from the ax of the lumberman, the pick of the miner, and the greed of avaricious men. Some pine trees are still waving their arms for joy.

BIBLIOGRAPHY

GPO: Government Printing Office, Washington, D.C.

BOOKS

Albright, Horace A., and Frank J. Taylor. *"Oh Ranger!": A Book about the National Parks.* Stanford, Calif.: Stanford University Press, 1929.

Allen, Edward Frank. *A Guide to the National Parks of America.* New York: R. McBride, 1918.

Allen, Eugene T., and Arthur L. Day. *Hot Springs of the Yellowstone National Park.* Washington: Carnegie Institute, 1935.

Alter, Cecil J. *Jim Bridger.* Norman: University of Oklahoma Press, 1962.

Atwood, John H. *Yellowstone Park in 1898.* Kansas City, Mo.: Smith Grieves, 1918.

Augspurger, Marie M. *Yellowstone National Park: Historical and Descriptive.* Middletown, Ohio: Naegele-Auer Printing Co. (published by the author), 1948.

Badé, William Frederic (ed.). *The Life and Letters of John Muir.* 2 vols. Boston and New York: Houghton Mifflin, 1923.

Bancroft, Hubert Howe. *History of Washington, Montana, and Idaho.* San Francisco: The History Co., 1896.

Barrus, Clara (ed.). *The Life and Letters of John Burroughs.* 2 vols. Boston and New York: Houghton Mifflin, 1925.

Batchelder, James. *Notes from the Life and Travels of James Batchelder.* San Francisco: Pacific Press, 1892.

Beal, Merrill D. *The Story of Man in Yellowstone.* Rev. ed. Yellowstone Park: The Yellowstone Library and Museum Association, 1960.

Bingaman, John W. *Guardians of Yosemite: Story of the First Rangers.* Washington: National Park Service, 1961.

Blaine, James G. *Twenty Years in Congress.* Norwich, Connecticut: Henry Bill Publishing Co., 1884–1886.

Blau, Joseph L. (ed.). *Men and Movements in American Philosophy.* New York: Prentice-Hall, 1952.

Bonney, Orrin H. and Lorraine. *Battle Drums and Geysers: The Life and Journals of Lt. Gustavus Cheyney Doane.* Chicago: Swallow Press, 1970.

Born, Wolfgang. *American Landscape Painting: An Interpretation.* New Haven: Yale University Press, 1948.

Brockman, Christian F. *Recreational Use of Wild Lands.* New York: McGraw-Hill, 1959.

Bruffey, George A. *Eighty-one Years in the West.* Butte, Mont.: Butte Miner Printing Press, 1925.

Bryant, Harold C., and Wallace W. Atwood. *Research and Education in the National Parks.* GPO, 1932.

Bunnell, Lafayette H. *Discovery of the Yosemite, and the Indian War of 1851 Which Led to That Event.* Chicago: F. H. Revell, 1880.

Burlingame, Merrill G. *The Montana Frontier.* Helena, Mont.: State Publishing Co., 1942.

Burroughs, John. *Camping and Tramping with Roosevelt.* Boston: Houghton Mifflin, 1907.

Cameron, Jenks. *The National Park Service: Its History, Activities and Organization.* (Institute for Government Research, Service Monographs of the United States Government, No. 11.) New York and London: Appleton, 1922.

Carstensen, Vernon (ed.). *The Public Lands.* Madison: University of Wisconsin Press, 1963.

Carvalho, S. H. *Incidents of Travel and Adventure in the Far West: With Colonel Fremont's Last Expedition Across the Rocky Mountains.* New York: Derby and Jackson, 1857.

Catlin, George. *Letters and Notes on The Manners, Customs, and Condition of the North American Indians.* 2 vols. London: George Catlin, 1841.

Chittenden, Hiram M. *The American Fur Trade of the Far West.* 2 vols. New York: Press of the Pioneers, 1935.

————. *The Yellowstone National Park.* 7th ed. Cincinnati: Stewart and Kidd, 1912.

————. See Le Roy, Bruce.

Clampitt, John W. *Echoes From the Rocky Mountains.* Chicago: Belford, Clarke and Co., 1889.

Coutant, C. G. *History of Wyoming.* Vol. 1. Laramie: Chaplin, Spafford and Mathison, 1899.

Cramton, Louis C. *Early History of Yellowstone National Park and its Relation to National Park Policies.* GPO, 1923.

Darling, F. Fraser, and Noel D. Eichorn. *Man and Nature in the National Parks: Reflections on Policy.* Washington: Conservation Foundation, 1967.

Dellenbaugh, Frederick S. *Breaking the Wilderness.* New York and London: Putnam's, 1905.

Driggs, B. W. *History of Teton Valley Idaho.* Caldwell, Idaho: Caxton Printers, 1926.

Elliott, L. Louise. *Six Weeks on Horseback through Yellowstone Park.* Rapid City, North Dakota: privately printed, 1913.

Farquhar, Francis P. *Yosemite, The Big Trees, and the High Sierra.* Berkeley: University of California Press, 1948.

———— (ed.). *Yosemite in 1896.* Berkeley: Tamalpais Press, 1962.

Folsom, David E. *Folsom-Cook Exploration of the Upper Yellowstone in the Year 1869.* St. Paul: privately printed, 1894.

Fry, Walter, and John R. White. *Big Trees.* Stanford, Calif.: Stanford University Press, 1930.

Gillis, Charles J. *The Yellowstone Park and Alaska.* New York: privately printed, 1893.

Greeley, Horace. *An Overland Journey, from New York to San Francisco, in the Summer of 1859.* New York: C. M. Saxton, Barker and Co., 1860.

Grinnell, George Bird (ed.). *American Big Game Hunting; The Book of the Boone and Crockett Club.* New York: Forest and Stream Publishing Co., 1901.

———— (ed.). *American Big Game in Its Haunts; The Book of the Boone and Crockett Club.* New York: Forest and Stream Publishing Co., 1904.

Grinnell, George Bird, and Charles Sheldon (eds.). *Hunting and Conservation; The Book of the Boone and Crockett Club.* New Haven: Yale University Press, 1925.

Hague, Arnold. *The Yellowstone Park as a Game Reservation.* New York: Forest and Stream Publishing Co., 1893.

Hall, Ansel F. (ed.). *Handbook of Yosemite National Park.* New York: Putnam, 1921.

Hamilton, William Thomas *My Sixty Years on the Plains.* New York: Forest and Stream Publishing Co., 1909.

Harris, Burton. *John Colter: His Years in the Rockies.* New York: Scribner's, 1952.

Henderson, G. L. *Yellowstone National Park, Past, Present and Future.* Washington: Gibson Brothers, 1891.

Hill, Cary LeRoy. *Forests of Yosemite, Sequoia and General Grant Parks.* GPO, 1917.

Hoar, George R. *Autobiography of Seventy Years.* New York: Scribner's, 1903.

Holmes, Burton. *Lectures.* 10 vols. Battle Creek, Mich.: Little-Preston Co., 1901.

————. *Travelogues.* New York: McClure, 1908.

Hornaday, William T. *Our Vanishing Wild Life.* New York: New York Zoological Society, 1913.

Howe, George F. *Chester A. Arthur; A Quarter Century of Machine Politics.* New York: Dodd, Mead, 1934.

Hutchings, James M. (ed.). *In the Heart of the Sierras; The Yosemite Valley.* Oakland: Pacific Press, 1886.

Huth, Hans. *Nature and the American.* Berkeley: University of California Press, 1957.

Ise, John. *Our National Park Policy—A Critical History.* Baltimore: Johns Hopkins Press, 1961.

Jarrett, Henry (ed.). *Resources for the Future: Comparisons in Resource Management.* Baltimore, Md.: Johns Hopkins Press, 1961.

Johnson, Robert Underwood. *Remembered Yesterdays.* Boston: Little, Brown, 1923.

Kipling, Rudyard. *American Notes.* New York: F. F. Lovell Co., c. 1893.

Kuykendall, Ralph S. *Early History of Yosemite Valley California.* GPO, 1919.

Langford, Nathaniel P. *Discovery of Yellowstone Park.* St. Paul: J. E. Haynes, 1905.

———. *Vigilante Days and Ways, The Pioneers of the Rockies, The Makers and Making of Montana, Idaho, Oregon, Washington and Wyoming.* 2 vols. New York: D. D. Merril Co., 1893.

Le Roy, Bruce (ed.). *H. M. Chittenden, A Western Epic. Being a Selection from His Unpublished Journals, Diaries, and Reports.* Tacoma, Wash.: Washington State Historical Society, 1961.

Lippman, Jean, and Alice Winchester. *Primitive Painters in America, 1750–1950: An Anthology.* New York: Dodd, Mead, 1950.

Mattes, Merrill. *Colter's Hell and Jackson's Hole.* Yellowstone Park: Yellowstone Library and Museum Association, 1962.

Mills, Enos A. *Your National Parks.* Cambridge: Houghton Mifflin, 1917.

Muir, John. *My First Summer in the Sierra.* Boston: Houghton Mifflin, 1911.

———. *The Mountains of California.* New York: Century Press, 1911.

———. *The National Parks: Sketches from the Atlantic Monthly.* Boston: Houghton Mifflin, 1901.

———. *Our National Parks.* Boston: Houghton Mifflin, 1901.

———. *Steep Trails, California, Utah, Nevada, Washington, Oregon, The Grand Canyon.* Boston: Houghton Mifflin, 1918.

———. *The Yosemite.* New York: Century, 1912.

Nash, Roderick. *Wilderness and the American Mind.* New Haven: Yale University Press, 1967.

Noble, Louis L. (ed. Elliot S. Vesell). *The Life and Works of Thomas Cole.* Cambridge: Harvard University Press, 1964.

Norris, P. W. *The Calumet of the Coteau, and other Poetical Legends of the Border Together with a Guide-Book of the Yellowstone National Park.* Philadelphia: Lippincott, 1884.

Oberholtzer, Ellis Paxson. *Jay Cooke, Financier of the Civil War.* 2 vols. Philadelphia: G. W. Jacobs, 1907.

Olmsted, Frederick Law, Jr., and Theodora Kimball. *Frederick Law Olmsted, Landscape Architect.* 2 vols. New York: Putnam's, 1922.

Peattie, Donald C. *Audubon's America.* Boston: Houghton Mifflin, 1940.

Phillips, Paul C. *The Fur Trade.* 2 vols. Norman: University of Oklahoma Press, 1961.

Porter, T. C. *Impressions of America.* London: C. A. Pearson, 1899.

Quick, Herbert. *Yellowstone Nights.* Indianapolis: Bobbs-Merrill, 1911.

Remington, Frederick. *John Ermine of the Yellowstone.* New York: Macmillan, 1902.

―――. *Pony Tracks.* New York: Harper, 1898.

Richardson, Elmo R. *The Politics of Conservation.* (University of California Publications in History, Vol. 70) Berkeley: University of California Press, 1962.

Riley, William C. *Grand Tour Guide to the Yellowstone National Park—A Manual for Tourists.* St. Paul: privately printed, 1889.

Robbins, Roy M. *Our Landed Heritage: The Public Domain 1776–1936.* Lincoln: University of Nebraska Press, 1962.

Roosevelt, Theodore, and George Bird Grinnell (eds.). *Hunting in Many Lands; The Book of the Boone and Crockett Club.* New York: Forest and Stream Publishing Co., 1895.

Russell, Carl P. *One Hundred Years in Yosemite.* Berkeley: University of California Press, 1932.

Russell, Osborne. *Journal of a Trapper, 1834–1843.* Boise, Idaho: Syms-York, 1921.

Schwatka, Frederick, and John Hyde. *Through Wonderland with Lieut. Schwatka.* St. Paul: Northern Pacific Railroad, 1886.

Settle, Raymond W. (ed.). *The March of Mounted Riflemen.* Glendale, Calif.: Arthur H. Clark, 1940.

Shankland, Robert. *Steve Mather of the National Parks.* New York: Knopf, 1951.

Sheridan, Michael V. *The Memoirs of General Phil Sheridan.* New York: C. L. Webster and Co., 1888.

Skinner, M. P. *The Yellowstone Nature Book.* Chicago: A. C. McClurg, 1924.

Smith, F. Dumont. *Book of a Hundred Bears.* Chicago: Rand McNally, 1909.

Smith, Hugh M., and William C. Kendall. *Fishes in Yellowstone National Park.* GPO, 1921.

Stanley, Edwin James. *Rambles in Wonderland; or, Up the Yellowstone and Among the Geysers and other Curiosities of the National Park.* New York: D. Appleton and Co., 1878.

Stoddard, John L. *John L. Stoddard's Lectures.* Chicago: Shuman, 1911.

Strahorn, Carrie A. *Fifteen Thousand Miles by Stage.* New York: Putnam's, 1911.

Strong, W. E. *A Trip to the Yellowstone National Park in 1875.* GPO, 1876.

Stuart, Granville. *Forty Years on the Frontier.* 2 vols. Cleveland: Arthur H. Clark, 1928.

Swain, Donald. *Wilderness Defender: Horace M. Albright and Conservation.* Chicago: University of Chicago Press, 1970.

Taft, Robert. *Artists and Illustrators of the Old West 1850–1900.* New York: Scribner's, 1953.

Taylor, Charles M., Jr. *Touring Alaska and the Yellowstone.* Philadelphia: George W. Jacobs, c. 1901.

Topping, E. S. *The Chronicles of the Yellowstone.* St. Paul: Pioneer Press Co., 1888.

Trefethen, James B. *Crusade for Wildlife, Highlights in Conservation Progress; A Boone and Crockett Club Book.* Harrisburg, Pa.: Stackpole, 1961.

Turrill, Gardner S. *A Tale of the Yellowstone; or, In a Wagon Through Wyoming and Wonderland.* Jefferson, Iowa: privately printed, 1901.

Victor, Mrs. Frances Fuller. *The River of the West; Life and Adventure in the Rocky Mountains and Oregon; Embracing Events in the Life-time of a Mountain-man and Pioneers; With The Early History of The North-western Slope.* Hartford, Conn.: R. W. Bliss and Co., 1870.

Vinton, Stallo. *John Colter, Discoverer of Yellowstone Park.* New York: Edward Eberstadt, 1926.

Weed, William H. *Geysers.* GPO, 1912.

Wheeler, Olin D. *Sketches of Wonderland.* St. Paul: Northern Pacific Railroad, 1895.

———. *Yellowstone National Park.* St. Paul: W. C. Riley, 1901.

White, John R., and Samuel J. Pusateri. *Sequoia and Kings Canyon National Parks.* Stanford, Calif.: Stanford University Press, 1949.

Wilbur, R. L., and W. A. DuPuy. *Conservation in the Department of the Interior.* GPO, 1931.

Wingate, George W. *Through the Yellowstone Park on Horseback.* New York: O. Judd Co., 1886.

Wolfe, Linnie Marsh (ed.). *John of the Mountains—The Unpublished Journals of John Muir.* Boston: Houghton Mifflin, 1938.

Wolfe, Linnie Marsh (ed.). *Son of the Wilderness: The Life of John Muir.* New York: Knopf, 1946.

Wood, Edwin O. *Historic Mackinac.* 2 vols. New York: Macmillan, 1918.

Wood, Francis E. *Yosemite, Sequoia, and Kings Canyon, Hawaii.* Chicago: Follett, 1963.

_____. *Yellowstone, Glacier, Grand Teton.* Chicago: Follett, 1963.

Yard, Robert S. *Our Federal Lands.* New York: Scribner's, 1928.

ARTICLES AND PERIODICALS

"About Buffalo," *Forest and Stream,* XLV (Nov. 1895), 127–131.

"Amateur Management of Yosemite Scenery," *Century Magazine,* XL (Jan. 1890), 797–798.

Anderson, A. A. "The Foundation and Development of Yellowstone National Park Forest Reservation," *Annals of Wyoming,* IV (Apr. 1927), 378–388.

"An Immense Tree," *Gleason's Pictorial Drawing-Room Companion,* V (Nov. 1853), 216.

Archibald, J. F. "A Cavalry March to the Yosemite," *Illustrated American,* VII (Nov. 1896), 27–34.

Athearn, Robert G. "The Great Plains in Historical Perspective," *Montana, Magazine of Western History,* VIII (Jan. 1958), 13–29.

Baker, Ray Standard. "A Place of Marvels," *Century Magazine,* LXVI (Aug. 1903), 481–501.

Bowden, Martyn J. "The Perception of the Western Interior of the United States, 1800–1870: A Problem in Historical Geosophy," *Proceedings* of the Association of American Geographers, I (1969), 16–21.

Brockman, C. Frank. "Administrative Officers of Yosemite," *Yosemite Nature Notes,* XXIII (June 1944), 13–18.

Bryce, James. "National Parks, The Need for the Future," *The Outlook,* CII (Dec. 1912), 135–141.

Bunnell, Lafayette H. "The Discovery of the Yosemite," *Century Magazine,* XL (Sept. 1890), 795–797.

"Care of the Yosemite Valley," *Century Magazine,* XXIX (Jan. 1890), 474–475.

Chittenden, Hiram M. "Early History of the Yellowstone," *The Nation,* LXII (May 1896), 415.

Colby, William E. "Yosemite and the Sierra Club," *Sierra Club Bulletin,* XXII (Apr. 1938), 12–19.

"Conditions under Which Yosemite Valley Was Given to California in 1864," *The Nation,* L (Mar. 1890), 204.

Comstock, Theodore B. "Points of Interest, Yellowstone National Park," *Transcripts,* American Institute of Mining Engineering, XVI (1888), 46–49.

Cook, C. W. "Valley of the Upper Yellowstone," *Western Monthly,* IV (July 1870), 60–67.

Cope. E. D. "Present Condition of the Yellowstone National Park," *American Naturalist,* XIX (Nov. 1885), 1037–1040.

DeLacy, Walter E. "A Trip up the Snake River in 1863," *Contributions,* Historical Society of Montana, I (1876), 113–143.

Deming, Lucius. "Destructive Tendencies in the Yosemite Valley," *Century Magazine,* XXXIX (Jan. 1890), 476–477.

Dudley, William Russell. "Forest Reservations," *Sierra Club Bulletin,* I (Jan. 1896), 254–267.

Driscoll, Charles F. "The Yellowstone National Park," *American Architect,* XIII (Mar. 1873), 130–131.

Eldridge, Maurice O. "Government Highways in Yellowstone National Park," *World Today,* XIX (Nov. 1910), 1263–1272.

Ellsworth, Fred W. "Through Yellowstone National Park with the American Institute of Banking," *Moody's Magazine,* XIV (Nov. 1912), 368–375.

Emerson, Ralph Waldo. "The Young Americans," *The Dial,* XVI (Apr. 1844), 489.

Everts, Truman C. "Thirty Seven Days of Peril,"*Scribner's Monthly,* III (Nov. 1871), 1–17.

Farquhar, Francis P. "Colonel Benson," *Sierra Club Bulletin,* XII (Apr. 1925), 175–179.

———. "Walker's Discovery of Yosemite," *Sierra Club Bulletin,* XXVII (Jan. 1942), 35.

Fenneman, N. M. "Yellowstone National Park," *Journal of Geography,* XI (June 1913), 314–320.

Finck, Henry T. "A Week in Yellowstone Park," *The Nation,* XLV (Sept. 1887), 166–169.

———. "Yellowstone Park in 1897," *The Nation,* LXV (Oct. 1897), 276–277.

———. "Yellowstone Park as a Summer Resort," *The Nation,* LXXI (Sept. 1900), 248–250.

Folsom, David E. "Folsom-Cook Exploration of the Upper Yellowstone in the Year 1869," *Contributions,* Montana Historical Society, V (1904), 349–355.

Freeman, L. R. "Protect the Game in Yellowstone Park," *Forest and Stream,* XV (Dec. 1901), 425–429.

———. "Ski-runners of the Yellowstone," *Nature Magazine,* XIX (Feb. 1904), 611–614.

Grant, Roland D. "Changes in Yellowstone National Park," *American Geographical Society Bulletin,* XL (Jan. 1908), 244–282.

Hague, Arnold. "The Yellowstone National Park," *Scribner's Magazine,* XXXV (May 1904), 513–527.

Haines, Aubrey, "Archival Material in Yellowstone Park," *Proceedings,* Montana Academy of Sciences, XXII (1962), 98.

Hall, Ansel. "The Early Days in Yosemite," *California Historical Society Quarterly,* V (Jan. 1923), 47–63.

Hayden, F. V. "On the Yellowstone National Park," *American Journal of Science,* III (Apr. 1872), 294–97.

———. "The Wonders of the West—More About the Yellowstone," *Scribner's Monthly,* III (Feb. 1872), 388–96.

Haynes, Jack Ellis. "The Expedition of President Chester A. Arthur to Yellowstone National Park in 1882," *Annals of Wyoming,* XIV (Jan. 1942), 31–38.

Hedges, Cornelius. "Journal of Cornelius Hedges," *Contributions,* Montana Historical Society, V (1904), 370–94.

Hedges, W. A. "Cornelius Hedges," *Contributions,* Montana Historical Society, VII (1910), 181–196.

Henderson, C. Hanford. "Through Yellowstone on Foot," *Outing,* XXXIV (May 1899), 161–167.

Hough, Emerson. "Forest and Stream's Yellowstone Park Game Exploration," *Forest and Stream,* XLIII (a series of thirteen articles printed in the spring and summer of 1894—May 5, to August 25).

Huth, Hans. "The American and Nature," *Journal of the Warburg and Courtauld Institutes,* XIII (July 1950), 101–149.

———. "Yosemite, the Story of an Idea," *Sierra Club Bulletin,* XXXIII (Mar. 1948), 47–78.

Jackson, W. Turrentine, "The Cook-Folsom Exploration of the Upper Yellowstone, 1864," *Pacific North-west Quarterly,* XXXII (July 1941), 307–322.

———. "The Creation of Yellowstone National Park," *Montana, Magazine of Western History,* VII (July 1957), 52–66.

Joffe, Joseph. "John W. Meldrum," *Annals of Wyoming,* XIII (No. 1, Jan. 1941), 5–47; (No. 2, Apr. 1941), 105–140.

Johnson, Robert Underwood. "Destructive Tendencies in Yosemite Valley," *Century Magazine,* XXXIX (Jan. 1890), 477–478.

Koch, Peter. "Discovery of Yellowstone Park," *Magazine of American History,* II (June 1884), 497–512.

Koch, F. J. "Protecting National Parks against Poachers," *Overland Monthly,* LXV (Feb. 1915), 117–122.

Kuppens, Francis X. "On the Origin of the Yellowstone National Park," *Jesuit Bulletin,* XLI (Oct. 1962), 6–7, 14.

Langford, Nathaniel P. "Yellowstone," *Scribner's Monthly*, II (May 1871), 1–17, 113–128.

Lewis, Henry H. "Managing a National Park," *Outlook*, LXXIV (Aug. 1903) 1036–1040.

Lockwood, John A. "Uncle Sam's Troopers in the National Parks of California," *Overland Monthly*, XXXIII (Apr. 1899), 356–368.

Logan, Olive. "Does it Pay to Visit Yo Semite?," *Galaxy*, X (Oct. 1870), 498–509.

Lowell, James Russell. "Humanity to Trees," *Crayon*, LV (Oct. 1857), 96.

Mackenzie, George G. "California's Interest in Yosemite Reform," *Century Magazine*, XLIII (Feb. 1891), 154–164.

———. "Destructive Tendencies in the Yosemite Valley," *Century Magazine*, XXXIX (Jan. 1890), 475–476.

Mattes, Merrill. "Behind the Legend of Colter's Hell: The Early History of Yellowstone National Park," *Mississippi Valley Historical Review* XXVI (Sept. 1949), 251–282.

Matthews, Albert. "The Word 'Park' in the United States," *Transcripts*, Colonial Society of Massachusetts, VIII (1902–1904), 373–399.

Mitchell, S. Weir. "Through Yellowstone to Fort Custer," *Lippincott's Magazine*, XXV (June 1880), 688–704.

Muir, John. "Creation of the Yosemite National Park," *Sierra Club Bulletin*, XXIX (Oct. 1944), 49–60.

———. "Features of the Proposed Yosemite National Park," *Century Magazine*, XL (Sept. 1890), 656–67.

———. "Forest Reservations and National Parks," *Harper's Weekly*, CLXIII (June 5, 1897), 19–26.

———. "Treasures of the Yosemite," *Century Magazine*, XL (Aug. 1890), 483–500.

———. "Yellowstone National Park," *Atlantic Monthly*, LXXXI (Apr. 1898), 509–522.

———. "Yosemite National Park," *Atlantic Monthly*, LXXXIV (Aug. 1899), 145–152.

Mulford, Prentice. "The East at Yosemite," *Overland Monthly*, VII (Aug. 1871), 191–194.

O'Brien, Bob R. "The Roads of Yellowstone—1870–1915," *Montana: Magazine of Western History*, XVII (July 1967), 30–39.

Olmsted, Frederick Law. "The Yosemite Valley and the Mariposa Big Trees, A Preliminary Report, 1865," reproduced with a forword by Laura Wood Roper, *Landscape Architecture*, XLIII (Oct. 1952), 14–18.

———. "Governmental Preservation of Natural Scenery," (1890), reproduced in *Sierra Club Bulletin*, XXIX (Oct. 1944), 61–66.

Owen, W. O. "First Bicycle Tour of the Yellowstone National Park," *Outing,* XVIII (June 1891), 191–195.

Palmer, T. S. "Obituary of Harry Copeland Benson," *Auk,* XLII (Oct. 1925), 619–620.

Potts, Daniel T. Open Letter in *Niles Weekly Register,* 3rd Series, IX, No. 6, (July 8, 1827) 90.

"Preservation of Yosemite Valley," *The Nation,* L, No. 1284, (Feb. 1890), No. 1288 (Mar. 1890).

Raftery, J. H. "Historic and Descriptive Sketch of Yellowstone National Park," *Annals of Wyoming,* XV (Apr. 1943), 101–132.

Rainsford, W. S. "Camping and Hunting in the Shoshone," *Scribner's Monthly,* XI (Sept. 1887), 292–311.

Reich, Charles A. "Bureaucracy in the Forests," *Occasional Papers,* Center for the Study of Democratic Institutions, (Oct. 1962).

"Reservation of the Yosemite Valley," *The Nation,* L (Feb. 1890), 106.

Rhoda, Jean. "Uncle Sam in the Yosemite," *Overland Monthly,* LXI (June 1913), 590–594.

Richardson, Alfred T. "Something about the Yellowstone Park," *Out West,* XXII (May 1905), 325–331.

Roosevelt, T. R. "A National Park Service," *Outlook,* CII (Feb. 1912).

———. "Wilderness Reserves," *Forestry and Irrigation,* X (June 1904), 250–259; (July 1904), 300–309.

———. "An Elk-Hunt at Two-Ocean Pass," *Century Magazine,* XLIV (Sept. 1892), 713–719.

Russell, Carl P. "Early Years in Yosemite," *California Historical Society Quarterly,* V, (Dec. 1926), 328–341.

Sargent, Charles S. "The Yosemite Valley," *Garden and Forest,* II (Jan. 1889), 1–2.

Shinn, Charles H. "The Yosemite National Park," *Garden and Forest,* V (Feb. 1892), 74.

Sovulewski, Gabriel. "Letter," *Sierra Club Bulletin,* XXI (Feb. 1936), 85–86.

"Standing Menace, Cooke City Vs. Yellowstone National Park," *Forest and Stream,* XXXIX (Dec. 1892), 485–487.

Strong, Douglas. "History of Sequoia," *Southern California Quarterly,* (June, Sept., Dec. 1966).

Thayer, Wade W. "Camp and Cycle in Yellowstone Park," *Outing,* XXXII (Apr. 1898), 17–24.

Thoreau, Henry D. "Chesuncook," *Atlantic Monthly,* II (Aug. 1852), 134.

Toll, Roger. "Wilderness and Wildlife Administration in Yellowstone National Park," *American Planning and Civic Annual* (1936), 65–72.

Van Blarcom, W. D. "The Yellowstone National Park," *National Magazine*, VI (Sept. 1897), 541–550.

Villard, Oswald G. "A Park, a Man, and the Rest of Us," *Survey*, LV (Feb. 1926), 542–544.

Warner, Charles D. "The Yellowstone National Park," *Harper's* XCIV (Jan. 1897).

Wheeler, Olin D. "Game in the Yellowstone National Park," *Recreation*, IV (May 1896), 43–48.

————. "Nathaniel Pitt Langford," Minnesota Historical Society *Contributions*, XV (May 1915), 631–668.

Wiley, H. B. "Yellowstone Park in 1883," *Montana: Magazine of Western History*, III (Jan. 1953), 8–19.

Wister, Owen. "Old Yellowstone Days," *Harper's Magazine*, CLVII (Mar. 1936), 37–48.

Worswick, F. H. "The Yellowstone National Park," *Manchester* (England) *Geographical Society Journal*, XV (Jan.–Mar. 1899), 15–55.

Yard, Robert Sterling. "Twenty-First Annual Report," *American Scenic and Historical Preservation Society* (1916), 673–678.

"Yosemite Recession," *The Nation*, LXXX (Apr. 1905), 325.

NEWSPAPERS

The Anaconda Standard (Montana). Clippings, 1903.

The Cheyenne Weekly Leader (Wyoming). Clippings, 1883.

The Chicago Tribune. Clippings, 1894.

The Daily Herald (Helena, Montana). 1870–1871.

Helena Weekly Herald. 1870–1873.

Montana Post (Virginia City). 1867–1886.

The New NorthWest (Deerlodge, Montana). Clippings, 1870–1872.

The Livingston Enterprise (Livingston, Montana). 1884–1890.

The Daily Enterprise (Livingston, Montana). 1882–1884.

The New York Times. Clippings, 1870.

Niles Weekly Register. 1827.

Rocky Mountain Weekly Gazette (Helena, Montana). Clippings, 1871.

UNPUBLISHED MATERIAL

Anderson, E. C. Diary. 1909. Yellowstone National Park Library, Yellowstone National Park.

Anderson, Henry. Diary. 1910, 1911. Yellowstone National Park Library.

Brown, Jesse R. Diary. 1909, 1910. Yellowstone National Park Library.

Buck, Paul Herman. "The Evolution of the National Park System of the United States." M. A. thesis, Ohio State University, 1921.

Burgess, Felix. Diary. 1898, 1899. Yellowstone National Park Library.

Fitzgerald, S. M. Diary. 1907. Yellowstone National Park Library.

Furey, Jane. "Tourism in the Pikes Peak Area 1870–1880." M. A. thesis, University of Colorado, 1958.

Gourley, James. "The 1870 Expedition into the Cooke City Region." MS, Yellowstone National Park Library.

Grinnell, George B. Diaries. 1870–1923. Southwest Museum Archives. Los Angeles, California.

Haines, Aubrey L. "A Review of Certain Attempts to Make Adverse use of Yellowstone National Park." MS, Yellowstone National Park Library.

Hamilton, James M. "History of Yellowstone National Park, Previous to 1895." MS, Yellowstone National Park Library.

Holmes, W. H. Diary. 1872, 1878. Yellowstone National Park Library.

Jackson, William Turrentine. "The Early Exploration and Founding of Yellowstone National Park." Ph. D. dissertation, University of Texas, 1940.

Joyner, Newell F. "History of Improvements in Yellowstone National Park." MS, Yellowstone National Park Library.

Kettlewell, Edith G. "Yosemite; The Discovery of Yosemite Valley and the Creation and Realignment of Yosemite National Park." M. A. thesis, University of California, 1930.

Mitchell, Carroll Lowell. "Federal Conservation of Natural Resources Prior to 1901." M. A. thesis, University of Colorado, 1941.

Rogers, Edmund B. "History of Legislation Relating to the National Park System Through the 82d. Congress." 12 vols., photostated replicas of legislation bound in loose-leaf folders. Yellowstone National Park Library.

White, John G. "A Souvenir of Wyoming, Being a Diary of a Fishing Trip in Jackson Hole and Yellowstone Park." MS, Yellowstone National Park Library.

Public Documents

Acker, W. B. (compiler). *Laws and Regulations Relating to Yellowstone National Park.* GPO, 1908.

Annual Reports of the Acting Superintendents, Yellowstone National Park, 18 86–1916; *Yosemite, Sequoia and General Grant National Parks,* 1890–1914. *GPO.* 1886–1916.

Annual Reports of the Secretary of the Interior, 1870–1920. GPO, 1871–1921.

Annual Reports of the Secretary of War, 1872–1919. GPO, 1873–1922.

Annual Reports of the Superintendent of Yellowstone National Park, 1872, 1877–1886. GPO, 1873, 1878–1886.

Appendix to the Journals, Senate and Assembly of California, 1864–1924. Sacramento: State Printing Office, 1865–1925.

Assembly Hearings, "Investigations of Yosemite Commissioners," California Legislature, 1889. Sacramento: State Printing Office, 1890.

Biennial Message of Governor R. W. Waterman to the Legislature of California, 28th Session. Sacramento: State Printing Office, 1889.

Biographical Directory of the American Congresses, 1774–1927. GPO, 1928.

Blaine, John E. *Annual Report of the Surveyor-General of Montana Territory, 1871.* GPO, 1873.

California State Board of Trade, "Yosemite Valley: History, Description, and Statement of Conditions Relative to Proposed Recession to the National Government." Sacramento: Board of Trade, 1904.

Circulars, Yellowstone National Park, 1912–1917. GPO, 1913–1918.

Congressional Globe, 1863–1874. GPO, 1863–1874.

Congressional Record, 1875–1920. GPO, 1875–1920.

General Information Circulars, National Parks, 1918, 1919. GPO, 1919, 1920.

Hayden, F. V. *Preliminary Report of the United States Geological Survey of Montana and Adjacent Territories, Being a Fifth Annual Report of Progress.* GPO, 1872.

————. *Twelfth Annual Report of the United States Geological Survey of the Territories.* GPO, 1883.

Heitman, Francis B. *Historical Register and Dictionary of the United States Army.* Volumes 1 and 2. GPO, 1903.

Jones, William A. *Report Upon the Reconnaissance of Northwestern Wyoming, Including Yellowstone National Park; Made in the Summer of 1873.* GPO, 1875.

Laws and Judicial Decisions Relating to the Yosemite Valley and the Mariposa Big Tree Grove. San Francisco: Correy, 1874.

Low, F. F., and others. *By-Laws of the Board of Commissioners in Charge of Yosemite Valley and Mariposa Big Tree Grove.* San Francisco: Edward Basqui, 1866.

Miscellaneous Documents, United States Senate and House of Representatives, 1865–1920. GPO, 1866–1921.

Proceedings of the National Park Conferences. GPO, 1912, 1913, 1915, 1917.

Reports of the Commissioners to Manage the Yosemite Valley and the Mariposa Big Tree Grove, 1866–1904. Sacramento: Superintendent of State Printing, 1867–1905.

Rules, Regulations and Instructions for the Information and Guidance of Officers and Enlisted Men of the United States Army, and of the Scouts in the Yellowstone National Park. GPO, 1907.

Rules and Regulations and By-Laws of the Board of Commissioners to Manage the Yosemite Valley and the Mariposa Big Tree Grove. Sacramento: State Printing Office, 1885.

Rules and Regulations of the Yellowstone and the Yosemite National Parks, 1912. GPO, 1912.

Russell, Carl P. *A Concise History of Scientific Investigations in the Yellowstone National Park.* GPO, 1930.

Senate Committee, State of California, "In the Matter of the Investigation of the Yosemite Valley Commissioners." Sacramento: State Printing Office, 1889.

Sheridan, W. T. *Reports on Explorations of Parts of Wyoming, Idaho, and Montana.* GPO, 1882.

Statutes of California, 1866. Sacramento: State Printing Office, 1877.

Sullivan, Thomas Alan (compiler). *Proclamations and Orders Relating to the National Parks, Up to January 1, 1945.* GPO, 1947.

Tolson, Hillory A. (compiler). *Laws Relating to the National Park Service.* GPO, 1933.

United States Statutes at Large, 1864–1920. GPO, 1947.

ARCHIVAL MATERIAL

National Archives, Washington, D. C.

Correspondence Received and Sent, Office of the Secretary of the Interior, 1864–1870.

Correspondence Received and Sent, Superintendents and Acting Superintendents, Yellowstone National Park, 1872–1920; Acting Superintendents, Yosemite, Sequoia, and General Grant National Parks, 1890–1914.

File Microcopies of Records Number 62: Records of the Office of the Secretary of the Interior Relating to the Yellowstone National Park, 1872–1886. Six Reels. (Communications Received and Sent by the Patents and Miscellaneous Division; Communications Received and Sent by the Appointments Division.)

General Correspondence Relating to Yosemite National Park, 1890–1907.

Miscellaneous Correspondence Received and Sent, General Land Office, 1864–1870.

Records of Fort Yellowstone, Wyoming, 1891–1916. (Records consist of copies of letters sent, 1903–1906; stubs of telegrams sent, 1901–1902; copies of telegrams sent, 1916; registers of letters received, 1906–1909; letters received, 1905–1910; telegrams received, 1905–1908, 1916; document file, 1910–1915; orders, 1891–1894, 1896–1916; record of Post schools, 1902–1904; descriptive book of noncommissioned staff, 1893–1906; descriptive lists of enlisted men, 1908–1916; sick reports, 1913–1916; morning reports and muster rolls, 1905–1916; post returns, 1915–1916; recruiting returns, 1903; records of summary courts, 1909–1916; letters received by a detachment of "Troop 2," Yellowstone Park, 1914–1916.)

Record Group 77, Documents pertaining to the United States Army Engineers, 1890–1907.

Record Group 79, Records of the National Park Service, Parks, Reservations and Antiquities, 1907–1914.

Record Group 92, United States Army Quartermaster Corps, Consolidated File, Fort Yellowstone, Wyoming, 1886–1917.

Record Group 94, The Adjutant General's Office, Select Documents pertaining to National Parks, 1886–1917.

Record Group 98, The Adjutant General's Office, Documents of Commands and Posts, 1886–1916.

Yellowstone National Park Archives

Correspondence Received, Yellowstone National Park, 1882–1908. 32 volumes.

Correspondence Sent, Yellowstone National Park, 1886–1907. 19 volumes.

Correspondence Received and Sent, Yellowstone National Park, 1908–1918. 76 boxes.

Correspondence Received From the Secretary of the Interior, 1897–1908. 7 volumes.

Court Records, United States Commissioner: Criminal Docket, 1894–1898; Reports of Trials, 1910–1917; Record of Violations of Rules and Regulations, 1887–1921; Letters Sent, 1894–1907, 1907–1918.

Monthly Station Reports, 1894–1917. 18 boxes.

Permanent Station Records, 1898–1918. 18 volumes.

Weekly Station Reports, 1910–1916. 16 boxes.

NOTES

Abbreviations used in notes are given below. Full references will be found in the Bibliography, if not given in the note.

CR: Congressional Record

Dept. Int., P&M, LR: Department of the Interior, Patents and Miscellaneous Division, Letters Received (or LS, Letters Sent)

GPO: Government Printing Office, Washington, D. C.

NA: National Archives, Washington, D. C.

Report, Act. Supt., Yosemite (or Sequoia): Report of the Acting Superintendent of the Yosemite (or Sequoia) National Park, GPO

SL: U.S. Statues at Large

SN: Serial Number

YNPA: Yellowstone National Park Archives, Mammoth Hot Springs, Wyoming

1. *The Genesis of an Idea*

1. Brockman, *Recreational Use of Wild Lands*, pp. 51–53; Trefethen, *Crusade for Wildlife*, p. 74.

2. Hans Huth in his *Nature and the American* traces the influence of early 19th-century poetry upon the changing views toward nature. The pattern established by Huth is closely followed by Roderick Nash, *Wilderness and the American Mind*.

3. Catlin, I, 261–62. Catlin's italics and parenthesis.

4. Ibid., p. 262.

5. Ralph Waldo Emerson, "The Young American," lecture reproduced in the *Dial;* Thoreau's *Walden* was published in 1854 and gained immediate acceptance by the reading public. Henry Thoreau, "Chesuncook," *Atlantic Monthly.* Other writers were also extolling the virtues of nature during this period. Washington Irving's *Sketchbook* appeared in 1819–1820, Cooper's *Pioneers* in 1823, and *The Last of the Mohicans* in 1826. Numerous nature essays by Emerson, Hawthorne, and Lowell appeared in the *Dial* between 1840 and 1844. See Huth, *Nature and the American,* Ch. 6, for additional detail.

6. Noble, *The Life and Works of Thomas Cole,* p. 299. Originally published under the title *The Course of Empire, Voyage of Life and Other Pictures of Thomas Cole* (1853).

7. Fitz-Hugh Ludlow, *The Heart of the Continent* (New York: Hurd and Houghton, 1871), p. 178. Quoted by Jane Furey, "Tourism in the Pikes Peak Area" (unpublished), pp. 4–5.

8. Huth, "The American and Nature," pp. 101–149. For a full discussion of Olmsted's activities on behalf of New York Central Park, see Olmsted and Kimball, passim.

9. Tolson, *Laws Relating to the National Park Service,* p. 221; 4 SL 505.

10. Huth, *Nature and the American,* pp. 129–131.

11. For a full historical description of the "Desert Theory" see Athearn, "The Great Plains in Historical Perspective," pp. 13–29. For a conflicting view see Bowden, "The Perception of the Western Interior of the United States, 1800–1870," pp. 16–21.

12. Carvalho, *Incidents of Travel and Adventure,* passim.

13. Born, *American Landscape Painting;* Benjamin P. Draper, *Art in America,* vols. XXVIII, XXIX (1940–41); Lipman and Winchester, *Primitive Painters in America;* Peattie, *Audubon's America;* Taft, *Artists and Illustrators of the Old West;* all passim.

14. "An Immense Tree," p. 216; "The Mammoth Trees of California," *Hutchings' California Magazine,* III (Mar. 1859), reproduced by R. R. Olmsted (ed.), *Scenes of Wonder & Curiosity from Hutchings' California Magazine 1856–1861* (Berkeley: Howell-North, 1962), p. 211.

15. James Russell Lowell, *Crayon,* LV (Oct. 1857), p. 96; "The Big Trees of California," *Harper's Weekly,* II (Sept. 1858), p. 357.

16. Russell, *One Hundred Years in Yosemite,* pp. 1–8; Farquhar, "Walker's Discovery of Yosemite," p. 35. Some early letters describing the discovery and subsequent publicity of the area are reproduced by Kuykendall, *Early History of the Yosemite Valley,* passim.

17. Russell, *One Hundred Years in Yosemite,* p. 37.

18. Huth, "Yosemite, the Story of an Idea," p. 64.

19. *The Country Gentleman*, XIV (Oct. 8, 1856), p. 243; Horace Greeley, *An Overland Journey*, p. 307. Greeley, visiting the valley in the late summer, thought the Yosemite Falls "a humbug" and the various names for the scenic wonders "maladroit and lackadaisical."

20. Russell, *One Hundred Years in Yosemite*, p. 56.

21. Huth, "Yosemite, The Story of an Idea," p. 65.

22. Russell, *One Hundred Years in Yosemite*, pp. 13–14.

23. *Congressional Globe*, 38th Cong., 1st Sess., Part 2, p. 1310.

24. Olmsted, "The Yosemite Valley and the Mariposa Big Trees," p. 16.

25. I. W. Raymond to John Conness, Feb. 20, 1864, NA, General Land Office, Miscellaneous Letters Received, File number 033572.

26. John Conness to J. W. Edmonds, Mar. 6, 1864, ibid.

27. *Congressional Globe*, 38th Cong., 1st Sess., Part 3, pp. 2300–2301.

28. *Congressional Globe*, 38th Cong., 1st Sess., Part 3, pp. 2300, 2301, 2695; Part 4, pp. 3378, 3388, 3389, 3444; Appendix, p. 240; "An Act Authorizing a grant to the State of California of the 'Yo Semite Valley' and of the land embracing the 'Mariposa Big Tree Grove,' approved June 30, 1864" (13 SL 325).

29. 13 SL 325.

30. The Other Commissioners so appointed were: Galen Clark, William Ashburner, Alexander Deering, George W. Coulter, E. S. Holden, I. W. Raymond, and J. D. Whitney. *Statutes of California*, 1866, p. 710.

2. *The Nation's First National Park*

1. Hiram M. Chittenden, in his *The Yellowstone National Park* (5th ed. rev.; Cincinnati: Stewart & Kidd, 1912), pp. 15–27, devoted an entire chapter to Colter. Unfortunately there exists no written account of Colter's trek, and his exact route has given rise to some dispute among historians. See Harris, *John Colter;* Vinton, *John Colter;* Mattes, *Behind the Legend of Colter's Hell: The Early History of Yellowstone National Park*, reprinted from the *Mississippi Valley Historical Review*, XXXVI (Sept. 1949); Mattes, *Colter's Hell and Jackson's Hole*.

2. N. W. Norris to Carl Schurz, Nov. 10, 1878, NA, Dept. Int., P&M, LR; "Report of the Superintendent of Yellowstone National Park," 1880, in *House Executive Document* 1, 46th Cong., 3d Sess. (Serial Number 1960), p. 573.

3. Daniel T. Potts to his family, *Niles Weekly Register,* Oct. 6, 1827. The original Potts letter is on file in the Yellowstone Park Library, Mammoth Hot Springs, Wyoming.

4. Journal entries made by Warren Angus Ferris, a clerk in the employ of the American Fur Company, appeared in the Mormon publication *The Wasp* (Nauvoo, Illinois), Aug. 13, 1842, and several articles by him were published by the *Western Literary Messenger* under the title "Life in the Rocky Mountains"in the early 1840's. Chittenden, *The Yellowstone National Park* (1912 ed.), footnote, p. 39. The experiences of Joseph Meek, including rather vivid descriptions of "blue flames and molten brimstone," were published by Mrs. Frances Fuller Victor in *The River of the West.* In the *Weekly Independent* (Helena, Montana), the *Wasp* article was reproduced under the heading, "Visit to the Yellowstone Geysers, 1833," in the May 1, 1874, issue of that paper.

5. Chittenden devotes a chapter to Bridger and his stories of the Yellowstone in *The Yellowstone National Park,* all editions, as does Beal, *The Story of Man in Yellowstone;* see also Alter, *Jim Bridger,* passim.

6. *Journal of a Trapper, 1834–1843,* passim.

7. For a full discussion of the trappers and traders see Chittenden, *The American Fur Trade,* and Phillips, *The Fur Trade.* For those men specifically linked to the Yellowstone region: Chittenden, *Yellowstone National Park,* pp. 15–55; Beal, *Man in Yellowstone,* pp. 71–83, 92–115; Augspurger, *Yellowstone National Park,* pp. 19–41.

8. W. F. Raynolds, "Report to the Secretary of War 1868," in *Senate Executive Document* 77, 40th Cong., 2nd Sess. (SN 1318), pp. 10, 77. Raynolds, even though he considered most of these descriptions "Munchausen tales," wrote, "I have little doubt that he [Bridger] spoke of what he had actually seen."

9. Chittenden, *The Yellowstone National Park,* p. 58.

10. Even though Raynold's report did not reach the public until later, there were many reports concerning the various phenomena found in the Yellowstone area. In 1867, Dr. James Dunley, Surgeon of the Montana Volunteers, provided descriptions of the geysers for the *Montana Post* (Virginia City), Aug. 31, 1867, and a few months later "An astonished tourist" wrote to the *Frontier Index* (Green River City, D. T.) and accurately described the Yellowstone Lake and Falls. (Reported in the *Virginia Tri-Weekly Post* [Virginia City and Helena], Feb. 4, 1868).

11. *The Montana Post* (Virginia City), July 29, 1867.

12. Charles W. Cook, David E. Folsom, and William Peterson, *The Valley of the Upper Yellowstone,* ed. Aubrey L. Haines (Norman: University of Oklahoma Press, 1965); N. P. Langford, "The Folsom-Cook Exploration of the Upper Yellowstone," *Contributions,* Montana Historical

Society, V (1905); Jackson, "The Cook-Folsom Exploration of the Upper Yellowstone," pp. 307–322; Cramton, *Early History of Yellowstone National Park* pp. 10–12. Folsom's article was rejected by *The New York Tribune, Scribner's,* and *Harpers,* editors of which "had a reputation that they could not risk with such unreliable material." Cramton, p. 10.

13. Langford, "Yellowstone," *Scribner's Monthly,* p. 1.

14. *Helena Herald,* Sept. 26, 27, 28, 30, Oct. 8, 15, 19, 28, Dec. 3, 1870; Jan. 28, 30, 1871; *Helena Daily Herald,* Oct. 21, Nov. 9, 14, 1870; *Rocky Mountain Gazette* (Helena), Oct. 3, 24, 31, 1870; *New York Times,* Oct. 14, 1870. Articles appeared in the May, June and November, 1871, issues of *Scribner's* and the May and June, 1871, issues of *Overland Monthly.*

15. F. V. Hayden, *Preliminary Report* of the United States Geological Survey of Montana and portions of adjacent Territories, being a fifth annual report of Progress (GPO, 1872). Doane's report, "The Report of Lieut. Gustavus C. Doane upon the so-called Yellowstone Expedition of 1870 to The Secretary of War," transmitted to Gen. Hancock Dec. 15, 1870, was sent to the Secretary of War, who forwarded it to the Senate, where it was ordered published as *Senate Executive Document* 51, 41st Cong., 3d Sess. (SN 1440). Doan's complete report appears in Orrin H. and Lorraine Bonney, *Battle Drums and Geysers* (Chicago: Swallow Press, 1970).

16. J. W. Barlow, "Reconnaissance of the Yellowstone River," *Senate Executive Document* 66, 42nd Cong., 2nd Sess., (SN 1479); F. V. Hayden, *Preliminary Report. . . .* Fifth Annual Report of Progress.

17. Chittenden, *The Yellowstone National Park,* pp. 89–90. In the first edition of this work, 1895, Chittenden notes that George Catlin had suggested the setting aside a large tract of land in the West as a "Nation's Park" and also credits Folsom with suggesting the idea to Gen. Washburn, but dismissed both with the statement that "no direct results can be traced" from either suggestion. Cornelius Hedges was a Yale-educated lawyer who had moved in 1865 to Helena, where he became prominent in civic and political affairs. He was United States District Attorney for Montana in 1871 and 1872, Judge of Probate from 1875 to 1880, a member of the Territorial Constitutional Convention in 1884, and president of the Montana State Historical Society and president of the Montana State Pioneers. Hedges died Apr. 29, 1907. Cramton, *Early History,* p. 13.

18. Hedges, "Journal of Cornelius Hedges," p. 372.

19. See Cramton, *Early History,* pp. 12–24; Huth, "Yosemite, the Story of an Idea," p. 72; Huth, "The American and Nature," pp. 146–47.

20. Kuppens, "On the Origin of the Yellowstone National Park," reprinted from *The Woodstock Letters,* XXVI, No. 3 (1897).

21. N. P. Langford, Preface to "The Folsom-Cook Exploration of the Upper Yellowstone in the year 1869," *Contributions, Historical Society of Montana, V* (1905), p. 351.

22. In a note to the third and subsequent revisions of Chittenden's *The Yellowstone National Park* (1899), p. 73; (1903, 1905, et al., pp. 89–90). "In the manuscript of his [Folsom's] article in the *Western Monthly* was a reference to the Park idea; but the publishers cut out a large part of his paper . . . and this reference was cut out with the rest."

23. Josiah D. Whitney, *The Yosemite Book,* 1868, p. 22, as noted by Matthews, "The Word Park in the United States," p. 25.

24. *The New Northwest* (Deer Lodge, Montana Territory), Dec. 23, 1871, p. 2.

25. At least Hayden thought the survey thorough. In a letter to the Secretary of the Interior, Aug. 28, 1871, Hayden stated: "The exploration of the Yellowstone basin is now completed . . . We think no portion of the West has been more carefully surveyed than the Yellowstone basin." Reproduced in *Helena Daily Herald*, Sept. 23, 1871, p. 1.

26. The creation of Yellowstone National Park, though undoubtedly due to the unselfish work of men like Langford, Hedges, Hayden, and interested Congressmen, may, to some extent, owe its success to the business minds of the Northern Pacific Railroad. Thomas Moran was able to join the Hayden exploration party only through the efforts of one A. B. Nettleton, who, writing from the firm of Jay Cooke & Co., "Financial Agents, Northern Pacific Railroad Co." prompted Hayden to extend an invitation to the noted painter to join his party. This same A. B. Nettleton also asked Hayden to include in his official report a recommendation that the "Great Geyser Basin" be reserved as a public park forever just as "that far inferior wonder the Yosemite Valley and big trees" had been reserved. Nettleton's words were duly incorporated in an article prepared by Hayden and published in *Scribner's Monthly,* II (1872), p. 396. A. B. Nettleton to F. V. Hayden, Oct. 27, 1871, NA, Records of the Department of the Interior, Geological Survey, LR by F. V. Hayden, 1871.

27. Henry L. Dawes, Representative and Senator from Massachusetts. Dawes represented Massachusetts in the House of Representatives for eight terms, Mar. 4, 1857 to Mar. 3, 1875. He served in the Senate from Mar. 4, 1875 to Mar. 3, 1893, declining to stand for re-election in 1892. He will be referred to herein either as a Representative or Senator, depending upon his office at the time alluded to.

28. Cramton, *Early History;* N. P. Langford, *Discovery of Yellowstone Park,* p. 40.

29. The House bill, H.R. 764, was introduced by Delegate Clagett, while Senator Samuel Pomeroy of Kansas introduced S. 392, an identical

bill, in the Senate. *Congressional Globe,* 42nd Cong., 2nd Sess., Part 1, pp. 159, 199.

30. *Congressional Globe,* 42nd Cong., 2nd Sess., Part 1, pp. 484, 520.

31. Ibid. p. 697.

32. *Congressional Globe,* 42nd Cong., 2nd Sess., Part 1, p. 697.

33. Langford, *Discovery of Yellowstone Park,* p. 41; Chittenden, *The Yellowstone National Park,* 1912 ed., p. 92.

34. F. V. Hayden, *Twelfth Annual Report* of the United States Geological Survey of the Territories (GPO, 1883), pp. xxii-xxix.

35. Hayden, "The Wonders of the West," p. 396.

36. Feb. 1872. Noted in Cramton, *Early History,* p. 24.

37. Council Joint Memorial No. 5, reproduced in the *Helena Weekly Herald* as "The National Park Memorial to Congress," Feb. 15, 1872. *The New North West* (Deer Lodge), Mar. 9, 1872. *Helena Daily Herald,* Oct. 6, 1871. Comments on the Yosemite Valley appear as early as July 14, 1866 in *The Montana Post* (Virginia City).

38. *Congressional Globe,* 42nd Cong., 2nd Sess., Part 2, p. 1243.

39. Ibid., p. 1244.

40. 17 SL 32; *Scribner's Monthly,* IV (May 1872), p. 120.

3. The Early Years in Yellowstone: 1872–1882

1. "An act to set apart a certain Tract of Land lying near the Headwaters of the Yellowstone River as a public Park," 17 SL, 32.

2. B. R. Cowen, Acting Sec. Int., to N. P. Langford, NA, May 10, 1872. Dept. Int., P&M, LS, 1872–1886.

3. N. P. Langford to C. Delano, Sec. Int., Feb. 3, 1873, NA, Dept. Int., P&M, LR, 1872–1882.

4. Ibid. See also W. H. Clagett to C. Delano, Sec. Int., same date and file.

5. J. V. Hayden to Carl Schurz, Sec. Int., Feb. 21, 1878, NA, Dept. Int., P&M, LR, 1872–1882. Hayden, writing six years after the fact, was explaining his role in establishing the Park.

6. *House Executive Document* 241, 42nd Cong., 3d Sess. (SN 1569), p. 1. See also Carl Schurz, Sec. Int., to Speaker of the House, Apr. 26, 1880, NA, Dept. Int., P&M, LS, 1872–1886, wherein subsequent Congressional action is reviewed.

7. N. P. Langford to C. Delano, Nov. 7, 1873, NA, Dept. Int., P&M, LR, 1872–1882.

8. H. R. Horr to Columbus Delano, Nov. 4, 1873; B. F. Potts to N. P. Langford, Nov. 27, 1873; J. A. Campbell to N. P. Langford, Sept. 26, 1873, NA, Dept. Int., P&M, LR, 1872–1882.

9. Petitioners to Sec. Int., 31 Dec. 1873, reproduced in *House Exec. Doc.* 147, 43d Cong., 1st Sess. (SN 1610), pp. 37–41.

10. F. V. Hayden to C. Delano, Feb. 9, 1874; James A. Garfield to Columbus Delano, Feb. 13, 1874, NA, Dept. Int., P&M, LR, 1872–1882.

11. C. Delano to James G. Blaine, Speaker of the House of Representatives, Feb. 17, 1874, NA, Dept. Int., P&M, LS, 1872–1886.

12. C. Delano to Wm. Sprague, Chairman, Committee on Public Lands, Mar. 4, 1874, NA, Dept. Int., P&M, LS, 1872–1886; *Senate Report* 216, 43d Cong., 1st Sess. (SN 1586), p. 1.

13. C. Delano to James G. Blaine, Dec. 8, 1874, NA, Dept. Int., P&M, LS, 1872–1886.

14. CR, 43d Cong., 2nd Sess., III, Part 3, p. 2017.

15. N. P. Langford to C. Delano, Aug. 28, 1875; Martin Maginnis, endorsement, NA, Dept. Int., P&M, LR, 1872–1882.

16. N. P. Langford to C. Delano, Feb. 17, 1874, NA, Dept. Int., P&M, LR, 1872–1882.

17. Strong, *A Trip to the Yellowstone National Park.* A newspaper account of the day deplored the practice of European nobility, particularly the "British sportsman" who demoralized "guides, trappers and hunters of the plains and mountains by his lordly manner of butchering buffalo and grizzly bears," and stated the fear that the "Yellowstone Park bids fair to become a very tame and civilized retreat" because of pressure from this type of sportsman. *Helena Weekly Herald* (Montana), Dec. 25, 1873, quoting *"The Daily Graphic* of a recent date."

18. *Report of the Chief of Engineers,* "Annual Report of Captain William Ludlow," Appendix NN. 44th Cong., 2nd Sess. (SN 1745), p. 605.

19. Ibid., p. 606.

20. "Report of the Secretary of War," Nov. 22, 1875, pp. 27–28, *House Exec. Doc.* 1, 44th Cong., 1st Sess. (SN 1674).

21. C. Schurz to N. P. Langford, Apr. 18, 1877, NA, Dept. Int., P&M, LS, 1872–1886.

22. P. W. Norris to C. Schurz, Apr. 13, 1877, NA, Dept. Int., P&M, LR, 1872–1882; C. Schurz to P. W. Norris, Apr. 18, 1877, NA, Dept. Int., P&M, LS, 1872–1886. Norris later presented a claim of $3,180.41 against the government for salary and expenses. This amount was subsequently appropriated in the sundry civil act of Aug. 7, 1882. 21 SL, 451; *House Exec. Doc.* 85, 47th Cong., 1st Sess. (SN 2027), p. 1.

23. P. W. Norris to J. C. McCartney, Apr. 19, 1877, NA, Dept. Int., P&M, LR, 1872–1882.

24. *Norris Suburban,* clipping, no date, in NA, Dept. Int., P&M, LR, 1872–1882.

25. Reproduced in *House Exec. Doc.* 85, 47th Cong., 1st Sess. (SN 2027), p. 18.

26. P. W. Norris to C. Schurz, Nov. 12, 1877, NA, Dept. Int., P&M, LR, 1872–1882.

27. T. B. Comstock to C. Schurz, Oct. 8, 1877, NA, Dept. Int., P&M, LR, 1872–1882. Members thus appointed were Professor Theo. B. Comstock, Joseph Henry. O. C. Marsh, Lt. Geo. M. Wheeler, and Maj. J. W. Powell.

28. "Petition to the Secretary of the Interior," reproduced copy in NA, Dept. Int., P&M, LR, 1872–1882.

29. C. Schurz to Samuel J. Randall, Speaker of the House, Mar. 6, 1878, NA, Dept. Int., P&M, LS, 1872–1886, and *House Exec. Doc.* 75, 45th Cong., 2nd Sess. (SN 1809), p. 1.

30. Act of June 20, 1878 (20 SL, 229); CR, 45th Cong., 2nd Sess., IV Part 3, p. 4557.

31. C. Schurz to P. W. Norris, July 6, 1878, NA, Dept. Int., P&M, LS, 1872–1886.

32. P. W. Norris to C. Schurz, Nov. 10, 1878, NA, Dept. Int., P&M, LR, 1872–1882.

33. Ibid.

34. F. V. Hayden to C. Schurz, Feb. 21, 1878, NA, Dept. Int., P&M, LR, 1872–1882.

35. P. W. Norris to A. Bell, Asst. Sec. Int., May 6, 1879, NA, Dept. Int., P&M, LR, 1872–1882.

36. Act of Mar. 3, 1879 (20 SL, 393).

37. Superintendent of the Yellowstone National Park, "Annual Report to the Secretary of the Interior, 1880," in *House Exec. Doc.* 1, 46th Cong., 3d Sess. (SN 1903), pp. 1–3.

38. Strahorn, *Fifteen Thousand Miles by Stage,* pp. 254–286; G. L. Henderson, *Yellowstone Park,* p. 8.

39. P. W. Norris to Sec. Int., Nov. 30, 1880, in *House Exec. Doc.* 1, 46th Cong., 3d Sess. (SN 1960), p. 576; C. Schurz to the Speaker of the House, Apr. 26, 1880, NA, Dept. Int., P&M, LS, 1872–1886.

40. Report of Harry Yount to P. W. Norris, Nov. 25, 1880, in Appendix A. *House Exec. Doc.* 1, 46th Cong., 3rd Sess. (SN 1960), p. 620; Yount to Norris, Sept. 30, 1881, in *House Exec. Doc.* 1, 47th Cong., 1st Sess. (SN 2018), pp. 807.

41. P. W. Norris to C. Schurz, Dec.1, 1881, *House Exec. Doc.* 1, 47th Cong., 1st Sess.(SN 2018), pp. 807–814.

42. "Journal of Lt. Col. James F. Gregory," reproduced in Sheridan's *Annual Report* of 1881, and quoted in *Senate Report* 911, 47th Cong., 2nd Sess. (SN 2087), pp. 3–4.

43. 1st Lt. G. C. Doane to Martin Maginnis, Member of Congress, Jan. 14, 1881, NA, Dept. Int., Appts. Div., LR Concerning Superintendents, 1872–1886.

44. James F. Gregory, "Journal," pp. 3–4.

45. Records of the Department of the Interior, NA, P&M, LS, 1872–1886.

46. P. W. Norris to Sec. Int., Dec. 1, 1881, reproduced in *House Exec. Doc.* 1, 47th Cong., 1st Sess. (SN 2018), p. 771.

47. CR, 47th Cong., 1st Sess., XIV, Part 1, p. 732; H. R. 3751, copy attached to letter, Thad. C. Pound to S. J. Kirkwood, Feb. 16, 1882, NA, Dept. Int., P&M, LR, 1872–1882.

48. S. J. Kirkwood to Thad. C. Pound, Mar. 4, 1882, NA, Dept. Int., P&M, LS, 1872–1886.

49. *The Calumet of the Coteau and other Poetical Legends of the Border . . . Together with a Guide-Book of the Yellowstone National Park* (Philadelphia: Lippincott, 1884).

4. The Early Years in Yellowstone: 1882–1886

1. Conger was required, as were his successors, to execute a $5,000 bond before entering upon his duties as Superintendent. His bond was received and approved on Mar. 2, 1882, but his appointment and salary did not begin until Apr. 1, 1882. S. J. Kirkwood to P. H. Conger, Feb. 3, Mar. 1, Mar. 20, 1882, NA, Dept. Int., P&M, LS, 1872–1886.

2. *Senate Report* 911, 47th Cong., 2nd Sess. (SN 2087), pp. 1–11.

3. P. H. Conger to Sec. Int., Sept. 20, 1882, NA, Dept. Int., P&M, LR, 1872–1882.

4. *Senate Report* 911, 47th Cong., 2nd Sess. (SN 2087), pp. 1–11.

5. P. H. Sheridan to Brig. Gen. R. C. Drum, Adjutant General, Nov. 1, 1882, NA, Dept. Int., P&M, LR, 1872–1882.

6. J. S. Crosby to George C. Vest, Dec. 29, 1882. Appendix D, *Senate Report* 911, 47th Cong., 2nd Sess. (SN 2087), pp. 1–2.

7. D. B. Sacket to G. C. Vest, Jan. 3, 1883, Appendix D, *Senate Report* 911, 47th Cong., 2nd Sess. (SN 2087), pp. 2–4.

8. During his long term in the Senate, Vest introduced much legislation designed to aid the Park, fought all proposed encroachments, and

became recognized "as the outstanding champion of proper protection and development of the park." On Mar. 1, 1883, he stated what was to be a guiding principle for himself and others of a like mind: "There should be to a nation that will have a hundred million or a hundred and fifty million people a park like this as a great breathing place for the national lungs." Born in Kentucky in 1830, he served as Judge Advocate in General Price's Confederate force in Missouri in 1862; he served in the House of Representatives of the Confederate Congress from 1862 to 1865, and thereafter in the Confederate Senate; elected as a Democrat to the U. S. Senate, he served in that capacity from Mar. 4, 1879 to Mar. 3, 1903; he died Aug. 9, 1904. Cramton, *Early History,* pp. 59–60; CR, 47th Cong., 2nd Sess., XIV, Part 4, p. 3488.

9. CR, 47th Cong., 2nd Sess., XIV, Part 1, p. 193. *Senate Report* 911, 47th Cong., 2nd Sess. (SN 2087), p. 5.

10. G. C. Vest to Henry M. Teller, Jan. 13, 1883, NA, Dept. Int., P&M, LR, 1883–1884.

11. Henry M. Teller to Supt., Yellowstone National Park, Jan. 15, 1883, NA, Dept. Int., P&M, LR, 1883–1884.

12. H. M. Teller to G. C. Vest, Jan. 15, 1883, NA, Dept. Int., P&M, LS, 1872–1886.

13. M. C. Brown, U. S. Attorney, Wyoming, to Benjamin Harris Brewster, Attorney General, Feb. 3, 1883; Governor Hale to H. M. Teller, Feb. 13, 1883, NA, Dept. Int., P&M, LR, 1883–1884.

14. CR, 47th Cong., 2nd Sess., XII, Part 3, pp. 2835–2836; *Senate Miscellaneous Document* 41, 47th Cong., 2nd Sess. (SN 2083), p. 1.

15. CR, 47th Cong., 2nd Sess., XII, Part 3, pp. 2890, 3214, 3268.

16. CR, 47th Cong., 2nd Sess, XIV, Part 4, pp. 3193–3194.

17. Ibid., p. 3195.

18. CR, 47th Cong., 2nd Sess, XIV, Part 4, pp. 3193, 3194, 3195, 3482, 3483, 3488; Act of Mar. 3, 1883 (22 SL, 626).

19. "Report of the Secretary of the Interior on the Administration of Yellowstone National Park," *Senate Exec. Doc.* 47, Part 3, 48th Cong., 1st Sess. (SN 2162), p. 3.

20. P. H. Conger to Sec. Int., Mar. 7, 1883, YNPA, Vol. 1, LS, File No. 164.

21. Reproduced in *Chicago Evening Journal,* Mar. 19, 1883, clipping in NA Dept. Int., P&M, LR, 1883–1884.

22. Jas. H. Dean, Asst. Supt., to P. H. Conger, July 31 and Aug. 31, 1883, YNPA, Vol. 9, File Nos. 1367, 1368, LR.

23. P. H. Conger to H. M. Teller, June 27, 1883, NA, Dept. Int., P&M, LR, 1883–1884.

24. H. B. Wiley, "Yellowstone Park in 1883," Diary form, entries of July 8 and July 11, 1883. Reproduced in *Montana; Magazine of Western History,* III (Summer, 1953), pp. 12, 14.

25. C. T. Hobart to H. M. Teller, Oct. 27, 1883, NA, Dept. Int., P&M, LR, 1883–1884; H. M. Teller to P. H. Conger, Dec. 20, 1883, YNPA, Vol. 1, File No. 151; P. H. Conger to Teller, Jan. 27, 1884, NA, Dept. Int., P&M, LR, 1885–1886.

26. W. Scott Smith, Special Agent, Department of the Interior, to H. M. Teller, Oct. 15, 1883, NA, Dept. Int., P&M, LR, 1883–1884.

27. P. H. Conger to Sec. Int., Nov. 4, 1883, NA, Dept. Int., P&M, LR, 1883–1884.

28. D. E. Sawyer to Hon. H. B. (illegible), Washington, D. C., Dec. 23, 1883, NA, Dept. Int., P&M, LR, 1883–1884.

29. P. H. Conger to H. M. Teller, Nov. 27, 1883, NA, Dept. Int., P&M, LR, 1883–1884.

30. *Senate Bill* 221, 48th Cong., 1st Sess., Dec. 4, 1883. Copy in NA, Dept. Int., P&M, LR, 1883–1884.

31. Cramton, *Early History,* pp. 42–43.

32. 22 SL, 626.

33. Special Order No. 73, Headquarters Military Division of the Missouri, Chicago, July 6, 1883; H. M. Teller to P. H. Conger, July 14, 1883, YNPA, Vol. 1, No. 85, LR.

34. CR 47th Cong., 1st Sess., XIV, Part 1, p. 732; Thad. C. Pound to S. J. Kirkwood, Feb. 16, 1882, NA, Dept. Int., P&M, LR, 1883–1884.

35. *Coulson Post* (Montana), Sept. 7, 1882, as quoted in Aubrey Haines, "A Review of Certain Attempts to Make Adverse use of Yellowstone National Park," MS, Yellowstone National Park Library, Mammoth Hot Springs, Wyoming.

36. P. H. Conger to Sec. Int., Dec. 20, 1883, NA, Dept. Int., P&M, LR, 1883–1884.

37. Lt. Kingman to Chief of Engineers, Nov. 1, 1883, NA, Dept. Int., P&M, LR, 1883–1884.

38. J. S. Crosby, "Report of the Governor of Montana Territory," Department of Interior *Report,* 1884, II (GPO, 1885), p. 562.

39. B. P. Van Horne to Sec. Int., Feb. 24, 1884, NA, Dept. Int., P&M, LR, 1883–1884.

40. L. B. Carey to Halton Frank, 1st Asst. Post Master General, Feb. 2, 1884, NA, Dept. Int., P&M, LR, 1883–1884.

41. Jas. Dean to P. H. Conger, Aug. 26, 1884, YNPA, Vol. 9, LR, File No. 1355.

42. Edmund L. Fish to P. H. Conger, May 12, 1884, YNPA, Vol. 9, LR, File No. 1418.

43. Edmund L. Fish to P. H. Conger, June 4, 1885, YNPA, Vol. 9, LR, File No. 1420.

44. *The Daily Enterprise* (Livingston, Montana), Sept. 5, 1884.

45. L. B. Carey to Halton Frank, 1st Asst. Post Master General, Feb. 2, 1884, NA, Dept. Int., P&M, LR, 1883–1884.

46. B. P. Van Horne to Sec. Int., Feb. 24, 1884, NA, Dept. Int., P&M, LR, 1883–1884.

47. H. M. Teller to the President, *pro tempore,* of the Senate, Jan. 9, 1884, NA, Dept. Int., P&M, LS, 1872–1886.

48. *Senate Exec. Doc.* 51, 49th Cong., 1st Sess. (SN 2333), p. 1; A. T. Babbitt to Sec. Int., Jan. 30, Mar. 7, 1884, NA, Dept. Int., P&M, LR, 1883–1884; Governor of Wyoming to P. H. Conger, Mar. 13, 1884, YNPA, Vol. 5, LR, File No. 929.

49. H. M. Teller to P. H. Conger, July 12, 1884, NA, Dept. Int., P&M, LS, 1872–1886.

50. *The Daily Enterprise* (Livingston, Montana), July 19, July 21, Sept. 2, 1884.

51. M. L. Joslyn, Act. Sec. Int., to R. E. Carpenter, Aug. 5, Aug. 28, 1884, NA, Dept. Int., P&M, LS, 1872–1886; R. E. Carpenter to Sec. Int., Sept. 18, 1884, NA, File 1906, Dept. Int., P&M, LR, 1883–1884.

52. R. E. Carpenter was a brother of C. C. Carpenter, a former member of Congress from Iowa.

53. M. L. Joslyn, Act. Sec. Int., to Supt., Yellowstone National Park, Nov. 6, Nov. 22, 1884, YNPA, Vol. 1, File Nos. 42 and 156, LR.

54. *The Daily Enterprise* (Livingston, Montana), June 6, 1884.

55. Senate Document 752, 60th Cong., 2nd Sess. (SN 5409), p. 18; Chittenden, *Yellowstone National Park,* p. 113.

56. *Livingstone Enterprise,* Jan. 31, Feb. 21, 1885. (Changed from *The Daily Enterprise,* Nov. 8, 1884.)

57. G. C. Vest to H. L. Muldrow, Asst. Sec. Int., Apr. 17, 1885, NA, Dept. Int. P&M, LR, 1872–1886.

58. L. Q. C. Lamar to D. W. Wear, June 1, 1885; J. J. Hassler, Chief, Appointment Div., Dept. Int., to D. W. Wear, June 20, 1885, NA, Dept. Int., P&M, LS, 1872–1886.

59. D. W. Wear to L. Q. C. Lamar, July 2, 1885, NA, Dept. Int., P&M, File No. 541, LR, 1872–1886; D. W. Wear to G. C. Vest, July 5, 1885, NA, Dept. Int., P&M, LR, 1885–1886.

60. D. W. Wear to L. Q. C. Lamar, Aug. 12, 1885, NA, Dept. Int., P&M, LR, 1885–1886, File No. 3694.

61. Ibid.

62. D. W. Wear to L. Q. C. Lamar, Sept. 7, 1885, NA, Dept. Int., Appts. Div., Concerning Supts., LR, 1886, File No. 86.

63. D. W. Wear to L. Q. C. Lamar, Nov. 2, 1885, NA, Dept. Int., P&M, LR, 1885–1886, File No. 4650. George B. Grinnell, later to play a significant role in the development of national parks, noted the activities of both the poachers and the Superintendent: "Last year [1885] Supt. Wear sent his family out of the Park Sept. 27 and remained all winter in the Park devoting his time and attention to keeping the skin hunters off the reservation. This has been quite common in the past the hunters coming in on snowshoes and running the elk into the deep drifts where they are easily butchered. In the autumn of 1884 a man named Ira Dodge and another named Rogers killed in this way 47 elk in one evening. . . ." Diary, 1886, No. 324, Grinnell Collection, Southwest Museum, Los Angeles.

64. *House Report* 1076, 49th Cong., 1st Sess., Vol. 4 (SN 2438), p. liv.

65. Ibid., pp. lii and lxiii.

66. Ibid., pp. liv, lv. Had this suggestion been followed (and there was strong precedent for it in the Yosemite Grant to the State of California in 1864) the experiment of National Parks might well have ended there. The later proven success of national control and administration in the Yellowstone provided a basis for the establishment of National Parks in California and the subsequent end of state control of the Yosemite Valley by recession of the original grant to the federal government. See Chapter VIII.

67. L. Q. C. Lamar to W. H. Phillips, July 20, 1885, NA, Dept. Ing., P&M, LS, 1872–1886.

68. W. H. Phillips to H. L. Muldrow, Act. Sec. Int., Sept. 21, 1885, NA, Dept. Int., P&M, 1885–1886, File 4072. In response to a Senate Resolution, Jan. 12, 1886, the Acting Secretary forwarded the Phillips report to the Senate, where, on Feb. 1, 1886, it was referred to the Committee on Territories and ordered to be printed as *Senate Exec. Doc.* 51, 49th Cong., 1st Sess. (SN 2333), pp. 1–29.

69. W. H. Phillips to H. L. Muldrow, Act. Sec. Int., Sept. 21, 1885, NA, Dept. Int., P&M, 1885–1886, File 4072.

70. D. W. Wear to Sec. Int., Mar. 26, 1886, NA, Dept. Int., P&M, LR, 1885–1886, File 1275.

71. *Senate Exec. Doc.* 51, 49th Cong., 1st Sess. (SN 2333), pp. 1–300; *House Report* 1076, 49th Cong., 1st Sess. (SN 2438), p. 1.

72. CR, 49th Cong., 1st Sess., XVII, Part 6, p. 5830.

73. L. Q. C. Lamar to Chairman, Committee on Appropriations, Senate and House, June 29, 1886, NA, Dept. Int., P&M, LS, 1872–1886.

74. CR, 49th Cong., 1st Sess., XCII, Part 7, pp. 7220, 7473.

75. Ibid., pp. 7546, 7586.

76. Ibid., Part 8, pp. 7667, 7839.

77. Ibid., p. 7841.

78. Ibid., p. 7842.

79. Ibid., p. 7844. Henry M. Teller of Colorado had been Secretary of the Interior during the Arthur administration.

80. Ibid., pp. 7844–7846.

81. D. B. Henderson was later Speaker of the House for two terms; his brother, G. L. Henderson, had been an Assistant Superintendent under Conger and during his position in office was responsible for many defamatory statements about his superior. In 1866 he was operating a hotel within the Park in competition with the newly formed Yellowstone Park Association and evidently asserted some influence over his brother to advocate military control over the Park, since he probably believed such control would be nominal. Representative Henderson was later to change his views concerning Park matters and in 1894 exerted considerable effort in the House in support of the Park.

82. D. W. Wear to General John C. Black, Commissioner of Pensions, Aug. 26, 1886, NA, Dept. Int., Special Appointments Division "Complaints"; W. Hallett Phillips to L. Q. C. Lamar, Aug. 7, 1886, NA, Dept. Int., P&M, LR, 1885–1886, File 3480.

83. The Congressman's memory was rather faulty in this case. Mackinac National Park, excluding old Fort Mackinac, was set aside in 1875 for the "health, comfort, pleasure, benefit and enjoyment of the people." (28 SL, 517). As in Yellowstone, the natural curiosities, timber, game, and fish were to be protected. Administration and protection of the area were entrusted to the Secretary of War, who appointed the Superintendent of the Park, usually the commander of the historic fort. His duties were confined mainly to letting leases to private parties for the purpose of building summer homes and cabins. When established, it was suggested that the area be ceded to Michigan, but the example set by the California State Commissioners in charge of the Yosemite grant, an example of abuse and corruption, persuaded Congress to ignore it. Senator Holman should have remembered the situation, for it was he who opposed the establishment of the Park, basing his argument upon the expense incurred in the establishment of Yellowstone. His argument in 1875 was no better than the one in 1886 for at that time, 1875, no moneys had been appropriated for Yellowstone. In 1895 the Mackinac National Park was turned over to the State of Michigan and became an element in that state's sytem of parks. (28 SL, 945).

84. CR, 49th Cong., 1st Sess., XVII, Part 8, pp. 7866–7867.

85. Ibid., p. 7915.

86. Ibid., pp. 7915–7918.

87. 24 SL, 240.

88. 22 SL, 627.

89. L. Q. C. Lamar to Secretary of War, Aug. 6, 1886, NA, AGO, File 4735, in File 3997, AGO 1886, RG 94.

90. P. H. Sheridan to Sec. of War, Aug. 9, 1886, NA, File 3997, AGO 1886, RG 94.

91. Special Orders No. 79, Headquarters, Dept. of Dakota, Ft. Snelling, Minn., Aug. 13, 1886, NA, File 3997, AGO, 1886, RG 94.

5. *The Saving of a Park and a System: 1886–1889*

1. Joseph K. Toole, as quoted in *The Livingston Enterprise,* Aug. 14, 1886.

2. Capt. Moses Harris to Assist. Adj. Gen., Dept. of Dakota, Sept. 13, 1886, NA, Document File, Office of the Adjutant General, Box No. 1448, File 1886, Doc. No. 5187. Telegrams, D. W. Wear to H. L. Muldrow, Act. Sec. Int., Aug. 13, Aug. 17, 1886, NA, Dept. Int., P&M, LR, 1885–1886.

3. Capt. Moses Harris to Sec. Int., Oct. 4, 1886, YNPA, Vol. I, LS.

4. Telegram, H. L. Muldrow, Act. Sec. Int., to Capt. Moses Harris, Aug. 18, 1886, YNPA, Vol. I, No. 106, LR.

5. Harris to Sec. Int. Oct. 4, 1886, YNPA, Vol. I, No. 29, LS; *Senate Exec. Doc.* 40, 49th Cong., 2nd Sess. (SN 2448), pp. 1–5.

6. By direction of the President, the name was changed from Camp Sheridan to Fort Yellowstone in accordance with General Orders No. 45, Headquarters of the Army, May 11, 1891. Fort Yellowstone was abandoned on Oct. 26, 1916, in compliance with Post Orders No. 62, Oct. 23, 1916. NA, *Records of the United States Army Commands* (Army Posts), Fort Yellowstone, RG 98.

7. Harris' regulations are reproduced in *Senate Exec. Doc.* 40, 49th Cong., 2nd Sess. (SN 2448), Appendix A, p. 7.

8. Capt. Moses Harris, quoted in *The Livingston Enterprise,* Aug. 28, 1886.

9. Harris to Sec. Int., Aug. 27, Sept. 29, 1886; Harris to H. L. Muldrow, Act. Sec. Int., Aug. 28, 1886; YNPA, Vol. I, LS, Nos. 3, 4, 10, 22–23, 182.

10. Harris to Adj. Gen., Dept. of Dakota, Aug. 18, 1886, and 5th endorsement thereto, P. H. Sheridan to Secretary of War, Sept. 4, 1886, NA, RG 94, AGO File No. 4524 in File 3997. C. J. Baronett, one of

Wear's former Assistant Superintendents and a long-time resident of the Park, was hired as a "scout and guide" by Harris.

11. Harris to Commanding General, Dept. of Dakota, Aug. 24, 1886, 5th endorsement thereto by Act. Sec. of War, Sept. 7, 1886; telegram, J. C. Kelton, Act. Adj. Gen., to Maj. Gen. Terry, Sept. 25, 1886, NA, RG 94, AGO, File 4735 in File 3997.

12. *Senate Exec. Doc.* 40, 49th Cong., 2nd Sess. (SN 2448), Appendix B; CR, 49th Cong., 2nd Sess., VIII, Part 8, p. 7868; telegram, J. C. Kelton, Act. Adj. Gen., to Lt. Col. Cochran, 5th Infty., Ft. Keogh, M. T., Aug. 17, 1886, NA, RG 94, AGO Doc. File, Box No. 1446, Doc. No. 4165, File 1886.

13. Chittenden, *The Yellowstone National Park,* p. 115.

14. Harris to Sec. Int., Oct. 4, 1886, YNPA, Vol. I, LS, pp. 26–48; *Senate Exec. Doc.* 40, 49th Cong., 2nd Sess. (SN 2448), Appendix B, p. 27. The military commander of the troops assigned to the Yellowstone National Park actually served in two capacities. As Acting Superintendent he reported directly to the Secretary of the Interior. As a military commander he reported directly to his regimental commander on purely military matters.

15. Ibid., p. 29.

16. These suggested rules were adopted *in toto* and published in 1892, under the date July 1, 1889, and over the signature of John W. Noble, Secretary of the Interior. *House Report* 1956, 52nd Cong., 1st Sess. (SN 3051), p. 172. They had previously been put forth as a Directive of the Department of the Interior by Sec. of the Int. L. Q. C. Lamar, Apr. 4, 1887, YNPA, Vol. I, LR, No. 154.

17. Harris to Sec. Int., Oct. 4, 1886, YNPA, Vol. I, LS, p. 41.

18. Harris to Asst. Adj. Gen., Dept. of Dakota, Sept. 13, NA, RG 94, AGO Docs., Box No. 1448, Doc. No. 5187 in File 1886.

19. W. Hallett Phillips to L. Q. C. Lamar, Sec. Int., Oct. 4, 1886, NA, Dept. Int., P&M, LR, No. 4123, 1885–1886.

20. Harris to E. C. Dawson, Chief Clerk, Dept. Int., July 31, 1887, YNPA, Vol. II, LS, No. 57.

21. W. S. Rainsford, "Camping and hunting in the Shoshone," *Scribner's Monthly,* XI, No. 3 (1887), p. 298.

22. "Minutes of the Boone and Crockett Club," 1888–1960, reproduced in Trefethen, *Crusade for Wildlife,* pp. 19–20. The Boone and Crockett Club, founded in New York by Theodore Roosevelt, George Bird Grinnell, and others, became one of the foremost elements in conservation advocation. All of the military Acting Superintendents of the Yellowstone National Park were members of this organization.

23. CR, 50th Cong., 1st Sess., XIX, Part 2, p. 2602. There were 262 of these petitions presented at this session of Congress.

24. *Senate Report* 315, Senate Territorial Committee on *Senate Report* 283, 50th Cong., 1st Sess. (SN 2519), *House Report* 3071, House Committee on Public Lands, on *Senate Report* 293, 50th Cong., 1st Sess. (SN 2605), p. 1.

25. Harris to H. L. Muldrow, Act. Sec. Int., Aug. 20, 1887, YNPA, Vol. II, LS, p. 81.

26. Harris to H. L. Muldrow, Apr. 24, 1887, July 7, 1887, YNPA, Vol. II, LS, pp. 11–15, 42–43; J. W. Ponsford, Deputy U. S. Marshal, Bozeman, Mont., to Harris, Oct. 31, 1887, Nov. 2, 1887, YNPA, Vol. VI, LR, No. 1263; "List of Expulsions from Park by Post Orders, 1886–1893," YNPA, Vol. 78.

27. Thomas Garfield, addressee unknown, Sept. 24, 1888, NA, Dept. Int., P&M, LR, 1885–1886 (no file number and evidently misfiled).

28. Harris to Muldrow, Aug. 2, 1887, YNPA, Vol. II, LS, pp. 59–63.

29. Professor Charles S. Sargent, as quoted in Johnson, *Remembered Yesterdays,* p. 296. Sargent established the publication *Garden and Forest* in 1887, and through this medium suggested and supported many movements in the field of forestry and conservation.

30. Harris to Muldrow, Aug. 20, 1887, UNPA, Vol. II, LS, pp. 122–24.

31. Harris to Murdock Deckson and Co., Toronto, Canada, Aug. 24, 1888, YNPA, Vol. II, LS, pp. 314–315. The policy of declining to purchase domestic animals to restore a vanishing species, as well as that of protecting carnivores, was later to be reversed and the opposite inaugurated: the extermination of carnivores and the purchase of buffalo. These in turn were reversed, and what was advocated by Harris eventually became an integral element of National Park policy.

32. L. Q. C. Lamar, Sec. Int., to Act. Supt. Harris, Nov. 1, 1887, YNPA, Vol. I, LR, No. 102.

33. Harris to Muldrow, Aug. 20, 1887, YNPA, Vol, II, LS, pp. 113–114.

34. Harris to Commanding Officer, Dept. of Dakota, June 23, 1888, with endorsements thereto. NA, RG 94, AGO, File 3027–1888 in File 3997–1886.

35. Harris to Muldrow, Jan. 12, 1887, YNPA, Vol. I, LS, pp. 70–72.

36. H. L. Muldrow, Act. Sec. Int., to Sec. War, Apr. 1, 1887, YNPA, copy in Vol. I, LR, No. 38.

37. Wm. C. Endicott, Sec. War, to Sec. Int., Apr. 14, 1887, YNPA, copy in Vol. I, LR, No. 40. J. C. Kelton, Act. Adj. Gen., to Maj. Gen.

Terry, Sept. 15, 1886, NA, RG 94, AGO, File 4735 in File 3997; Harris to Muldrow, Aug. 20, 1887, YNPA, Vol. II, LS, pp. 110–111.

38. Harris to Phillips, Mar. 7, June 28, 1888, YNPA, Vol. II, LS, pp. 216–222, 278–290. The men who Harris thought might aid in obtaining the appropriations were: "Senators Vest, Farwell, Cameron, and Sabin and Representatives Hitt of Illinois, Reece of Maine and Rice of Minnesota."

39. *House Report* 1956, 52nd Cong., 1st Sess. (SN 3051), pp. 171–172; 25 SL, 534. The first appropriation made for improvement and *protection* came in 1891, and was followed by similar appropriations. R. Tracewell, Comptroller, to Sec. Int., Jan. 11, 1900, YNPA, Vol. 16, LR (no p. no.).

40. H. L. Muldrow to Harris, Oct. 31, 1887, YNPA, Vol. I, LR, No. 54.

41. George S. Anderson, "Protection of The Yellowstone National Park," in Roosevelt and Grinnell (eds.), *Hunting in Many Lands,* p. 387.

6. *The Development of a Policy: 1889–1894*

1. 1st Lt. G. C. Doane to Martin Maginnis, Jan. 14, 1881, NA, Dept. Int., Appts. Div., LR Concerning Supts. 1872–1886, File 189, LR, 1881; correspondence urging Doane's appointment is extensive.

2. Special Orders No. 47, Headquarters, Dept. of Dakota, May 8, 1889, NA, File 2276, AGO, 1889, in File 3997, AGO, 1886.

3. Boutelle to Sec. Int., July 27, 1889, YNPA, Vol. II, LS, p. 469.

4. Boutelle to Sec. Int., July 31, 1889, YNPA, Vol. II, LS, pp. 478–481.

5. Ibid., Aug. 18, 1899, pp. 491–494.

6. D. B. May to Sec. Int., Mar. 28, 1889, YNPA, Vol. VI, LR, No. 1162.

7. Sec. Int. to Boutelle, Sept. 6, 1889, YNPA, Vol. II, LR, No. 406, 600.

8. Boutelle to Sec. Int., Oct. 3, 1889, YNPA, Vol. III, LS, pp. 28–29.

9. Sec. Int. to Boutelle, Aug. 2, 1890, YNPA, Vol. II, LR, No. 403.

10. Boutelle to Sec. Int., July 5, 1890, YNPA, Vol. III, LS, pp. 122–125.

11. Sec. Int. to Boutelle, Aug. 2, 1890, YNPA, Vol. II, LR, No. 403.

12. Sec. Int. to Boutelle, Aug. 22, 1890, YNPA, Vol. II, LR, No. 258; Boutelle to Sec. Int., Aug. 29, 1890, YNPA, Vol. III, LS, pp. 155–167.

13. Sec. Int. to Boutelle, Oct. 15, 1890, and copy, letter Sec. Int. to D. B. May, Oct. 15, 1890, YNPA, Vol. II, LR, No. 405. The elevator scheme was later resurrected and the Assistant Secretary of the Interior

threw his support behind it, maintaining that the construction of an elevator would "not detract from the natural grandeur of the landscape." Senator George Vest immediately secured the adoption of a Senate Resolution requesting the withholding of "any action in the premises until it can be determined by Congress as to the propriety of the granting of any such privilege." The principle proposed by Acting Superintendent Boutelle, that of protecting the Park from "commercialization" and defacement, came to the fore and this second attempt met the fate of the first. CR, 54th Cong., 2nd Sess., XIX, Part 2, pp. 1919, 2223.

14. Boutelle to Col. Marshall McDonald, Fish Commissioner, June 13, 1889, YNPA, Vol. II, LS, p. 441, Sept. 25, 1889, Vol. III, p. 26. Boutelle, Adj. Gen., State of Washington, to Capt. George Anderson, Act. Supt., Yellowstone National Park, Nov. 18, 1895, YNPA, Vol. X, LR, no file no.

15. During the summer of 1889, 61 separate fires were extinguished by Troops "A" and "K," then detailed to the Park on a seasonal basis. Capt. D. A. Bomus to Boutelle, Dec. 15, 1889, YNPA, Vol. IX, "Employees," No. 1407.

16. Boutelle to Sec. Int., Sept. 11, 1890, Vol. III, LS, pp. 168–169; Sec. Int. to Boutelle, Sept. 24, 1890, YNPA, Vol. II, LR, No. 236.

17. Boutelle to Sec. Int., Dec. 8, Dec. 11, 1899, YNPA, Vol. III, LS, pp. 56–58, 59–62; Boutelle to Governor Warren, Boutelle to Secretary, Territory Idaho, Nov. 25, 1889, pp. 48, 53; Boutelle to Sec. Int., Dec. 12, 1890, pp. 206–210. Boutelle's interest in game protection and preservation extended beyond his tenure as Acting Superintendent. He was a member of the Boone and Crockett Club and served as Vice President of that organization the year preceding his death in 1924.

18. Boutelle to Charles S. Fee, General Passenger and Ticket Agent, Northern Pacific Railroad, Aug. 21, 1889, YNPA, Vol. III, LS, pp. 9–10.

19. Boutelle to E. E. VanDyke, Cooke City, Dec. 2, 1890, ibid., p. 199.

20. Boutelle to Sec. Int., Oct. 13, Nov. 5, 1889, YNPA, Vol. III, LS, pp. 34, 35.

21. Clipping from *Omaha World* (date, 1889 only); Boutelle to Charles S. Fee, Aug. 21, 1889, YNPA, Vol. III, LS, pp. 9–15. All commendatory letters filed as Doc. No. 1316, Vol. IX, YNPA.

22. Sec. Int. to Sec. War, Dec. 18, 1890, NA, RG 94, File 8923, War Dept., in File 3997, AGO, 1886.

23. W. F. Sanders to Sec. War, Jan. 8, 1891; Gen. William E. Strong to Sec. War, Jan. 7, 1891; Sec. War to W. F. Sanders and Gen. Wm. E. Strong, Jan. 24, 1891, NA, AGO, File 610, PRD, 1891, filed in 3997, AGO, 1886. Doane, whose health was failing, did not give up hope that

he might still be named to the Park detail. He applied for transfer to General Miles' command so that he might be on hand for the next Park command change, but this too was denied. He died at Bozeman, Montana, in May, 1892.

24. Nelson A. Miles to Adj. Gen., Jan. 30, 1891, NA, File 1206/3, AGO, PRD, 1891 in File 3887, AGO, 1886. The overland march was not made and the Sixth Cavalry troops traveled by rail to the Park. Adj. Gen. to Commanding General, Div. of the Missouri, Feb. 5, 1891, NA, File 1206/3, AGO, PRD, 1891, in File 3997, AGO, 1886.

25. Special Orders No. 17, Headquarters of the Army, AGO, Jan. 21, 1891, as amended by S. O. No. 21, paragraph 18; Capt. George Anderson to Sec. Int., Feb. 15, 1891, YNPA, Vol. III, LS, pp. 218–225; NA, 1206, AGO, PRD, 1891, in File 3997, AGO, 1886.

26. Sec. Int. to Sec. War, Feb. 27, 1891, YNPA, Vol. II, LR, No. 402, 413; Brig. Gen. Thomas H. Ruger, C. O. Dept. Dakota, to Adj. Gen., Jan. 16, 1891, YNPA, Vol. II, LR, No. 301. The area of the reservation was 43.39 acres. An additional company of cavalry was permanently stationed at the post in 1893, and by 1904 three companies were stationed there. For three years, 1911–1913, there was a full squadron (four companies) with a machine gun platoon attached stationed in the Yellowstone. From 1914 to 1916, 200 cavalrymen assigned to the Yellowstone Park detachment were in garrison at Fort Yellowstone. When the reservation was finally abandoned by the Army in 1918, the jurisdiction of the area reverted to the Department of the Interior. For additional information concerning structures, year of construction, etc., see Ray H. Mattison, "Report on the Historical Structures at Yellowstone National Park," MS, mimeographed copy, Yellowstone National Park Library.

27. Frank Chatfield to Capt. Boutelle, June 29, 1890, YNPA, Vol. IV, LR, No. 736.

28. George S. Anderson, "Protection of the Yellowstone Park," in Theodore Roosevelt and George Bird Grinnell (eds.), *Hunting in Many Lands; The Book of the Boone and Crockett Club,* pp. 389–90.

29. W. S. Mellen to Anderson, July 27, 1892, YNPA, Vol. VI, LR, No. 1202.

30. Anderson, "Protection of the Yellowstone Park," p. 390.

31. Ibid., p. 393.

32. Anderson to Sec. Int., May 24, 1894, YNPA, Vol. V, LS, p. 58.

33. Eugene F. Weigel to Sec. Int., Aug. 8, 1892; Sec. War to Sec. Int., Sept. 28, 1892; copies in NA, File 39086, PRD, 1892, located in File 3997, AGO, 1886.

34. Anderson to Hosea Ballou, May 21, 1895; Anderson to John W. Whitson, June 25, 1894, YNPA, Vol. V, LS, pp. 245, 74–75; Frederick

Remington, "Policing the Yellowstone," in *Pony Tracks* (New York: Harper, 1898), pp. 114–115.

35. Ibid., p. 109.

36. Sec. Int. to Anderson, Sept. 14, 1891, YNPA, Vol. I, LR, No. 248.

37. Anderson to Sec. Int., Apr. 8, 1891, YNPA, Vol. III, LS, pp. 277–281. E. VanDyke to Capt. Anderson, Sept. 8, 1893, Vol. III, LR, No. 545; Mar. 31, 1894, YNPA, Vol. VII, No. 792.

38. Telegram, Anderson to Sec. Int., Aug. 10, 1892, Sec. Int. to Anderson, Aug. 11, 1892, YNPA, Vol. IV, LS, pp. 46, 47.

39. John Krachy, Wyoming Game Keeper, to Anderson, May (n.d.), 1893, YNPA, Vol. V, LR, No. 110; Anderson to Sec. Int., Jan. 8, 1894, YNPA, Vol. IV, LS, pp. 412–414; Anderson to Sec. Int., Dec. 16, 1895, Vol. V, LS, p. 324; Dunham Cameron to Anderson, July 7, 1893, Vol. IV, LR, No. 821.

40. Anderson to 1st. Lt. William W. Forsyth, June 4, 1894, YNPA, Vol. IV, LS, No. 826. Anderson to Sec. Int., Sept. 14, 1893, YNPA, Vol. IV, LS, pp. 333–334.

41. Anderson to Sec. Int., Oct. 8, 1891, YNPA, Vol. III, LS, pp. 398–404; Sept. 22, 1895, Vol. V, LS, p. 294.

42. Joffe, "John W. Meldrum," p. 190.

43. Anderson to D. L. Tremblay, Apr. 21, 1895, YNPA, Vol. V, LS, p. 219.

44. Anderson to Sec. Int., June 29, 1894, YNPA, Vol. V, LS, pp. 80–83. Between 1889 and 1895 some 82,685 game fish were stocked in the streams of the Park. In the following years, an additional 9,319,650 were stocked under military supervision, the largest annual plants being made in 1908 (2,626,500) and 1912 (3,969,000). "Memoranda of Game and Fish in Yellowstone National Park," YNPA, Vol. 168.

45. G. Brown Goode, Act. Sec., Smithsonian Institution, to Sec. Int., Sept. 30, 1891, copy in YNPA, Vol. V, LR, No. 260.

7. *The Development of a Legal Structure*

1. CR, 47th Cong., 2nd Sess., XV, Part 1, p. 193.

2. *Senate Report* 221, 48th Cong., 1st Sess.; *Senate Report* 101, 49th Cong., 2nd Sess.; *Senate Report* 283, 50th Cong., 1st Sess.; *Senate Report* 491 and 1275, 51st Cong., 1st Sess.; *Senate Report* 428, 52nd Cong., 1st Sess.; *Senate Report* 43, 53rd Cong., 1st Sess.; NA, Dept. Int., P&M, LR, 1883–1884. *House Exec. Doc.* 1, 52nd Cong., 1st Sess. (SN 2933), p. cxxxvii; G. B. Grinnell, "The Yellowstone National Park Act," in Roosevelt and Grinnell (eds.), *Hunting in Many Lands*, p. 409; Aubrey Haines, "A Re-

view of Certain Attempts to Make Adverse Use of Yellowstone National Park," pp. 4–7.

3. CR, 47th Cong., 1st Sess., XIII, Part I, p. 732. See also Chapter IV of this book.

4. Anderson to Sec. Int., Oct. 30, 1893, YNPA, Vol. IV, LS, pp. 373–376.

5. *Senate Report* 2373; CR, 52nd Cong., 1st Sess., XXIII, Part 2, p. 1472.

6. Ibid., Part 5, p. 4120.

7. Ibid., pp. 4121, 4124, 4125.

8. Ibid., pp. 4126, 4122.

9. Ibid., pp. 4120–4125; CR, 52nd Cong., 1st Sess., XXIII, Part 6, pp. 4170, 5012, 5027; *House Report* 1574.

10. Anderson to Sec. Int., Dec. 3, 1892, Jan. 22, Feb. 3, 1894, YNPA, Vol. IV, LS, pp. 140–145, 422–424; *House Report* 1956, 52nd Cong., 1st Sess. (SN 3051), pp. 18–22.

11. Theodore Roosevelt to the Editor, *Forest and Stream,* Dec. 3, 1892, reproduced in pamphlet, "A Standing Menace: Cooke City vs. the National Park," copy in Yellowstone National Park Library.

12. CR, 53rd Cong., 2nd Sess., XXVI, Part I, p. 3879.

13. Oakes' statement related by Anderson in letter to Sec. Int., Dec. 3, 1892, YNPA, Vol. IV, LS, pp. 140–145.

14. CR, 53rd Cong., 1st Sess., XXV, pp. 1271, 1341; XXVI, p. 8233; Anderson to Sec. Int., Oct. 28, 1890, YNPA, Vol. IV, LS, pp. 367–370; W. Hallett Phillips to Act. Supt., Nov. 10, 1893, YNPA, Vol. VI, LR, No. 1219. Similar bills were introduced in 1895, 1896, and 1897, but all were reported out of committee adversely and "indefinitely postponed." CR, 54th Cong., 1st Sess., XXVIII, Part 1, pp. 33, 51, 3799, and 55th Cong., 1st Sess., XXX, Part 1, o. 97.

15. CR, 53rd Cong., 1st Sess., XXV, Part 1, pp. 209, 212, 1138, 1271, Part 2, p. 1341; 53rd Cong., 2nd Sess., XXVI, Part I, pp. 321, 561, Part 3, p. 8288; 53rd Cong., 1st Sess. (Special Session), L, Part 1, p. 876; M. B. Murphy to Col. P. T. Severine, C.O., Ft. Keogh, referred to the C.O., Ft. Yellowstone, May 17, 1893, YNPA, Vol. VI, LR, No. 1187; *Livingston Post* (Montana) Nov. 30, 1893.

16. CR, 63rd Cong., 1st Sess., XXV, Part 1, pp. 209, 212; Anderson to Sec. Int., Jan. 7, 1894, YNPA, Vol. IV, LS, pp. 407–408.

17. Anderson to Sec. Int., Mar. 17, 1894, YNPA, Vol. V, LS, pp. 1–9. Somewhat more melodramatic accounts of this arrest appeared in the *Chicago Tribune,* Dec. 23, 1894, written by Emerson Hough; and in Anderson's "Protection of the Yellowstone Park." The story was also related by Hough in *Forest and Stream,* XLII, No. 18 (1894).

18. Anderson to Sec. Int., Mar. 17, 1894, YNPA, Vol. V, LS, pp. 1–9.

19. CR, 53rd Cong., 2nd Sess., XXVI, Part 5, p. 3252.

20. Ibid., pp. 3252, 3457, 3503, 3631.

21. Editorial, "Save the Park Buffalo," *Forest and Stream,* XLII, No. 15, (1894), pp. 307, 309.

22. Theodore Roosevelt to George A. Anderson, Mar. 30, 1894, YNPA, Vol. VI, LR, No. 1286.

23. W. Hallett Phillips to George A. Anderson, Mar. 31, 1894, YNPA, Vol. VI, LR, No. 1217–A.

24. CR, 53rd Cong., 2nd Sess., XXVI, Part 5, pp. 3457, 3688, 3751, 3939, 3961, 3962, 4019, 4296, 4541. The law as passed by Congress was, and is, known as the "Lacey Act." In view of Senator Vest's long legislative interest in the Park, and his continual introduction of essentially the same legislation, it should perhaps more properly be termed the "Vest Act."

25. Act of May 7, 1894, 28 SL, 73.

26. Meldrum's career is traced by Joffe, "John W. Meldrum," pp. 5–47, 105–140. 28 SL, 73. This Act was amended and made more practicable by the Act of June 28, 1916 (39 SL, 238) when punishment was reduced to "a fine of not more than $500 or imprisonment not exceeding six months, or both. . . ."

27. Theodore Roosevelt to George A. Anderson, Apr. 30, 1894, YNPA, Vol. VI, LR, No. 1284.

28. Edward A. Bowens to Anderson, May 12, 1894, YNPA, Vol. IV, LR, No. 741.

29. W. Hallett Phillips to Anderson, May 13, 1894, YNPA, Vol. VI, LR, No. 1217. Phillips was wrong in reference to Idaho and correct as far as Montana was concerned. Idaho had ceded exclusive jurisdiction to the United States over all those lands within that state that were included within the Park boundaries on February 7, 1891 (*Session Laws of Idaho,* 1890–1891, p. 40). Montana did not cede jurisdiction over her lands similarly situated until Mar. 3, 1917 (*Revised Code of Montana,* I, 1921, p. 232.)

30. W. Hallett Phillips to Anderson, July 2, 1894, YNPA, Vol. VI, LR, No. 1216; W. Hallett Phillips to G. C. Vest, Feb. 2, 1895, copy in YNPA, Vol. VI, LR, No. 1215.

31. Gibson Clark to Anderson, Nov. 2, 1894, YNPA, Vol. IV, LR, No. 727.

32. Anderson to Howell, July 24, YNPA, Vol. VI, LS, p. 7; Maj. J. W. Pope, QMC, to Col. S. B. M. Young, Act. Supt., Nov. 3, 1897, Vol. IX, LR, No. 1490; James R. Erwin, Capt., 4th Cavalry, to Ed Howell, Nov. 17, 1897, Vol. IX, LR, No. 1443.

8. *The Extension of a System: Yosemite, Sequoia, and General Grant National Parks*

1. *Congressional Globe,* 38th Cong., 1st Sess., Part 4, p. 3444 (13 SL, 325). For a full discussion of the Congressional debates on this act, see Chapter I.

2. *Report of the Commissioners to Manage the Yosemite Valley and the Mariposa Big Tree Grove, 1891–1892* (Sacramento: Superintendent of State Printing, 1893), Appendix 19. These reports were published under separate covers with variations in title: *Biennial Report of the Commissioners . . .; Report of the Yosemite Commissioners . . .* They are also contained in the *Appendix to the Journals of the Senate and Assembly of the . . . Session of the Legislature of the State of California.* Hereafter cited as *Report Yosemite Commissioners,* and *Appendix, Journals of the Calif. Leg.* For a more complete account of the Commissioner's activities see Edith G. Kettlewell, "Yosemite; The Discovery of the Yosemite Valley and the Creation and Realignment of Yosemite National Park," unpublished M.A. thesis, University of California, 1930.

3. *Statutes of California,* 16th Sess. of the State Legislature, Apr. 2, 1866, Chapter DXXXVI, p. 710.

4. F. L. Olmsted, "Governmental Preservation of Natural Scenery," as quoted by Brockman, "Administrative Officers of Yosemite," p. 54. The surveying of the boundaries of the two grants was accomplished with the aid of the United States Geological Survey. *Report, Yosemite Commissioners,* 1867–1868, 1874–1875, pp. 4, 6; 1891–1892, p. 20.

5. Olmsted, "The Yosemite Valley and the Mariposa Big Trees," p. 17.

6. Olmsted and Kimball, *Frederick Law Olmsted, Landscape Architect,* 1, 12.

7. *Report, Yosemite Commissioners,* 1874–1875, p. 9; "A Report of the Special Committee of the Assembly in Relation to the Grant of Land in Yosemite Valley," *Appendix, Journals of the Calif. Leg.,* II, 17th Sess.; *Low et al. v. Hutchings,* 15 Wall (U. S.) 77; Hutchings, *In the Heart of the Sierras, pp. 153–163; Hutchings v. Low,* 41 Cal. 634.

8. *Report, Yosemite Commissioners,* 1874–1875, p. 3. Russell, "Early Years in Yosemite," pp. 328–341.

9. The new Board of Commissioners consisted of I. W. Raymond (the only holdover from the old Board), J. P. Jackson, W. H. Mills, George S. Ladd, J. L. Sperry, W. C. Priest, A. J. Meany, and M. C. Briggs. James

Hutchings, one of the original settlers in the Valley, was named to replace Galen Clark as Guardian. *Senate Constitutional Amendments, Joint and Concurrent Resolutions of the California State Legislature,* 24th Session, 1880, *Concurrent Resolution* No. 20; *Report, Yosemite Commissioners,* 1880; Hutchings, *In the Heart of the Sierras,* pp. 162–165.

10. *Appendix to the Journals of the California Legislature,* 24th Sess. (1880), Vol. 1, p. 26.

11. Ibid., Vol. III; *Report, Yosemite Commissioners,* 1880–1882, p. 4.

12. *Appendix to the Journals of the California Legislature,* 29th Sess. (1886), Vol. II, "Report of William Ham Hall, State Engineer, 1882," passim.

13. Bills designed to enlarge the original grant were introduced into Congress in 1882, 1885, and 1886. None was reported out of committee. CR, 47th Cong., 1st Sess., XIII, Part 1, p. 68; Part 4, p. 3076; 48th Cong., 2nd Sess., XVI, Part 1, p. 230; 49th Cong., 1st Sess., XVII, Part 2, p. 1443. Mackenzie, "Destructive Tendencies in the Yosemite Valley," p. 475.

14. Results of the legislative investigation were published as "In the Matter of the Investigation of the Yosemite Valley Commissioners," *Journals of the California Legislature,* Senate, 1889, 40 pages; Assembly, 1889, 430 pages. Portions also quoted by Farquhar, *Yosemite, The Big Trees, and the High Sierra,* p. 93.

15. *Report, Yosemite Commissioners,* 1889–1890, p. 7.

16. Mackenzie, "California's Interest in Yosemite Reform," p. 155; editorial, "The Care of the Yosemite Valley," *The Century,* XXXIX (Jan. 1890), p. 474; *Report, Yosemite Commissioners,* 1889–1890; Farquhar, *Yosemite, The Big Trees, and the High Sierra,* p. 93.

17 George G. Mackenzie, "California's Interest in Yosemite Reform," *The Century,* XLII (Nov. 1891), pp. 154–155.

18. W. F. Badé, *Life and Letters of John Muir,* II, 394–395; Johnson, "Destructive Tendencies in the Yosemite Valley," pp. 477–478; Johnson, *Remembered Yesterdays,* p. 289.

19. San Francisco *Bulletin,* June 21, 1889; Wolfe (ed.), *Son of the Wilderness,* pp. 245–246.

20. Deming, "Destructive Tendencies in the Yosemite Valley," pp. 476–477.

21. George G. Mackenzie, "Destructive Tendencies in the Yosemite Valley," pp. 475–476.

22. Deming, p. 477.

23. Editorial, "The Care of the Yosemite Valley," *The Century,* XXXIX (Jan. 1890), pp. 474–475.

24. John Muir to Robert Underwood Johnson, Mar. 4, 1890, as reproduced in Badé, *The Life and Letters of John Muir,* II, pp. 237–238.

25. Editorial, "Preservation of the Yosemite Valley," *The Nation,* L, Feb. 6, 1890, p. 106; Mar. 6, 1890, p. 204.

26. Muir, "Treasures of the Yosemite," pp. 438–500.

27. Muir, "Features of the Proposed Yosemite National Park," pp. 665–667.

28. *Report, Yosemite Commissioners,* 1885–1886; 1887–1888; 1889–1890; Letter Sec. Int. to President of the Senate, Jan. 30, 1891, reproduced in *Senate Executive Doc.* 22, 52nd Cong., 2nd Sess. (SN 3056), p. 2. The Commissioners had urged that 1,000 acres of land on the floor of the Valley be so cultivated, thus diverting nine-tenths of the valley floor from use as a public resort to a source of state revenue.

29. Editorial, "Amateur Management of the Yosemite Scenery," *The Century,* XL (Sept. 1890), pp. 797–798.

30. Ibid., p. 798.

31. CR, 51st Cong., 1st Sess., XXI, Part 10, pp. 10297–10298.

32. "Report of Major Eugene F. Weigel, Special Land Inspector," letter, Sec. Int. to President of the Senate, Jan. 30, 1891, Dec. 29, 1892; *Senate Exec. Doc.* 22, 52nd Cong., 2nd Sess. (SN 3056), pp. 1–5.

33. CR, 47th Cong., 1st Sess., XIII, Part 1, p. 78.

34. George W. Stewart to Col. John R. White, June 8, 1929, reproduced in Fry and White, *Big Trees,* pp. 23–29; "Resolution of the California Academy of Science," in *Report of the Secretary of the Interior,* I (GPO, 1890), Appendix E, pp. clvii–clviii, clix–clxii.

35. CR, 51st Cong., 1st Sess., XXI, Part 8, p. 7834; Part 9, p. 9072.

36. Ibid., Part 9, p. 9137; Part 10, pp. 9829, 10170, 10189; Part 11, p. 10641.

37. The inclusion of the General Grant area in the bill may have been due to the efforts of one man. Writing in 1929, George W. Stewart, one of the men responsible for the establishment of Sequoia National Park, stated, "The creation of General Grant National Park was due to the timely suggestion of D. K. Zumwalt of Visalia [California] at the psychological moment . . . Mr. Zumwalt happened to be in Washington at the time . . . the bill creating Yosemite Park was up for passage, and his recommendation that the General Grant Grove be also made a park was acted upon favorably . . . by Congress." George W. Stewart to Col. John R. White, June 8, 1929, reproduced in Fry and White, *Big Trees,* p. 29.

38. CR, 51st Cong., 1st Sess., XXI, Part 3, p. 2372, Part 11, p. 10752.

39. Ibid., pp. 10740, 10794.

40. John Muir to Robert Underwood Johnson, Mar. 4, Apr. 20, June 9, 1890, reprinted in full in *The Sierra Club Bulletin,* XXIX, No. 5, pp.

50–60. Muir later worked ceaselessly, and successfully, for the recession by the state of the Yosemite Grant to the Federal Government. The grant was finally re-ceded in 1906, but not without the bitter opposition prophesied by Muir in 1890.

41. Act of Mar. 1, 1872 (17 SL, 32); Act of Sept. 25, 1890 (26 SL, 478); Act of Oct. 1, 1890 (26 SL, 650).

42. 26 SL, 1103; CR, 51st Cong., 2nd Sess., XXII, Part 4, pp. 3545–3547, 3611–3616, 3685. Differentiation between forest reserves and National Parks was made the following year. On March 3, 1891, Congress authorized the President "to set apart and reserve . . . any part of the public lands wholly or in part covered with timber or undergrowth . . . as public reservations." Forest reserves were established by executive proclamation; National Parks were specific statutory creations. 26 SL, 1103; CR, 51st Cong., 2nd Sess., XXII, Part 4, pp. 3545–3547, 3611–3616, 3685.

43. *Annual Report of the Secretary of the Interior,* I (GPO, 1890), pp. cxxii–cxxv.

44. Ibid., p. cxxv.

45. Sec. Int. to Sec. War, Oct. 21, 1890, NA, RG 94, AGO, "General Correspondence Relating to Yosemite National Park," 1890–1907, LS, Part 1; Sec. Int. to President of the U. S., Dec. 4, 1890; Sec. Int. to Sec. War, Dec. 22, 1890; Special Orders, No. 30, Headquarters, Dept. of California, Apr. 6, 1891; NA, RG 94, AGO, "Memorandum" Misc. Div., Doc. 4.

46. Ibid., 1901.

47. Series of letters, A. E. Wood to "Stockowners," June 7, 1891, A. E. Wood to "W. T. T.," July 14, 1891, Yosemite National Park Library, Record of Letters Sent, 1891–1900, Vol. 6, pp. 1–2, 4–5; A. E. Wood to Sec. Int., Aug. 31, 1891, *Report, Act. Supt., Yosemite,* 1891, p. 3.

48. A. E. Wood to Sec. Int., Aug. 31, 1891, *Report, Act. Supt., Yosemite,* 1891, pp. 4–5.

49. A. E. Wood to Sec. Int., July 15, 1893; ibid., 1893, pp. 3–5; *Reports, Act. Supts., Yosemite, Sequoia,* 1893–1905, passim.

50. Capt. J. H. Dorst to Sec. Int., Sept. 11, 1892, *Report, Act. Supt., Sequoia,* 1892, p. 17; Capt. Alex Rodgers to Sec. Int., Aug. 22, 1895, *Report, Act. Supt., Yosemite,* 1895, p. 5.

51. Translation, des Portes to Elihu Root, Sept. 2, 1905, NA, RG 94, AGO, "Select Documents Relating to National Parks."

52. Capt. J. Lockett to Sec. Int., Sept. 1, 1895, *Report, Act. Supt., Sequoia,* 1895, p. 4.

53. Capt. H. C. Benson to Sec. Int., Oct. 10, 1905, *Report, Act. Supt., Yosemite,* 1905, p. 8; "Board of officers appointed to investigate charges

of Ranger Charles Shinn, of the Forest Reserve, to the effect that soldiers had been bribed and that herds of sheep had summered in Yosemite Park," NA, RG 94, AGO, "Selected Documents Relating to National Parks."

54. John Muir to Robert Underwood Johnson, Sept. 12, 1895, reproduced in Badé, *Life and Letters of John Muir,* II, 294–295; Wolfe (ed.), *John of the Mountains,* p. 352.

55. Johnson, *Remembered Yesterdays,* pp. 288–289; Dudley, "Forest Reservations," pp. 266–267.

56. Maj. John Bigelow, Jr. to Sec. Int., Sept. 23, 1904, *Report, Act. Supt., Yosemite,* 1904, pp. 10–11.

57. Lt. Col. S. B. M. Young to Sec. Int., Aug. 15, 1896, ibid., 1896, p. 8.

58. A. E. Wood to Sec. Int., Aug. 31, 1891, *Report, Act. Supt., Yosemite,* 1891, p. 10.

59. Capt. G. H. G. Gale to Sec. Int., Aug. 28, 1894, *Report, Act. Supt., Yosemite,* 1894, p. 4; Lt. Col. S. B. M. Young to Sec. Int., ibid., 1896, pp. 10–11, quoting remarks of John Muir that appeared in "Sierra Club Bulletin No. 7."

60. Lt. Col. Joseph A. Garrard to Sec. Int., Oct. 1903, *Report, Act. Supt., Yosemite,* 1903, pp. 12–23; CR, 52nd Cong., 2nd Sess., XXIV, Part 2, pp. 1092, 1093, 1049, 1466–1475; *Senate Report* 1248, 52nd Cong., 2nd. Sess., I (SN 3072), pp. 1–82.

61. "An Act making appropriations for sundry civil expenses to the Government for the fiscal year ending June 30, 1904, and for other purposes," approved Apr. 28, 1904 (33 SL, 487); "An Act to exclude from the Yosemite National Park, California, certain lands therein described . . . ," approved Feb. 7, 1905 (33 SL, 702). The segregation of these lands was vehemently opposed by the Acting Superintendent, who maintained that such a move was proposed and urged by "a syndicate of lumber men" and that the reduction of boundaries, once started, might well continue, to the great detriment of the Park. Maj. John Bigelow, Jr., to Sec. Int., Sept. 23, 1904, *Report, Act. Supt., Yosemite,* 1904, p. 16. The problems presented by private land holdings in the Park have continued to the present day, since the boundary change of 1905 did not exclude all of the patented land. Some 15,570 acres were purchased in 1930 at an approximate cost of $3,300,000, half of which was supplied by John D. Rockefeller, Jr. In 1939, after several years of negotiation, another 7,200 acre tract was purchased by the government for a price of $1,495,500. Russell, *100 Years in Yosemite,* pp. 161–163.

62. Capt. A. E. Wood to Sec. Int., Aug. 31, 1891, *Report, Act. Supt., Yosemite,* 1891, p. 10.

63. Capt. J. H. Dorst to Sec. Int., Sept. 11, 1892, *Report, Act. Supt., Sequoia,* 1892, p. 15.

64. Capt. G. H. G. Gale to Sec. Int., Aug. 28, 1894; Capt. Alex Rodgers to Sec. Int., Aug. 26, 1897, *Report, Act. Supt., Yosemite,* 1894, p. 5, 1897, p. 8.

65. CR, 58th Cong., 2nd Sess., XXXVIII, pp. 228, 4592, 5449, 5502, 5672; XXXIX, pp. 1627, 2008. Frank Pierce, Asst. Sec. Int., to C. C. Smith, Mar. 21, 1905, NA, RG 79, "Parks, Reservations and Antiquities," File 12–9–15; Secretary of the Interior to Capt. John O'Shea, Apr. 18, 1905, RG 94, AGO, "Select Documents Relating to National Parks." *Public Law* No. 46, approved Feb. 6, 1905, copy YNPA, Vol. 23.

66. 35 SL, 1098, approved Mar. 4, 1909. *Report, Act. Supt., Yosemite,* 1910–1912; 36 SL, 857, approved June 25, 1910. *Report, Act. Supt., Sequoia,* 1910–1912.

67. Capt. A. E. Wood to Sec. Int., Aug. 31, 1891, *Report, Act. Supt., Yosemite,* 1891, p. 8; Capt. J. H. Dorst to Sec. Int., Aug. 31, 1891, *Report, Act. Supt., Sequoia,* 1891, pp. 7–9.

68. 1st Lt. Alex Dean to Sec. Int., Aug. 20, 1894, *Report, Act. Supt., Sequoia,* 1894, p. 16.

69. Lt. Col. S. B. M. Young to Sec. Int., Aug. 15, 1896, *Report, Act. Supt., Yosemite,* 1896, p. 4; Capt. Alex Rodgers to Sec. Int., Aug. 26, 1897, *Report, Act. Supt., Yosemite,* 1897, p. 4; B. Broemmel to Representative Julius Kahn, Nov. 9, 1901; Thomas Ryan, Act. Sec. Int., to Sec. War, July 17, 1902, NA, RG 94, AGO, "Select Documents relating to National Parks"; Capt. Frank C. Barton to Sec. Int., Aug. 14, 1902, *Report, Act. Supt., Sequoia,* 1902, pp. 5, 6.

70. Capt. H. C. Benson to Sec. Int., Oct. 10, 1905, *Report, Act. Supt., Yosemite,* 1905, p. 11.

71. Capt. A. E. Wood to Chairman, U. S. Fish Commission, Aug. 17, 1892, Vol. 1, LS, 1891–1900, No. 3, p. 10, Yosemite National Park Library; Capt. James Parker to Sec. Int., Aug. 26, 1893, *Report, Act. Supt., Sequoia,* 1893, p. 6, 1894, p. 4; Capt. Alex Rodgers to Sec. Int., Aug. 22, 1895, ibid., *Yosemite,* 1895, p. 5; Lt. Col. S. B. M. Young to Sec. Int., Aug. 15, 1896, ibid., 1896, pp. 5–8; Capt. L. C. Andrews to Sec. Int., Oct. 13, 1901, ibid., *Sequoia,* 1901, p. 8; Capt. H. C. Benson to Sec. Int., Oct. 10, 1905, ibid., *Yosemite,* 1905, p. 12.

72. Daniel Lamont, Sec. War, to Sec. Int., Apr. 22, 1896; Hoke Smith, Sec. Int., to Sec. War, Apr. 24, 1896; Sec. Int. to Sec. War, Feb. 17, 1897, NA, RG 94, AGO, "Select Documents Relating to National Parks."

73. Maj. Gen. [illegible] Merriam to Adj. Gen., May 14, 1898, C. N. Bliss, Sec. Int., to Sec. War, Feb. 10, 1899, NA, RG 94, AGO, "Select Documents"; 2nd Lt. Henry B. Clark to Sec. Int., Aug. 31, 1899, Capt. E. F. Willcox to Sec. Int., Oct. 28, 1899, *Reports, Act. Supt., Sequoia, Yosemite,* 1899, pp. 3–4.

74. W. Dickenson to Sec. War, June 20, 1898, NA, RG 94, AGO, "Select Documents Relating to National Parks."

75. J. C. Needham to Sec. War, Jan. 15, Mar. 5, 1900; Adj. Gen. to J. C. Needham, Apr. 6, 1900, NA, RG 94, AGO, "Select Documents . . ."

76. "Memorandum," NA, Misc. Div., AGO, Feb. 6, 1900.

77. Sec. War to Sec. Int., Feb. 9, 1900; Sec. Int. to Sec. War, Mar. 3, Mar. 22, 1900; in a letter to the Secretary of the Interior dated June 31, 1900, the Secretary of War suggested that "special agents of the General Land Office, known as Forest Rangers," be utilized for the purpose of park protection, ibid.; 31 SL, 618.

78. The events leading up to and the actual recession of the grants is treated by Colby, "Yosemite and the Sierra Club," pp. 11–19. For activities that took place in the national legislature, see CR, 58th Cong., 3rd Sess., xxxix, pp. 3962–3963; 59th Cong., 1st Sess., XL, Part 9, pp. 8144–8148, 8218; *The Nation,* LXXX (Apr. 27, 1905), pp. 325–326.

79. Troops had been withdrawn from the General Grant Park in 1902, and the Park had been placed in charge of a civilian guard. The entire Park had been fenced the previous year; and the evil of stock grazing and trespass thus abated. Capt. Frank C. Barton to Sec. Int., Aug. 14, 1902, *Report, Act. Supt., Sequoia,* 1902, p. 13.

80. 1st Lt. Hugh S. Johnson to Sec. Int., Sept. 1, 1913, NA, RG 94, AGO, "Select Documents relating to National Parks."

9. *The Culmination of an Idea*

1. Not all life was protected. The military was responsible for instigating the unfortunate policy of predator extermination. Mountain lions, wolves, and coyotes were killed.

2. Arnold Hague, "The Yellowstone National Park," in Roosevelt and Grinnell (eds.), *American Big Game Hunting,* p. 162. Letter, "National Park Game," *Forest and Stream,* XL, No. 7 (1893), p. 135; Capt. James O. Brown, Act. Supt., Yellowstone National Park, to Mark Sullivan, July 21, 1900, YNPA, Vol. 9, LS, p. 412.

3. Act. Supt. to Sec. Int., Feb. 14, 1902, YNPA, Vol. XI, LS, p. 191; John F. Lacey to Act. Supt., July 7, 1902, Vol. XVIII, LR; Act. Supt. to J. M. Keith, Conrad Bros., Douglas Carlin, Dick Rock, Feb. 10, 1902, Vol. XI, LS, pp. 181–184; Act. Supt. to Sec. Int., Mar. 29, 1902, Vol. XI, LS, p. 274, Nov. 19, 1902, Vol. XXI, LS, p. 94. The Pablo-Allard herd had been formed from two sources. In 1884 Michael Pablo had purchased from a Pend d'Oreille Indian ten bison that had been captured in Southern Alberta in 1873. These were released on the Flathead Indian Reservation in Montana. Five calves that had been captured by a Canadian fur trapper in Saskatchewan became the nucleus of the Charles Allard herd in Kalispell, Montana. The Charles Goodnight herd of Clarendon, Texas, traced its ancestry to some calves that had been captured from the rapidly disappearing Southern herd. James B. Trefethen, *Crusade for Wildlife,* pp. 93–94.

4. Act. Supt. to Sec. Int., May 26, 1905, YNPA, Vol. XV, p. 146; June 11, 1906, Vol. XVI, pp. 158–161; May 23, 1907, Vol. XVII, pp. 66–67, LS; B. P. Wells to C. A. Lindsley, June 25, 1907, Vol. XXVII, LR.

5. Act. Supt. to Supt. National Parks, July 10, 1916, YNPA, Vol. 89 (monthly reports). Of the 273 animals in the tame herd, 220 were adults, including 112 bulls and 108 cows; 53 were calves.

6. "Address of the Governor," reproduced in the *Cheyenne State Leader,* Feb. 15, 1911, clipping in YNPA, Vol. 40, File 29.

7. Act. Supt, to Sec. Int., Nov. 23, 1911; Act. Supt. to Dr. W. O. Stillman, Pres., Amer. Humane Assoc., Dec. 22, 1911; Act. Supt. to H. W. Henshaw, Chief, Biological Survey, Dec. 22, 1911, Jan. 3, 1912; all filed in YNPA, Vol. 40, File 29.

8. In 1816, 808 elk were live trapped and shipped to thirteen different states. Act. Supt. to Supt. National Parks, Feb. 5, 1916; Act. Supt. to Sec. Int., Sept. 30, 1916, YNPA, Vol. 65, File 310. The problem of too many animals and not enough feed was outlined in an article that appeared in the *Denver Post,* Feb. 23, 1964: "According to Bob Howe, park biologist, there isn't enough winter forage there for the 5,000 elk, 490 antelope, nearly 200 buffalo, 30 bighorn sheep, several hundred mule deer and a few head of moose. . . . In some areas there is less than half the natural feed there was 50 years ago. . . . In the past 30 years more than 5,500 elk and lesser numbers of other animals have starved to death. In 1914 there were 35,000 elk in the northern range . . . in 20 years two-thirds of that number perished—11,000 of starvation in the winter of 1919–20 alone . . . two winters ago park rangers shot 4,309 elk in a project that started a national controversy. In an attempt to keep the northern herd at about

5,000 animals, approximately 1,500 must be removed from the park annually or face starvation."

9. Remington, *Pony Tracks,* p. 112; Act. Supt. to Sec. Int., Sept. 30, 1898, Vol. VIII, LS, pp. 48–49; Cpl. Robert Ingersoll to C. O. Ft. Yellowstone, Jan. 19, 1902, Sgt. Frank Clark to C. O. Ft. Yellowstone, Sept. 15, 1905, Monthly Reports, YNPA; Act. Supt. to Sec. Int., June 3, 1909, YNPA, Vol. 103, File 302.

10. Act. Supt. Yosemite to Sec. Agric., Aug. 14, 1904, LS, 1901–1905, YNPA, pp. 301–304; Act. Supt. to Sec. Int., Sept. 15, Sept. 23, 1904, in *Report, Act. Supt., Yosemite,* 1904, pp. 13–14, 20–22: *Report, Act. Supt., Yosemite,* 1905, p. 18.

11. Act. Supt. Yellowstone to Sec. Int., Jan. 13, 1908, YNPA, Vol. XVIII, LS, p. 191, Nov. 4, 1913, Vol. 34 (no no.); M. P. Skinner to Act. Supt., Nov. 5, 1913, Dec. 6, 1913, Vol. 34 (no no.).

12. 2nd Lt. Henry B. Clark to Sec. Int., Aug. 31, 1899, *Report, Act. Supt., Sequoia,* 1899, pp. 10–12.

13. Yoshio Kinoshita to Act. Supt., Yellowstone, May 29, 1911, YNPA, Vol. 103, File 302; Theodor G. Wanner to Act. Supt., Yellowstone, Nov. 4, 1903, Vol. 22; Act. Supt. to C. V. R. Townsend, Nov. 25, 1906, Vol. 25; J. DuPratt White to Act. Supt., Mar. 12, 1908, Vol. 32; John Gifford to Act. Supt., Mar. 12, 1895, Vol. VI; James H. Cathey to Act. Supt., Feb. 2, 1904, Vol. 24.

14. Act. Supt. to Sec. Int., Nov. 4, 1913, YNPA, LS, Vol. 34. For additional information on road construction, see O'Brien, "The Roads of Yellowstone—1870–1915," pp. 30–39.

15. Act. Supt. to Gov. Wm. A. Richards, Aug. 25, 1897; Gov. Robert B. Smith to Act. Supt., Mar. 11, 1899, YNPA, Vol. 11; Miles R. Cahoon to Act. Supt., Feb. 17, 1897, Vol. 10; Act. Supt. To Sec. Int., Sept. 30, 1898, Vol. VIII, LS, pp. 22–23; Act. Supt. to Gov. Montana, Mar. 3, 1899, Vol. VIII, LS, p. 211; A. L. Palmer to Act. Supt., Dec. 22, 1900, Vol. 18; Act. Supt. to A. W. Miles, Jan. 12, 1905, Vol. 15; Roosevelt, "Wilderness Reserves," in *Forestry and Irrigation,* X (June, 1905), pp. 3–5.

16. John Meldrum, U. S. Commissioner, to Act. Supt., Sept. 25, Oct. 27, Nov. 3, 1913; copy, letter, Wm. R. Harr, Asst. Atty. Genl., to Hillard S. Ridgely, U. S. Atty., June 5, 1913, YNPA, Vol. 74, File 70. Act. Supt. to Sec. Int., Sept. 30, 1916, YNPA, Vol. 65, File 310; CR, 63rd Cong., 2nd Sess., LI, Part 2, 1328; 3rd Sess., LII, Part 1, 252; 64th Cong., 1st Sess., LIII, Part 1, 223, 437, 573; Part 2, 1135; Part 3, 2338; Part 7, 7247; Part 9, 9322; Part 10, 9447, 10253; 39 SL, 238.

17. S. B. M. Young to Theodore Roosevelt, Jan. 15, 1907, in *Senate Doc.* 752, 60th Cong., 2nd Sess. (SN 5409), p. 1. What prompted Roose-

velt to suggest an end to military rule is not known. His instructions to Young were repeated in the letter cited above and further documentation was not found.

18. S. B. M. Young to Gifford Pinchot, Sept. 7, 1907, YNPA, Vol. XVII, LS, p. 351; Young to James B. Adams, Oct. 1, 1907, Vol. XVII, LS, p. 422; Young to Sec. Int., Oct. 16, 1907, Vol. XVII, LS, pp. 6–9; Oct. 18, 1907, NA, RG 79, File 12–12–24, AGO; Young to Sec. Int., Nov. 20, 1907, YNPA, Vol. XVIII, LS, pp. 77–79. S. B. M. Young had previously served as Acting Superintendent of Yosemite National Park, 1896–1897, and of the Yellowstone, 1897–1898. He was a Major General commanding a division in the Spanish-American War, and, after observing the famous charge up San Juan Hill, he called the young Lieutenant Colonel of the Rough Riders aside and criticized him for the boisterous conduct and ragged charge of his men. When the Lieutenant Colonel became President of the United States he named Young, then a Lieutenant General, Chief of Staff of the United States Army. Francis P. Farquhar (ed.), *Yosemite in 1896*, p. 16.

19. Sec. Int. to Young, Nov. 21, 1907; "Memorandum" attached to Civil Guard Plan; both in NA, RG 79, File 12–12–24; Young to Sec. Int., Dec. 20, 1907, YNPA, Vol. XVIII, LS, p. 149.

20. Act. Supt. to Chief of Staff, Jan. 14, 1914, RG 79, Records of the National Park Service, File 12–12–24; Sec. War to Sec. Int., Mar. 14, 1914; Asst. Sec. Int. to Sec. War, Mar. 21, 1914; Adj. Gen. to Act. Supt., Mar. 31, 1914, May 11, 1914; all from NA, "Select Docs. pertaining to National Parks," Doc. No. 1834, File No. 5.

21. Act. Supt. to Commanding General, Western Dept., Apr. 17, 1914; AG, Western Dept. to Act. Supt., June 21, Aug. 29, Dec. 4, 1914; all from NA, RG 98, LR 1910–1915, Ft. Yellowstone, Box No. 6, Doc. No. 268, from File No. 1951.

22. "Hearings before the House Comm. on Approp. Sundry Civil Bill for 1916," pp. 677–679; Sec. Int. to Sec. War, Apr. 10, 1915, both in NA, RG 79, Records of the National Park Service, File 12–13–23.

23. Sec. War to Sec. Int., May 13, 1915, Act. Supt. to Stephen Mather, Asst. to Sec. Int., Nov. 26, 1915, "Memorandum on Troop Withdrawal," all in NA, RG 79, Records of the National Park Service, File 12–12–24. Act. Supt. to Asst. Sec. Int., Nov. 11, 1915, YNPA, Vol. 89, File 90.

24. *Proceedings of the National Park Conferences* (GPO, 1911, 1912, 1915), passim, 39 SL, 535, 40 SL, 20.

25. Twenty-one enlisted men chose to remain behind and were appointed park rangers at a salary of $100 per month, thus forming the nucleus of the new Park Service. Sec. Int. to Sec. War, July 18, 1916, Sec.

War to Sec. Int., July 20, 1916, Act. Supt. to Adj. Gen., Sept. 19, 1916, NA, RG 98, Commands, Posts, Ft. Yellowstone, LR, File 2273654E. Act. Supt. to Adj. Gen., Oct. 7, 1916, NA, RG 98, Commands, Posts, Ft. Yellowstone, Tel. Sent., Box No. 1, File 82; Special Order No. 229, War Dept., Sept. 30, 1916; No. 245, Oct. 19, 1916; C. A. Lindsley, Act. Supervisor, to Supt. National Parks, Nov. 14, 1916, YNPA, Vol. 89, Monthly Reports.

26. Asst. Sec. Int., to Sec. Int., Sept. 18, 1916, Sec. Int. to Asst. Sec. Int., Sept. 18, 1916, T. H. Walsh to Asst. Sec. Int., Sept. 18, H. L. Meyers to Asst. Sec. Int., Sept. 18, Asst. Sec. to Walsh and Meyers, Sept. 18, Walsh to Sec. Int., Sept. 19, Meyers to Sec. Int., Sept. 25, Woodrow Wilson to Sec. Int., Oct. 1, 1916, all in NA, RG 79, Records of the National Park Service, File 12–12–24. Tel. T. H. Walsh to Sec. War, Sept. 22, H. L. Meyers to Sec. War, Aug. 28, J. P. Tumulty to Sec. War, Oct. 1, Sec. War to Pres. U. S., Oct. 2, 1916, all in NA, RG 94, "Select Docs. pertaining to National Parks."

27. Sundry Civil Approp. Act. of June 12, 1917, 40 SL, 151; Sec. War to Chairman, Comm. on Approp., House, Feb. 21, Sec. War to Speaker of House, June 4, 1917, NA, RG 94, "Select Docs. Relating to National Parks," File 4; Sec. Int. to Sec. War, June 15, 1917, Sept. 25, 1917, NA, RG 79, Records of the National Park Service, File 12–12–24; Horace M. Albright to C. A. Lindsley, Maj. E. M. Leary, and Capt. John W. N. Schulz, July 5, 1917, YNPA, Vol. 70, File 341.

28. "Memo" by H. Albright to accompany letter to Sec. War from Sec. Int., Sept. 25, 1917, W. T. Judkins to Sen. F. E. Warren, May 31, 1919, W. F. Gossell to Sec. Int., Sept. 13, 1917, Chester A. Lindsley to H. Albright, Nov. 28, 1917, May 13, 1918; letter published in *New York Times,* Oct. 14, 1917, from "A Sergeant, Ft. Yellowstone," clipping; all in NA, RG 79, Records of the National Park Service, File 12–12–24. For a slightly different view of the political maneuvers relating to troops in Yellowstone, one stressing the role played by Representative John J. Fitzgerald, New York, see Robert Shankland, *Steve Mather of the National Parks,* pp. 104–105, and Donald Swain, *Wilderness Defender,* pp. 62–63.

Epilogue

1. Muir, *Our National Parks,* p. 40.
2. CR, 49th Cong., 2nd Sess., XVIII, Part 1, pp. 149–154.
3. Chittenden, *The Yellowstone National Park,* preface to 1918 edition (Chittenden's italics).

4. The sometimes contrasting roles of the politician, park supervisors, and the public are admirably presented by Reich in "Bureaucracy in the Forests."

5. Past and present national park policy has been, in recent years, more closely examined by several investigative committees. The results of this scrutiny and suggestions for future policy development appear in *Wildlife Management in the National Parks,* U. S. Department of the Interior Advisory Board on Wildlife Management, A. S. Leopold, Chairman (Washington: Interior Department, 1963, mimeographed); *Report,* National Academy of Sciences—National Research Council Advisory Committee to the National Park Service on Research, W. J. Robbins, Chairman, 1963; Darling and Eichhorn, *Man and Nature in the National Parks.*

6. *National Parks Magazine,* Vol. 42, No. 254 (Nov. 1968), p. 19; *National Geographic,* Vol. 133, No. 4 (May, 1968), pp. 642–667.

INDEX